THE ANTISLAVERY ORIGINS OF

THE FOURTEENTH AMENDMENT

The Antislavery Origins of the Fourteenth Amendment

By Jacobus tenBroek

1951
UNIVERSITY OF CALIFORNIA PRESS
Berkeley and Los Angeles

UNIVERSITY OF CALIFORNIA PRESS
BERKELEY AND LOS ANGELES
CALIFORNIA

◆

CAMBRIDGE UNIVERSITY PRESS
LONDON, ENGLAND

COPYRIGHT, 1951, BY
THE REGENTS OF THE UNIVERSITY OF CALIFORNIA

Contents

Part One: THE FORGING OF THE CONSTITUTIONAL DOCTRINE

Introduction to Part One 7

CHAPTER
    I. The District of Columbia 15
    II. The Fugitive Slave Law 32
    III. The Power and Duty of Congress 42
    IV. Paramount National Citizenship 71
    V. Conclusions; the Antislavery Origin 94

Part Two: THE DISSEMINATION OF THE CONSTITUTIONAL DOCTRINE

Introduction to Part Two 113
    VI. Party Platforms and Resolutions 115

CHAPTER

VII. John A. Bingham 125
VIII. The Victory of the Republican Party 129

Part Three: THE CONSUMMATION OF ABOLITIONISM—THE THIRTEENTH AMENDMENT

Introduction to Part Three 137
  IX. The First Two Congressional Debates 140
  X. The Third Congressional Debate 156

Part Four: RECONSUMMATION—THE FOURTEENTH AMENDMENT

XI. The Fourteenth Amendment 183
XII. The Fourteenth Amendment (*Continued*) . . . 192
XIII. Conclusions 218
Table of Cases 225
Source Material 226
Index 229

Introduction

SECTION 1. All persons born or naturalized in the United States, and subject to the jurisdiction thereof, are citizens of the United States and of the State wherein they reside. No State shall make or enforce any law which shall abridge the privileges or immunities of citizens of the United States; nor shall any State deprive any person of life, liberty, or property, without due process of law; nor deny to any person within its jurisdiction the equal protection of the laws. SECTION 5. The Congress shall have power to enforce, by appropriate legislation, the provisions of this article.—*Fourteenth Amendment, United States Constitution.*

SOCIALLY AND POLITICALLY as well as historically, there are no more important questions in American constitutional law today than those raised and reraised by eighty years of application of this language of the Fourteenth Amendment:

1. What were intended to be the privileges and immunities of citizens of the United States which the states were forbidden to abridge by law?

2. Was the equal protection clause merely procedural, a requirement of proper classification, or did it also have a substantive content?

3. Was the due process clause intended simply as a procedural guarantee or was it to be substantive as well? Was it intended to safeguard human rights only or economic rights also?

4. Was the amendment intended to apply the Bill of Rights to the states?

5. Was the legislative enforcement power vested in Congress by section 5 intended to be corrective only, that is, limited to the removal of offensive state action, or was a revolution in federalism to be accomplished by which the national government was authorized directly and affirmatively itself to protect the rights of individuals which were intended to be identified by section 1?

Eighty years of investigation and research by scholars, judges, and lawyers has cast surprisingly little light on these questions. In most respects, they are not only as crucial but virtually as puzzling today as they ever were. Part of the reason for this is doubtless the difficulty, if not impossibility, of determining either historically or contemporaneously the intentions of men and movements. Part of the reason, also, is the disproportionate weight given to judicial decisions in the writing of this as in other phases of the history of our constitutional law. But the greatest difficulty has come from the chronological limits of the research. When attention has properly focused on nonjudicial sources, it has been confined to the congressional, popular, and ratification debates at the time of the adoption of the Fourteenth Amendment and immediately thereafter. December, 1865, the date when the first draft proposals for the Fourteenth Amendment were introduced into Congress, has stood as an unassailed temporal barrier to almost all inquiry.[1] The pervasive limitation of the researches so far published has been the

---

[1] Howard Jay Graham, in his brilliant and basic articles, "The Conspiracy Theory of the Fourteenth Amendment," penetrated the barrier far enough to discover Bingham's congressional speeches of 1856–1859. *Yale Law Journal*, Vol. 47 (1938), p. 371; *ibid.*, Vol. 48 (1939), p. 171.

failure to push across "the great divide" of December, 1865, into the social, political, and economic background of the amendment; has been the implicit assumption that the constitutional theory and language embodied in the amendment was the spontaneous creation of the Joint Committee on Reconstruction of the Thirty-ninth Congress, or, at most, of that Congress and of that year.

The present work deals with the antecedents of the Fourteenth Amendment before December, 1865. The research has centered on the doctrines and political activities of the organized abolitionist movement, going back as far as the period of the formulation of the American Anti-Slavery Society in 1833.

Much help has been derived from general historians, with their new light upon the character, methods, location, and leading personalities of the antislavery movement.[2] These writers, however, were not particularly interested in constitutional law and thus missed the historical and present-day importance of the constitutional theories of the movement.[3] For those theories, it was necessary to explore the original sources: (1) the truly amazing and prolific pamphlet literature of the movement; (2) collections of letters, papers, and speeches of the leaders of the movement; (3) proceedings, reports, and resolutions of antislavery meetings; (4) selections from the abundant abolitionist press, especially *The Philanthropist, The Emancipator, The Albany Patriot, The Friend of Man,* and *The National Era.*

The upshot of these researches might be summarized as follows: (1) proponents of the Civil War amendments presumed and fell back on a constitutional theory and usage which was generally and popularly understood; (2) this theory and usage reached back to

---

[2] W. S. Jenkins, *Pro-Slavery Thought in the Old South* (1935); Dwight L. Dumond, *Anti-Slavery Origins of the Civil War* (1939); Clement Eaton, *Freedom of Thought in the Old South* (1940); T. Harry Williams, *Lincoln and the Radicals* (1941); Avery Craven, *The Coming of the Civil War* (1942); Russell B. Nye, *Fettered Freedom* (1949); Kenneth Stampp, *And the War Came* (1950).

[3] Dumond is an exception to this statement. He has an interesting chapter on the constitutional theories of the abolitionists, but he did not relate these to the Fourteenth Amendment.

the mid-thirties, and was evolved and widely propagandized by the abolitionist movement; (3) the central features of the theory were the equal protection of the laws, due process of law, privileges and immunities of citizens, and doctrines about the powers of the national government in relation to the states; (4) this theory was hammered into public consciousness by all forms of propaganda but principally by the platforms of minor and major political parties; (5) the discovery of the antislavery origins of the Civil War amendments dissipates much of the confusion resulting from the congressional and ratification debates; in fact, it settles the answers to some of the foregoing questions and casts new light on others.[4]

[4] In two articles Howard Jay Graham has presented the biographical, geographical, and motivational aspects of the abolition movement bearing on the genesis of their constitutional system. He has traced the gradual crystallization of equality, governmental protection, due process, and privileges and immunities from a religious-ethical, "higher law" system into a primitive system of constitutional right, concentrating on the period down to 1837. "The Early Anti-Slavery Backgrounds of the Fourteenth Amendment," *Wisconsin Law Review*, Vol. 1950, No. 3 (April, 1950), p. 479; No. 4 (May, 1950), p. 610. The present writer's chief concern is with the progressive evolution of this system—especially its crucial transformation into a system of constitutional power—and its popularization and eventual enactment in the Civil War amendments.

Part One

THE FORGING OF
THE CONSTITUTIONAL DOCTRINE

Introduction to Part One

WHEREAS we hold these truths to be self-evident, that all men are created equal ... —and whereas we believe slavery is contrary to the precepts of Christianity, dangerous to the peace and liberties of the country, and contrary to the spirit of our republican institutions; and believing that we not only have a right to protest against it, but are under the highest obligation to seek its removal by a moral influence, and believing that the entire abolition of slavery is not only expedient, but perfectly practicable, and that the unrighteously oppressed people of color stand in need of our sympathy and coöperation; therefore, recognizing the inspired declaration that "God hath made of one blood all nations of men to dwell upon the face of the earth" and in obedience to our Savior's Golden Rule ... we agree to form ourselves into a society to be governed by the following constitution ...

Article 2. The object of this society shall be to collect and diffuse information on the character of slavery, to convince our countrymen of its heinous criminality in the sight of God, to show that the duty, safety, and interest of all concerned, require its abandonment; to take all lawful, moral, and religious means, to effect a total and immediate abolition of slavery in the United States, using no weapon but reason and truth.

Article 3. This society shall aim to elevate the character and condition of the people of color, by encouraging their intellectual, moral, and religious improvement, by correcting the prejudices of public opinion, and by endeavoring to obtain for our colored citizens civil and religious privileges, but will never countenance the oppressed in vindicating their rights, by resorting to physical force.

THIS STATEMENT, taken from the preamble and constitution of the Anti-Slavery Society of Booneton, New Jersey,[1] formed in 1834, expressed the policy adopted by the American Anti-Slavery Society and all its auxiliaries in the early years of the organized movement. It was a policy of moving against slavery in the South, not by law or by compulsion, but by persuasion—the persuasion both of precept and northern example. "No weapons but reason and truth" were to be used. The abolition of slavery was to be accomplished "by a moral influence," by collecting and diffusing information on its true character, by convincing "our countrymen" that it ought to be abolished. This was to be done by a variety of arguments: by showing "the heinous criminality" of slavery "in the sight of God"; by appealing to the Christian conscience of slaveholders; by portraying its violations of religion, ethics, and humanity. It was to be done, too, by showing that slavery was contrary to the natural rights of man, "the spirit of our republican institutions," and "the peace and liberties of the country." Finally, slavery and the concomitant discriminations against free Negroes and abolitionists were to be described by abolitionists, as early as 1835,[2] as denials of rights to the equal protection of the laws, the safeguards of due process, and the privileges and immunities of citizens. This last argument, too, was adjusted to the policy of emancipation by persuasion. The rights denied were said to be constitutional rights. Therefore they constituted a rule of conduct for individuals and governments. But little was said of a means of enforcement. There was no invocation of state or federal judicial power; least of all,

---

[1] Published in *The Emancipator*, June 3, 1834.
[2] *Proceedings* of the Ohio Anti-Slavery Convention held at Putnam, April 22–24, 1835; report of the committee on the laws of Ohio.

the Fourteenth Amendment

any mention of congressional intervention or authority. The remedy for such violations was that men and governments should be persuaded to conform.

The policy of the American Anti-Slavery Society of emancipation by the conversion and repentance of slaveholders and the amelioration of the lot of the Negro in the North seemed reasonable. It was backed by the authority of the British example, by the antislavery proviso in the Northwest Ordinance and in the constitutions of the states carved out of the Northwest Territory, by the early success of the common-law attack in Massachusetts and of freedom suits in the middle and New England states, and by emancipation acts in other northern states. The policy was bolstered, too, by liberal decisions in the South.[3] It was immeasurably strengthened by the sensational growth of abolitionism in 1835 and 1836 in Ohio, Pennsylvania, and western New York.

Before long, however, the policy proved futile and the faith of the abolitionists in the revival and pamphlet campaign naïve and unwarranted. It soon became apparent that slavery could never be abolished nor emancipation visibly accelerated in the southern and the border states by these methods. Mob attacks upon abolitionists in North and South alike, gag laws in Congress, and angry threats of secession and disunion served notice that the majority of slaveholders were not to be converted to immediate abolition. Censorship of the southern mail and laws proscribing discussion of slavery and education of the slaves set at naught the tools of propaganda designed for "the great reform."

The commitment to isolation by the South ended all hope that the extinction of slavery could be effected "by moral and religious means, and by no other." Once the South had cut off the indispensable means of conversion by propaganda, the abolitionists were left with no alternative but intensive political action and, in

---

[3] *Harry and others* v. *Decker and Hopkins* (Miss. Sup. Ct., June term, 1818), Walker 36; *Forsyth et al.* v. *Nash*, 4 Martin's La. Reps. 385; *Merry* v. *Chexnaider* (1830), 20 Martin's La. Reps. 699, holding that slaves in the Northwest Territory at the time of the adoption of the Northwest Ordinance or Negroes born in the territory after the adoption of the ordinance were free.

the end, sectional struggle for control of the federal government and the instrumentalities of national power. In a comparatively short time, the organized movement underwent a complete reversal and reorientation—from one primarily personal, religious, and evangelical to one increasingly political in both aims and methods. The effects of the change were pervasive. The drama of revival and conversion, still reënacted daily in the North, ceased to be the sole preoccupation or the principal method of "the great reform." Increasingly, abolitionists waged their fight in the courtroom, the legislative hall, and the political arena. Constitutional invective and discourse rapidly assumed primacy over appeals to the Bible, "eternal principles of morality" and Christian ethics. Most important, political action is premised on the constitutional authority of the agencies of government to take the action urged. Another and the most crucial stage in the development of abolitionist constitutional theory had therefore become necessary. In its groping, uneven, but persistent advance toward a coherent constitutional system, abolitionism had moved easily from natural right to constitutional right. The next step—from constitutional right to constitutional power—was now to be taken.

In moving into political action, the abolitionists were faced with the problem of which front or fronts to activate. Their alternatives were, however, far from unlimited. Political action in the South was eliminated by the very means which prevented a personal appeal to slaveholders. Northern abolitionists or northerners suspected of abolitionism dared not enter the slaveholding states. Statements like those of Governor Lynch of Mississippi that "necessity will sometimes prompt a summary mode of trial and punishment unknown to the law," and of Governor McDuffie of South Carolina that "I would have those who oppose slavery, if caught in our jurisdiction, put to death without benefit of clergy," were no more warnings against prospective activity than epitaphs for past actors. Birney's question was almost entirely rhetorical when he asked: "Who dares go into the southern half of this Union and

the Fourteenth Amendment

speak of the Declaration of Independence, except in whispers, and publicly insist that the object of the Constitution—to establish justice—ought to be carried out in practice?"

Lobbying, pressure, and persuasion applied to the legislative representatives of the slave system, in these circumstances, were not merely futile but physically impossible. Equally denied was access to the southern courts, including the federal tribunals. That point was put at rest by the experience of Samuel Hoar, who was peremptorily ejected from South Carolina by a mob when, as the official representative of Massachusetts, he had gone to the southern state to test the constitutionality of its colored seamen laws in the federal courts. The abolitionists might continue to invoke, as indeed they did, constitutional ideas of protection, equal protection, and due process against the slave codes of the southern states,[4] but once the iron curtain had dropped, these could no more serve as the basis or instrument of abolitionist political action in the South than they could be used as an article of persuasion served up to the individual slaveowner.

The immediate need of the abolitionists in the free states was for

---

[4] An excellent summary statement, for example, appears in an unsigned article in the August, 1837, issue of the *Anti-Slavery Record,* official organ of the American Anti-Slavery Society. "Among Republicans," the argument runs, "it is a very common opinion that the object of government is to protect the rights of the governed ... The Sword of Justice cannot be very effectual protection to any unless it is an equal protection to all ... again the Constitution declares that 'no person shall be deprived of life, liberty, or property without due process of law.' Hence, it is obvious that no person, so far as the Constitution of the United States is concerned, can hold as property that which, without due process of law, deprives another of liberty. ... The Constitution, if it were to take the place of state laws, would open the way for the slaves to recover wages or damages in the courts of the United States, for not one of the two-and-a-half million has been deprived of liberty by any due process of law, if by any process whatever."

Elizur Wright, able editor of the *Quarterly Anti-Slavery Magazine* and secretary of the American Anti-Slavery Society, devoted much of his *Fourth Annual Report,* May, 1837, to these constitutional issues.

N. P. Rogers' article, "The Constitution," *Quarterly Anti-Slavery Magazine,* Vol. 2 (1837), describes the Constitution as "a warranty deed of universal liberty,—equal and absolute freedom to every mortal man who comes within its outmost protection." The phrases of the Preamble, the republican form of government guaranty, the comity clause, the rights of the First and Fourth amendments—all are arrayed in support of the unconstitutionality of slavery. But above all, the personality of the slave was said to entitle him in his property and his life as well as his liberty to the due process requirement of the Fifth Amendment.

protection against riot, arson, assault, and murder. These breaches of established rights were perpetrated almost daily in a context of bitter community and official hostility to the victims. They were conducted "with a knowledge of, and oft-times in the presence of, public officials whose sworn duty it was to uphold the law, in the presence of courts established and maintained to dispense justice, and under the eyes of governors and legislators who had ceased to reverence the majesty of the law." Consequently, in this area, it was for restoration of the protective power of the law, its supremacy over mob violence, private invasion, and official wrongdoing, that the abolitionists contended.[5] Enforcement of existing laws rather than the passage of new laws or the repeal of old ones was their crying need.

On the state level, these matters presented few constitutional issues. The obligation and constitutional authority of the state governments to supply protection would be admitted by all, once the popular hysteria had died down. The abolitionist appeal to the national Constitution—an appeal based upon the denial of the civil liberties guaranteed by the amendments to all citizens[6]—was

---

[5] "Law has lost its honor; it is in the dust; none do it reverence; its authority to restrain, to punish, to protect, is mocked at." Letter of James G. Birney to Joshua Leavitt and others, January 10, 1842, in Dwight L. Dumond, *Birney Letters* (1938), p. 645.

"The right of petition" (T. D. Weld in *The Power of Congress over Slavery in the District of Columbia*, New York, 1838) "ravished and trampelled by its constitutional guardians, and insult and defiance hurled in the faces of the sovereign people while calmly remonstrating with their servants for violence committed on the Nation's Charter and their own dearest rights!... 'The right of peaceably assembling' violently wrested—the rights of minorities, rights no longer—free speech struck dumb—free men outlawed and murdered—free presses cast into the streets and their fragments strewed with shoutings, or flourished in triumph before the gaze of approving crowds as proud mementoes of prostrate law!

"The spirit and power of our fathers, where are they? Their deep homage always and everywhere rendered to free thought, with its inseparable signs—free speech and a free press—their reverence for justice, liberty, rights, and all-pervading law, where are they?"

[6] Wrote William Goodell, editor of *The Emancipator*, after the New York riots in the summer of 1834 (July 22, 1834), "And so we are generously offered protection on condition that we shall renounce our principles and cease to disseminate them ... We are to be protected, not in the enjoyment of our civil and religious liberties as free citizens; but if we will relinquish those rights, then we are to be unmolested in our persons and our property....

"The protection we ask is a protection different from all this; and it is a pro-

the Fourteenth Amendment

the one fruitful source of development derived from the riotous upheavals in the free states. For some time to come, however, this appeal was but an anguished exhortation addressed to the general public. The demand for federal enforcement of the rights thus

tection we supposed we had a right to claim, as free American citizens. . . . We ask them (our opponents) to remember that all the protection we need is needed by them, and is due to every citizen. Above all, we ask them to remember that the protection most highly appreciated by us, is that which protects the freedom of speech and of the press; and not that which merely offers us a useless life and useless property, on condition that we shall not improve them, according to the dictates of our own consciences, in the service of our creator, and of our fellow men.

"Was it an imprudence in us; that we so far trusted to the constitution and laws under which we live that we took for granted our undisturbed and peaceable possession of that freedom of speech and of the press which is claimed by every American citizen?"

E. P. Lovejoy pleaded before a committee of the people of Alton who days later took his life: "I, Mr. Chairman, have not desired, or asked any compromise. I have asked for nothing but to be protected in my rights as a citizen—rights which God has given men, and which are guaranteed to me by the constitution of my country. Have I, sir, been guilty of any infraction of the laws? Whose good name have I injured? When and where have I published anything injurious to the reputation of Alton? . . . What, sir, I ask, has been my offence? Put your finger upon it—define it—and I stand ready to answer for it. If I have committed any crime, you can easily convict me. You have public sentiment in your favor. You have your juries, and you have your attorney (looking at the Attorney-General) and I have *no doubt* you can *convict* me. But if I have been guilty of no violation of law, why am I hunted up and down continually like a partridge upon the mountains? Why am I threatened with the *tar-barrel*? Why am I waylaid every day, and from night to night, and my life in jeopardy every hour? . . .

"I plant myself, sir, down on my unquestionable *rights,* and the question to be decided is, whether I shall be protected in the exercise and enjoyment of those rights—*that is the question, sir;*—whether my property shall be protected, whether I shall be suffered to go home to my family at night without being assailed, and threatened with tar and feathers, and assassination; whether my afflicted wife, whose life has been in jeopardy, from continued alarm and excitement, shall night after night be driven from a sick bed into the garret to save her life from the brickbats and violence of the mobs; *that sir, is the question?"* Joseph C. and Owen Lovejoy, *Memoir of the Rev. Elijah Lovejoy; Who Was Murdered in Defence of the Liberty of the Press, at Alton, Illinois, Nov. 7, 1837* (New York, 1838), pp. 279–280.

For a similar treatment of the right of free discussion and other rights of the amendments see: Speech of Gerrit Smith, Esq., in Peterboro', October 22, 1834; Defensor (Wm. Thomas), *Enemies of the Constitution Discovered* (New York, 1835); William Goodell, "An Appeal in Behalf of the American Anti-Slavery Society Addressed to the People of the City of New York," *The Emancipator* (special edition), August, 1834; *A Full Statement of the Reasons Which Were in Part Offered to the Committee of the Legislature of Massachusetts on the Fourth and Eighth of March, 1836, etc., Published by Order of the Managers of the Mass. ASS* (Boston, 1836); H. B. Stanton, *Remarks in the Representatives Hall on 23 and 24 February before the Committee of the House of Representatives of Massachusetts* (Boston, 1837); Elizur Wright, *Fourth Annual Report,* American Anti-Slavery Society, May, 1837; S. B. Treadwell, *American Liberties and American Slavery Morally and Politically Illustrated* (Rochester, N.Y., 1838).

guaranteed by the federal Constitution awaited the conception of political action on a national scale and the articulation of a theory of paramount national citizenship in the following decade. When that demand came, it would be important to remember that, in its origins, one of the immediate causes had been the violation of the rights of freemen as well as slaves, white men as well as blacks.

Since slavery did not exist in the northern states and protection of the person and property of the abolitionists could be secured only through a lessening of public animosity, antislavery political action on a state level was necessarily directed to the removal of the incidents and appendages of the slave system which did exist in the North. The elevation of the free Negro to a position of civil and religious equality, procuring for "our fellow colored citizens" "all of the privileges and immunities of white citizens" through the opening up of economic and educational opportunities and the elimination of legal discriminations—in short, the emancipation of the free colored people of the North—had from the beginning been an integral part of abolitionism and a propulsive force in the development of its constitutional power. It was emphasized in the constitutions and declarations of sentiments of the American Anti-Slavery Society and of state and local auxiliaries as well as in such notable documents as the Putnam report on the laws of Ohio and discussions about Judge Lawless and the McIntosh case. In the sweep of the total movement, this also became an area of political action. But here again, the removal of disabilities and discriminations by the repeal of the offending laws was within the admitted constitutional and protective power of the state; and the authority of the national Constitution to strike down the double standard in state laws and constitutions continued to be a claim of right and not of power.

CHAPTER I

The District of Columbia

An obvious and significant arena for abolitionist political action was the District of Columbia. As the capital of the nation, action there would have a great symbolic value. Nor could it be frustrated by lowering an iron curtain of isolation. Problems of federalism would not be raised. There was no particularly difficult constitutional language to be overcome, such as the fugitive slave clause, which clearly commanded, and undoubtedly was intended to command, rendition of fugitive slaves, quite apart from whether state, nation, or any agency of government was empowered to enforce it.

But above all, in the District of Columbia a direct assault could be made upon the institution of slavery itself. The city of Washington was "the Congo of America"; "the great government barricoon, whence coffles are driven across the country to Alabama or Texas." Slavery not only existed in the District of Columbia, but existed there by the acquiescence of the free states. The District was the common property of the nation, and North and South alike were responsible for the institutions in it. "Look again at the District of

Columbia," said James Birney to a convention of the American Anti-Slavery Society in May, 1835, "and see if you are not slaveholders, as much as the people of Kentucky."[1] A systematic campaign for the abolition of slavery in the District of Columbia by congressional enactment was the result.

In terms of antislavery origins of the Fourteenth Amendment, the all-important fact about the determined political opposition of the abolitionists to slavery in the District of Columbia is that it brought the antislavery movement into head-on collision with the constitutional theories of the South. The proslavery forces, as the possibility of an all-out political attack began to emerge, had evolved an elaborate constitutional argument designed to frustrate governmental action as isolation had been designed to frustrate private action. The collision of the antislavery movement with this constitutional argument forced and catalyzed a development of abolitionist constitutionalism. At no point can the basic elements of similarity and conflict in the contending theories better be seen. At no point is it more evident that due process and equal protection lay at the heart of the constitutional theories of both sides. At no point can we better trace the part played by these two concepts in transforming the constitutional system of the abolitionists from a mere argument in a policy of emancipation by persuasion to a mandatory requirement of compulsive legislation.

The constitutional system of proslavery forces in its early form was primarily the work of F. W. Pickens' congressional speech and H. L. Pinckney's congressional committee report in January and May, 1836, both dealing with resolutions respecting the power of Congress to abolish slavery in the District of Columbia. By that system, governments were instituted among men to safeguard and protect their natural and inalienable rights. Any governmental denial of those rights, any deprivation of life, liberty, or property without due process of law, any negation of the great objects specified in the Preamble or failure to sustain and promote them would be impolitic, unconstitutional, "repugnant to the principles of natural

---

[1] *The Emancipator*, May 19, 1835.

justice and of the social compact," and "totally subversive of all the purposes for which government is instituted." "The Union was formed... for the perfect and equal protection of the rights and interests of all of the citizens" and "the common and equal benefit of all the states." Property is one of the inalienable rights enjoying the manifold securities, and slaves are property.

Although the theory of the South was dominantly defensive in character because of the part played in it by the due process prohibition and the vested rights doctrine, it demanded something more than governmental abstinence and restraint. It claimed for citizens the right to the protection for which governments were created. It asserted the obligation of the federal government to "sustain and promote" the great objects of the Preamble, and to do these things perfectly and equally for all citizens.

Intended by its drafters as the last word in an episode, the Pickens-Pinckney doctrine was in reality the first word in an era. Thenceforward the struggle over slavery was a constitutional struggle, a struggle bearing irresistibly upon the nature and constitutional powers of the national government. For the doctrine and implications asserted spread far beyond the ten-mile-square seat of government. They reached as far as the issue of slavery reached; and eventually that was everywhere.

Once the constitutional lines had thus been clearly drawn, once Pickens and Pinckney had planted the defense of slavery in the Constitution itself, once the South had interposed what, if accepted, would be as ultimate a barrier to political action as isolation had been to private action, the abolitionists were forced to reread the constitutional document and to reorient and readapt their constitutional system. Lawyer and laymen alike took up the task with zest, ingenuity, and imagination. They produced not only an answer to Pickens and Pinckney but monuments in the constitutional history of the United States.

Three of the most important and elaborate of these[2] were the

---

[2] For the preconstitutional abolitionist argument on the District of Columbia, see

work of Henry B. Stanton in his address before the legislature of Massachusetts, February, 1837; Charles Olcott in his two lectures on the subject of slavery and abolition; and Theodore Dwight Weld in his newspaper article and separately published pamphlet on *The Powers of Congress over Slavery in the District of Columbia*.[3]

Olcott's lectures, published in 1838, are a 120,000-word compendium of abolitionist doctrine, covering everything from the Bible to the British experience, from slave breeding in the South to the Constitution of the United States. The constitutional argument is a refurbishing of the points made in the report to the Putnam convention, with important elaboration and some addition. The phrases of the Preamble, the common defense and general welfare clause, the republican form of government guarantee, and the interstate commerce power are analyzed one by one "to prove that the practice of slavery is utterly hostile, to the letter and spirit of the Constitution of the United States." The amendments also are invoked for this purpose. "By them, the rights of conscience, speech, the press, trial by jury, etc., are guaranteed in words, in the most solemn and ample manner, to the 'people' generally, without any proviso, restriction, exception, or qualification whatever . . . All slaves (who are 'people' also) are totally deprived of every one" of these rights in "all the amendments to the Constitution."

Olcott points to the laws against assault and battery, false imprisonment, mayhem, and murder as the white man's protection—"full and ample relief by due course of law"—against enslavement.

What abolitionists demand as naked justice is, that the benefit and protection of these just laws, be extended to all human beings alike, to the colored as well as the white...And that all mankind be allowed the same legal rights and protection without regard to color or other physical peculiarities. [The objective of abolitionism is] to abolish the laws, custom and practice of slavery, and restore the protection of the

---

"Petition of the American Anti-Slavery Society *re* Slavery in the District of Columbia," *The Emancipator*, December 16, 1834.

[3] The pamphlet was reprinted from the New York *Evening Post* with additions by the author signed by him under the pseudonym of "Wythe" (1838).

common law and all just statute laws to the slaves, thus making them to become free men with the whites, enjoying the same just, equal rights and privileges. It is to abrogate all unjust unequal laws and customs whatever, and restore the supremacy of all just and equal laws within the jurisdiction, over all persons alike....

The spirit of slavery leads to direct violations, [of the comity clause] in most of the states; and the practice itself will prevent its full operation.... Would anybody imagine [from the wording of the clause] that it was intended citizenship should depend on color! Or that free colored people were not intended to be as free (that is, to have as many "privileges and immunities") as other "citizens"? Or that if colored men are citizens, by the laws of one state, as some are, they are not to be "citizens," and have all the "privileges and immunities" of citizens, in every of the other states?

For these reasons, slavery violates the Constitution of the United States, but that instrument reserves jurisdiction over it and hence over its abolition to the states. In the District of Columbia and federal territories, however, "Congress has ... the undoubted legal right and duty, to abolish the crime...." Nor does the vested rights doctrine stand in the way: customary indulgence aggravates, it does not justify, sin. Finally, the due process clause of the Fifth Amendment does not stay the constitutional hand or interrupt the righteous duty of Congress.

The slaves (who are persons) have been deprived of liberty either with or without due process of law. If they have been thus deprived, then the law for their emancipation must also be "due process"; one law being as much "due process" as another. If they have not thus been deprived, there is an end to the objection of the want of "due process"; for the slaves having been deprived of liberty without due process are all free under the Constitution. And if it be further contended, that due process means writs and other judicial process, then I say, that as the slaves have never been deprived of liberty by such process, they are all free under the Constitution. And further I say, that by the words of this article, every slave in the U. S. is entitled to his freedom under the Constitution!⁴

---

⁴ Olcott also argued that "by emancipation, Congress will not take the slaves for 'public use'; and . . . as the Article expressly says 'just compensation,' we are not

Confining himself much more exclusively than Olcott to the question of the power of Congress to abolish slavery in the District of Columbia,[5] Stanton's argument is a direct and categorical counter-attack upon the main points of the Pickens-Pinckney doctrine—"compact," "violations of public faith," and vested property rights. The first two are negatived, he argued, by the terms in which the power over the District is granted to Congress; the third by the circumstance that, according to the laws of nature and "God's moral government," there can be no property in man.[6] Stanton's central thesis, however, was the protection of the laws, "a principle so self-evidently just, so necessary to the existence of human society in its most degraded forms, that even semi-barbarians acknowledge and act upon it." It was the absence of the protection of the laws which was the indispensable condition of slavery. The supplying of the protection of the laws would bring slavery to an immediate and absolute end.

Having robbed the slave of himself, and thus made him a thing, Congress is consistent in denying to him all the protection of the law as a man. His labor is coerced from him by laws of Congress: No bargain is made, no wage is given. His provender and covering are at the will of the owner. His domestic and social rights are as entirely disregarded in the eye of the law as if the Deity had never instituted the endearing relations of husband and wife, parent and child, brother and sister. There is not the shadow of legal protection for the family state

---

at liberty to suppose it applies to cases of unjust compensation, as all slave compensation clearly is . . ."

[5] Stanton argued that the Constitution expressly grants to Congress exclusive lawmaking power over the District of Columbia "in all cases whatsoever." With respect to the District, therefore, the question is whether a legislature with exclusive lawmaking power can abolish slavery. Stanton contended that it could because (1) the legislature had done so in Pennsylvania, Connecticut, Rhode Island, New Jersey, and New York; (2) the common law will not tolerate slavery and a legislature can adopt the common law; (3) slaves are made only by law and the legislature can repeal its own laws.

[6] In any event, property rights, as shown by statutes of limitation, laws regulating inheritance, and laws abolishing entail, are subject to legislative curtailment. Stanton also dealt with the Pickens-Pinckney just compensation argument: the just compensation clause "manifestly refers to the taking of individual property for governmental uses." Nothing like that is done in the case of abolition.

among the slaves of the District... neither is there any real protection for the limbs and lives of the slaves.... No slave can be a party before a judicial tribunal,... in any species of action against any person, no matter how atrocious may have been the injury received. He is not known to the law as a person: much less, a person having civil rights. The master may murder by system, with complete impunity, if he perpetrates his deeds only in the presence of colored persons! What think you as a legislator, sir, of such a system in the capital of the land of light and law, which boasts of equal rights, of trials by jury, of courts of justice, and whose Constitution says, "no person shall be deprived of life, liberty, or property without due process of law."

Congress should immediately restore to every slave, the ownership of his own body, mind and soul, transfer them from things without rights, to men with rights... The right of property, on the part of the master over the slave, should instantly cease. This being done... the slave should be legally protected in life and limb, in his earnings, his family and social relations, and his conscience. To give impartial legal protection in that District, to all its inhabitants would annihilate slavery. Give the slave then, equal legal protection with his master, and at its first approach slavery and the slavery trade flee in panic, as does darkness before the full-orbed sun.

Weld's fifty-seven-page monograph on *The Powers of Congress over Slavery in the District of Columbia* is a restatement and synthesis of the abolitionist constitutional theory as applied to the federal District. It is the work of an able mind—factual, closely reasoned, and free from sentimentality. In his argument Weld assumes that the power to legislate is limited by natural rights and natural law, and that, though the Constitution grants Congress "exclusive" law-making authority "in all cases whatsoever," the question still must be answered whether abolition is a power appropriate to legislation. He concludes that it is by the authority of many jurists, framers, and other writers and also by the fact that, in the Ordinance of 1787, Congress abolished slavery in the Northwest Territory, even freeing the slaves then held there, without compensation, and at a time when Congress, deriving its authority from the Articles of Confederation, had far less power than under the constitutional grant with respect to the District.[7]

In three succinct and powerful paragraphs Weld rephrases what was now the ark of the constitutional covenant for abolitionists: the protection of the laws.

The Preamble of the United States Constitution declares it to be a fundamental object of the organization of the government "to establish justice." Has Congress no power to do that for which it was made the depository of power? Cannot the United States Government fulfill the purpose for which it was brought into being?

To abolish slavery, is to take from no rightful owner his property; but to "establish justice" between two parties. To emancipate the slave, is "to establish justice" between him and his master—to throw around the person, character, conscience, liberty and domestic relations of the one, the same law that secures and blesses the other. In other words, to prevent by legal restraints one class of men from seizing upon another class, and robbing them at pleasure of their earnings, their time, their liberty, their kindred, and the very use and ownership of their own persons.

It has been already shown that allegiance is exacted of the slave. Is the government of the United States unable to grant protection where it exacts allegiance? It is an axiom of the civilized world, and a maxim even with savages, that allegiance and protection are reciprocal and correlative. Are principles powerless with us which exact homage of

---

[7] Weld also took the position that the power of Congress to abolish slavery in the District of Columbia followed "from the fact, that as the sole legislature there, it has unquestionable power to adopt the common law, as the legal system within its exclusive jurisdiction" and "the common law knows no slaves." "Congress may well be at home in common law legislation, for the common law is the grand element of the United States Constitution. All its fundamental provisions are instinct with its spirit; and its existence, principles, and paramount authority are presupposed and assumed throughout the whole. The Preamble of the Constitution plants the standards of the common law immovably in this foreground. 'We the people of the United States, in order to establish justice, etc. . . . do ordain'; thus proclaiming devotion to justice, as the controlling motive in the organization of the government, and its secure establishment the chief object of its aims. By this most solemn recognition, the common law, that grand legal embodiment of 'justice' and fundamental right was made the groundwork of the Constitution, and entrenched behind its strongest munitions. Clause 2 of Section 9 of Article I; section 4 of Article II and the last clause of section 2, Article III with Articles VII, VIII, IX, and XIII of the Amendments are also express recognitions of the common law as the presiding genius of the Constitution."

the Fourteenth Amendment

barbarians? Protection is the constitutional right of every human being under the exclusive legislation of Congress who has not forfeited it by crime.[8]

Weld deals next with the due process argument of Pickens and Pinckney by an adaptation of the dilemma contrived by Olcott. The seventh [i.e., fifth] of the amendments to the Constitution is alleged to withhold from Congress the power to abolish slavery in the District. "No person shall be deprived of life, liberty, or property, without due process of law." All the slaves in the District have been deprived of liberty by legislative acts. Now, these legislative acts depriving them of liberty were either due process of law or they were not. If they were, then a legislative act taking from the master that property which is the identical liberty previously taken from the slave, would be due process of law also, and of course a constitutional act; but if the legislative acts "depriving" them of liberty were not due process, then the slaves were deprived of liberty unconstitutionally, and these acts are void. In that case the Constitution emancipates them.

If the objector reply by saying that the import of the phrase "due process of law," is judicial process solely, it is granted, and that fact is our rejoinder; for no slave in the District has been deprived of his liberty by a judicial process, or, in other words, by due process of law; consequently, upon the objector's own admission, every slave in the District has been deprived of liberty unconstitutionally and is therefore free by the Constitution. This is asserted only of the slaves under the "exclusive legislation" of Congress.[9]

---

[8] Weld also contended that Congress derived power to abolish slavery in the District from its constitutional grant of power "to provide for the common defense and the general welfare."

[9] Weld turns his attention also to the Pickens-Pinckney just compensation argument: "Granting for argument's sake that slaves are 'private property,' and that to emancipate them, would be to 'take private property' for 'public use,' the objector admits the Power of Congress to do this, provided it will do something else, that is, pay for them. Thus, instead of denying the power, the objector not only admits but affirms it, as the ground of the inference that compensation must accompany it. So far from disproving the existence of one power, the objector asserts the existence of two—one, the power to take the slaves from masters, the other, the power to take the property of the United States to pay for them.

"If Congress cannot constitutionally impair the right of private property, or take it without compensation, it cannot constitutionally, legalize the perpetration of such acts, by others, nor protect those who commit them. . . . Congress not only impairs but annihilates the right of private property, while it withholds from the slaves of the District their title to themselves. What! Congress powerless to protect a man's right to himself, when it can make inviolable the right to a dog! But waiving this,

24   *The Antislavery Origins of*

These summaries and excerpts of the more important tracts of the antislavery movement[10] define a pattern of argument followed by many lesser speakers and pamphleteers. They make clear the constitutional consequences of abolitionist political action in the District of Columbia. In Stanton and Weld, especially, may be marked the adjustment of constitutional theory to the reoriented methods and aims of the movement. They show an immediate and pressing concern with questions of power, with the expediency and constitutionality of exercising governmental power to abolish slavery.

The words in which the Constitution vests power in Congress over the District of Columbia—"exclusive" law-making authority "in all cases whatsoever"—conferred on the abolitionists an apparent advantage. If taken literally and apart from other provisions of the Constitution, these words immediately dispose of all questions in favor of the power. Had the matter ended with an interpretation of these words standing alone, little of historical importance would have emerged from the discussion. The initial abolitionist advantage, however, turned out to be short-lived and insubstantial. It was sufficient to counteract the superficial and flimsy proslavery arguments about "compact" and "plighted public faith," but not much more. For both sides agreed that the power to legislate, however unqualified the constitutional grant, extended only to "appropriate subjects of legislation," that the power was curtailed by the extraconstitutional and unexpressed limitations of natural law and natural rights, and by the constitutional and ex-

---

I deny that the abolition of slavery in the District would violate this clause. What does the clause prohibit? The 'taking' of 'private property' for 'public use.' Suppose Congress could emancipate the slaves in the District, what would it 'take'? Nothing. What would it hold? Nothing. What would it put to public use? Nothing. Instead of 'taking private property,' Congress, by abolishing slavery, would say 'private property shall not be taken'; and those who have been robbed of it already, shall be kept out of it no longer; and since everyman's right to his own body is paramount, he shall be protected in it."

[10] For similar arguments see: William Slade, representative from Vermont, speeches of 1837 and 1840, *Cong. Globe*, 26th Cong., 1st sess., p. 129; Horace Mann, representative from Massachusetts, congressional speech of 1849, Horace Mann, *Slavery: Letters and Speeches* (Boston, 1851), p. 121.

the Fourteenth Amendment 25

pressed limitations in the amendments. The central issue thus lay in the effect of those limitations, expressed and unexpressed. The focal point of the first was the due process and just compensation clauses of the Fifth Amendment; of the second, the idea of the governmental obligation to supply protection.

In its implications and tendencies, the abolitionist due process argument amounted to this: slavery was created and could exist in the District only by positive enactment. The laws creating and sustaining it transcend the due process prohibition of the Constitution both because laws depriving men of their natural and inalienable right to liberty may not be passed at all (substantive due process) and because the deprivation was in fact accomplished without the requisite forms of jury trial and judicial process (procedural due process). The slave laws in the District of Columbia were therefore unconstitutional and void.

To this extent, following the lead of the Pickens-Pinckney doctrine, the abolitionists used the due process clause of the Fifth Amendment in both a procedural and substantive sense; and they used it, moreover, in defense of the human right of liberty and distinctly in opposition to the economic right of property claimed under it by the South. These, however, are implications and tendencies of the abolitionist due process argument, and not express avowals. Olcott and Weld do not particularly advance and rely upon a substantive conception of due process. Neither do they question or repudiate it in circumstances which called upon them to do so if they disagreed with it. They simply accept the position of Pickens-Pinckney that the clause contains certain absolute prohibitions. All they do is to maintain that, if this be so, the doctrine applies to liberty as well as to property. As stated by Weld and Olcott, accordingly, the abolitionist due process argument accepts and presupposes rather than asserts a substantive meaning. The antislavery origins of the Fourteenth Amendment, as revealed in the great constitutional debate over the power of Congress to abolish slavery in the District of Columbia, thus do not supply an unequivocal answer to the perennial question of constitutional historians and judges about the substantive nature of the due process clause; but they come close to doing so. They accept and presuppose the substantive meaning of due process expressly and avowedly relied upon by the Pickens-Pinckney argument.

The antislavery origins of the Fourteenth Amendment, as revealed by the District debate, do supply a firmly unequivocal answer to the even more important question of constitutional historians and judges about the substantive nature of the equal protection requirement. Both when conceived substantively and procedurely, the abolitionist due process argument was rebuttal in character and altogether negative in function. It was sufficient merely to prevent or nullify congressional laws creating and sustaining slavery. That would be enough, technically, to bring slavery to an end in the District. But broadly and forensically a more affirmative element was necessary, an element which would impose on Congress not merely a negative duty to refrain from acting but an affirmative duty to act. The abolitionists fully appreciated this need.

The affirmative element was supplied by the doctrine that it is the duty of the government to protect men in their natural rights by laws. That this element was a requirement both of the protection of the laws and of the *equal* protection of the laws is put beyond all doubt by the language quoted above from Olcott, Stanton, and Weld. Olcott would "restore the protection of the common law and all just statute laws to the slaves," for example, the laws against assault, battery, mayhem, and murder. This is a straightforward matter of the protection of the laws. But Olcott alternatively states his objective thus: "That the benefit and protection of these just laws be extended to all human beings *alike,* to the colored as well as the white . . . and that all mankind be allowed the *same* legal rights and protection without regard to color or other physical peculiarities." The protection of the laws has now become the equal protection of the laws.

the Fourteenth Amendment

Stanton follows an identical course. He first says that Congress denies slaves the protection of the laws in their rights as men. He next lists the rights of men which are not protected. He then says: "The slave should be legally protected in life and limb, in his earnings, his family, and social relations, and his conscience." So far, this is an unmixed plea for the protection of the laws. But since that protection is received by others, the same point can be made in another way. So Stanton continues or, just as accurately, repeats: "To give *impartial* legal protection in the District, to all its inhabitants, would annihilate slavery. Give the slave then, *equal* legal protection with his master, and at its first approach slavery and the slave trade flee in panic, as does darkness before the full-orbed sun." Could protection and equal protection be more interchangeably employed?

Weld, if anything, is even more explicit, certainly more concise. It is the duty of government, he says,

to throw around the person, character, conscience, liberty and domestic relations of the one, [class], the same law that secures and blesses the other. In other words, to prevent by legal restraints one class of men from seizing upon another class, and robbing them at pleasure of their earnings, their time, their liberty, their kindred, and the very use and ownership of their own persons.... to throw around ... the one, the *same* law that secures ... the other [is] in other words ... to prevent by legal restraints one class of men from seizing upon another class ...

Protection and equal protection are thus other words for the same thing. And so they are—once the obligation of government to supply protection is posited and once some persons are protected.

Olcott, Stanton, and Weld are explicit, too, about the particular rights which must receive the protection of government. Olcott flatly says that slaves "are totally deprived of every one of the rights" of "all of the amendments to the Constitution of the United States." This obviously is not intended strictly. The Tenth and the Twelfth amendments are not commonly thought to mention rights. And the rights to which Olcott particularly refers are the rights of conscience, speech, press, and trial by jury, not the total list of rights mentioned in the first eight amendments. To these four specifically identified rights, Olcott, by his emphasis on the fact that the ordinary laws of assault, battery, false imprisonment, mayhem, and murder do not apply to the slaves, adds the right of personal security. Later he also dwells on the right of petition and the due process clause of the Fifth Amendment.

Stanton is more expansive. His list includes the right to protection in life and limb; the right to self-ownership of one's body, mind, and soul; the right to one's earnings; the right to family and social relations; the right to conscience; the right to sue and be a party in court; the right to a jury trial; and the right not to be deprived of life, liberty, and property without due process of law.

According to Weld, the rights abrogated by slavery are the rights of person, character, conscience, earnings, self-ownership, liberty, domestic relations, and due or judicial process.

These are the natural rights of men which governments must protect and which slavery denies. They comprise not all the rights of the first eight amendments but a selected list of them together with some rights not mentioned in the amendments.

A number of highly significant propositions emerge from this debate in regard to the abolitionist idea of the equal protection of the laws:

1. Congress is under obligation to supply the protection of the laws to men in the District of Columbia. This duty is an unexpressed part of the Constitution. It is implicit in all governments, including constitutional governments; and certain words in the Preamble and elsewhere in the Constitution are evocative of it.

2. The protection is to be extended not only to citizens or those who stand in some peculiar relationship to the government. It extends to everyone within the jurisdiction, to all human beings, even to the lowly slave.

3. Since all men are equally entitled to the protection of the laws,

the Fourteenth Amendment

they are entitled to the equal protection of the laws. The full protection of the laws and the equal protection of the laws, in this context, are the same thing.

4. Governments alone are instituted to afford, and are capable of affording, the protection of the laws. Consequently, government denies the protection of the laws, the equal protection of the laws, when it withholds or fails to supply such protection. Denials of the protection or equal protection of the laws, accordingly, are most likely to occur because of the government's failure to act.

5. The rights which the government must protect are not the privileges and immunities of citizens. They are the rights of all men.

6. Nor are all these rights listed in the amendments. Some are listed; others are not.

7. They are natural rights. By virtue of that fact, the requirement of the protection or equal protection of the laws has a sweeping substantive meaning.

8. The meaning of the equal protection requirement which eighty years of Supreme Court decisions has made primary, namely, that it enjoins proper classification, never occurred to the abolitionists in this debate. The failure of protection, the unequal protection in the case of slavery, was so gross that refinements of this sort were irrelevant.

Finally, since the debate was over the powers of Congress with respect to the District of Columbia and did not relate particularly to citizenship, neither federalism nor the comity clause (United States Constitution, Art. IV, sec. 2) were at stake, though Olcott did mention that slavery and the comity clause were in spiritual conflict. The abolitionists therefore freely acknowledged that Congress could not abolish slavery in the states.

The battle that raged over the constitutional power of Congress with respect to slavery in the District of Columbia brought home the tremendous impact of the great slavery struggle upon our fundamental law, its constitutionally productive and creative force in our history, and the striking circumstance that, however crucial the constitutional points of difference between proslavery and antislavery men, the area of agreement was preponderant. Both sides agreed that governments were instituted among men to safeguard and protect their natural and inalienable rights. Both sides agreed that any governmental denial of those rights, any deprivation of life, liberty, or property without due process of law, any negation of the great objects specified in the Preamble or failure to sustain and promote them would be not only "impolitic" but unconstitutional, "repugnant to the principles of natural justice and of the social compact," and "totally subversive of all the purposes for which the government is instituted." "The Union was formed . . . for the perfect and equal protection of the rights and interests of all" persons—Pinckney said citizens—and "the common and equal benefit of all the states." The theory of both sides was dominantly defensive in character because of the part played by the due process prohibition and the natural rights doctrine. But both sides claimed something more than governmental abstinence and restraint; both claimed for persons the right to the protection for which governments were created, the obligation of the federal government to "sustain and promote the great objects of the Preamble," and to do these things "perfectly and equally for all." The South attempted to resolve the difficulty of asserting an absolute prohibition on the power of government to touch the "peculiar institution" simultaneously with a duty on the part of government to sustain and support it, by ignoring the difficulty and claiming both prohibition and duty. This was a difficulty that the abolitionists, speaking of liberty, were soon to meet in exactly the same way.

That the protagonists relied on the same doctrine as to the nature of society, the same theory of government, the same constitutional clauses and concepts to achieve their opposite ends, merely put the greatest constitutional struggle in the history of our country in the same class with many a lesser one. It emphasized, too, how largely

the Fourteenth Amendment

the constitutional struggle was a battle of premise. Once the constitutional starting point on either side was accepted, almost all else followed automatically. If slaves were things, chattels, property, then the purpose of government, the right to protection, the idea of equality, the due process and just compensation clauses of the Fifth Amendment—all were applicable to their owners as citizens or as persons and were designed to continue the servitude by safeguarding ownership. If the slaves were human beings, individuals with minds and souls, persons, then the just compensation clause was wholly irrelevant to the forcible termination of their slavery; their liberty was protected by the due process clause; and they were in the class of persons whose equal need for protection and equal possession of inalienable rights gave rise to government.

CHAPTER II

The Fugitive Slave Law

CONSTITUTIONAL developments in the District of Columbia did not stand alone. Development of abolitionist theory of constitutional power was occurring simultaneously in connection with the Fugitive Slave Act of 1793. This single act of Congress raised all the crucial issues which underlay the abolitionist movement. It did so, moreover, in a way that permitted the abolitionists to present those issues for settlement. The Fugitive Slave Act, by denying him protection in his status as a freeman, placed at stake the most basic of the rights of the free Negro—his freedom. It placed at stake, too, a basic right of the slaveowner—his right of ownership. Finally, it placed at stake the far-reaching constitutional issues of the scope of the powers of Congress, the distribution of powers as between the state and the nation, and the power of enforcement of constitutional injunctions and prohibitions.

Since the escaped or free Negro was physically present in the North, all these issues were raised and could be settled in the North, where abolitionist freedom of maneuver and instruments of action could not be frustrated by the South. The abolitionists could and did: (1) seek the repeal of the act by Congress, (2) challenge the constitutionality of the act in the courts, (3) insist on the right of the states to supplement the act by providing safeguards for the rights of free Negroes, and (4) withhold active participation in the enforcement of the act, if not actively conspire to defeat its execution.

The Fugitive Slave Act of 1793, though it mentioned neither Negro nor white but only "person," was designed by Congress to implement the fugitive slave clause of the Constitution forbidding the free states to discharge escapees from any obligation of service or labor existing under the laws of other states. The purpose of the act was plainly to facilitate the reclaiming of fugitive slaves, that is, Negroes seeking to escape their bondage by flight into or through free states. The act authorized the slaveowner or his agent personally and without warrant to recapture such persons wherever found. Only after the seizure was the owner or agent required to seek official sanction, and then by resorting to "any judge of the circuit or district courts of the United States residing or being within the state, or . . . any magistrate of a county, city, or town corporate, wherein such seizure or arrest shall be made." "Upon proof, to the satisfaction of such judge or magistrate, either by oral testimony or affidavit," of ownership, "it shall be the duty of such judge or magistrate to give a certificate thereof" to the claimant "which shall be sufficient warrant for removing" the Negro to the state of the owner. There was no provision for compulsory attendance of witnesses for the Negro; no obligation on the part of the judge or magistrate to investigate or assign counsel; and the vital issues of identity, slavery, escape, were finally determinable by the judge or magistrate, usually the local justice of the peace, without a jury.

The possibilities of abuse of power under this drastic statute, highly geared to the reception and restoration of property and not to the safeguarding of the rights of freemen, are now and were then readily apparent. The seizure of free Negroes, especially in the border states, who were unable in these circumstances to establish their freedom and who were hurried off into perpetual bondage under the forms of law, was a frequent occurrence if not a systematic business.

Elizur Wright's *Chronicles of Kidnapping,* published in the spring of 1834 and describing the operation of the Fugitive Slave Act in New York City, was the first and a sensational attack upon the law by the American Anti-Slavery Society. Wright denominated such proceedings "man-stealing," and applied the epithet "kidnapping" not merely to the seizure of the free but to the recapture of slaves whose escape had been made good for some time, and even to those taken in fresh pursuit. He maintained that the slaveholder had no more right to retake the slave who had achieved his freedom by flight than to commit the original act of enslavement. The *Chronicles,* though rigidly factual and untheoretical, doubtless had a tendency to inspire resistance to the law if they were not deliberately designed to "kindle an irregular and factious opposition against them," as critics of the movement asserted.[1]

The program of political action against the Fugitive Slave Act, begun before the sealing off of the South, represented the middle ground between two opposing theories of the movement. On the one hand, the most voluble, insistent, and strident demand of the abolitionists was for the protection of the laws. This demand was built on the obligation of mobs and individuals alike to submit themselves to the duly established provisions of the law and the duty of officers to enforce it against dissenters. On the other hand, there were inherently anarchical and socially disorganizing tendencies in the resistance of abolitionists to the slave laws, particularly the Fugitive Slave Act. This tendency was given virtually explicit statement in the Declaration of Sentiments of the American Anti-Slavery Society in December, 1833.[2] "All those laws," says the

---
[1] *The Emancipator,* March 24, 1835.
[2] American Anti-Slavery Society, New York, 1835.

declaration, "which are now in force, admitting the right of slavery, are, therefore, before God, utterly null and void."

The sharp and opprobrious criticism to which this extreme doctrine rendered abolitionists liable, much more than concern about its logical conflict with their claims for legal protection, drove the leaders of the movement to reconsider their position and tone down their statements.[3] Speaking through William Goodell, then editor of *The Emancipator,* they answered these criticisms at length, first, by cutting down the nullification doctrine to mean merely that individuals were not obliged to give "active obedience" but only "patient submission" to unjust laws, and second, by espousing the principle that individuals are bound to protest against wicked laws and labor for their repeal. The American Society did not intend to confine its efforts, said Goodell, "to mere moral suasion in such a sense as to exclude political action. . . . There is no principle of the Anti-Slavery Society that leads to the great moral error of discarding political action."[4]

Down to the time when the Fugitive Slave Act was wiped off the books during the Civil War, the abolitionists used both methods—individual nullification and political action, resistance and repeal. Nullification was in the ascendancy after the Supreme

---

[3] This criticism came not only from proslavery forces, colonizationists, and conservatives generally. Gerrit Smith, then on the verge of embracing abolitionism, reprobated this official stand of the American Society in the sharpest terms. In a series of articles published in *The Emancipator* and widely discussed in the movement, Smith described the stand as "the highest toned nullification" he had ever met with and as tending "to generate or justify a disorganizing spirit, and a contempt for that profound respect for the authority of human laws, in which the fabric of civil society is founded and by which it is ever after maintained." Once admit the doctrine, he argued, and "there is no longer any binding authority in human government and human laws. This doctrine not only clothes every individual with the highest judicial power of the land, by making him the final and conclusive interpreter of the laws; but even the legislature is a farce—a mere nullity—before the paramount and supreme authority, which this doctrine claims for his whims and conceits." The alternative view which Smith held out to the American Society was that the individual is bound to protest against wicked laws and labor for their repeal, but meanwhile to obey them. "As a citizen, and especially as one of the co-sovereigns of this Republican Nation," he said, "her unjust laws devolve a responsibility on me, of which I cannot rid myself by merely turning my back on them and pronouncing them 'null and void.' " *The Emancipator,* March 24, 1835.
[4] *Ibid.*

Court sided with slavery in the Prigg case[5] and after the Fugitive Slave Act was reënacted by Congress in the Compromise of 1850. Between these two methods lay the possibility of inducing the courts to invalidate the Fugitive Slave Act and the state legislatures to supplement it. Such efforts unavoidably raised constitutional questions and prompted constitutional arguments.

The fugitive slave clause itself contains no grant of power to Congress or to any other department of the federal government. Nor does it make any reservation of enforcement authority to the states. It simply forbids certain state action—that discharging escapees from their obligation to labor—and requires that they "shall ... be delivered up." Since Article I contains no grant of power

---

[5] *Prigg* v. *Pennsylvania* (1842), 16 Peters 539. Read, for example, this striking language in the Liberty party platform for 1843: *"Whereas,* the Constitution of these United States is a series of agreements, covenants, or contracts between the people of the United States, each with all and all with each; and

"Whereas, It is a principle of universal morality that the moral laws of the Creator are paramount to all human laws: or, in the language of an Apostle, that 'we ought to obey God rather than men'; and

"Whereas, The principle of common law, that any contract, covenant, or agreement to do an act derogatory to natural rights is vitiated and annulled by its inherent immorality, has been recognized by one of the justices of the Supreme Court of the United States, who in a recent case expressly holds that any 'contract that rests upon such a basis is void'; and

"Whereas, The third clause of the second section of the fourth article of the Constitution of the United States, when construed as providing for the surrender of a fugitive slave, does 'rest upon such a basis' in that it is a contract to rob a man of a natural right, namely, his natural right to his own liberty, and is, therefore, absolutely void; therefore

"Resolved, That we hereby give it to be distinctly understood by this nation and the world that, as Abolitionists, considering that the strength of our cause lies in its righteousness, and our hope for it in our conformity to the laws of God and our respect for the rights of man, we owe it to the Sovereign Ruler of the universe, as a proof of our allegiance to him in all our civil relations and offices, whether as private citizens or as public functionaries sworn to support the Constitution of the United States, to regard and to treat the third clause of the fourth article of that instrument, whenever applied to the case of a fugitive slave, as utterly null and void, and consequently as forming no part of the Constitution of the United States, whenever we are called upon or sworn to support it." Edward Stanwood, *History of the Presidency* (Cambridge, Mass., 1906), p. 219.

See also Lysander Spooner, *The Unconstitutionality of Slavery* (Boston, 1845); Joel Tiffany, *A Treatise on the Unconstitutionality of Slavery* (Cleveland, Ohio, 1849); Joshua Giddings, *Speeches in Congress* (Boston, 1853), pp. 335, 338, 346, 394, 398, 399, 434. The view that Seward's higher law doctrine popularized in the 'fifties was a new kind of moral appeal "quite unlike that of Garrison, Weld, and the other Abolitionists" (see Avery Craven, *The Coming of the Civil War* [1942], pp. 339–340) is not sustained by a comparison of Seward's formulation and the statements of abolitionists as early as the middle 'thirties.

to Congress on this subject, supporters of the Fugitive Slave Act were forced to maintain that Congress was the guardian of the limitations of the Constitution and under a duty to carry out its prohibitions against the states by affirmative and not merely corrective legislation. This thoroughly nationalistic doctrine, the abolitionist movement—which in all its other basic trends and implications was thoroughly nationalistic—was forced to repudiate in its attack upon the fugitive slave law. It turned instead to the Tenth Amendment and beyond that to the limitation in the due process clause of the Fifth Amendment and the common law provision of the Seventh Amendment.

Two of the earliest and most important arguments amplifying and illustrating these points were made by Salmon P. Chase and Senator Francis James.[6] The two arguments were neatly complementary. In seeking, by action in the Ohio courts, to free the colored woman Matilda who had been seized as a fugitive slave, Chase struck at the constitutional foundations of the Fugitive Slave Act.[7] Senator James, by sponsoring in the Pennsylvania legislature a state statute granting alleged fugitives the right of jury trial, contended for the power and duty of the state to supplement the federal act and thereby bring it into conformity with the Constitution.[8]

---

[6] The argument elaborated and refined by Chase in the Matilda case appeared two and a half years earlier in summary form in *The Emancipator*. In an article, presumably by Goodell, entitled "Constitution of the U. S. vs. Slavery," which appeared in the issue for November 4, 1834, the author argued that the Fugitive Slave Act of 1793 was unconstitutional. Nowhere among powers given to Congress was there a power to enforce the fugitive slave clause. In the absence of such grant the Tenth Amendment reserved enforcement to the states. Congress had no more power to enforce the fugitive slave clause than the comity clause, which appears in the same article of the Constitution. Moreover, the Fugitive Slave Act was unconstitutional because it denied the guarantees of jury trial and due process clause of the Fifth Amendment. The author attributes this argument to Robert Sedgwick in the case of *Jack* v. *Martin* before the New York Supreme Court.

Another approach taken by the abolitionists to the Fugitive Slave Clause was to deny that it had reference to such "service or labor" as was wrung from slaves. It applied rather "to free labor and hired services." Address of New England Anti-Slavery Society, *The Emancipator*, September 30, 1834.

[7] *Speech in the Case of the Colored Woman Matilda Who Was Brought before the Court of Common Pleas of Hamilton County, Ohio, by Writ of Habeas Corpus March 11, 1837* (Cincinnati, 1837).

[8] Published in part in the *Anti-Slavery Record*, August, 1837.

Chase stressed the federal character of our governmental system and argued that not by any granted power, and therefore not by the necessary and proper clause, was Congress authorized to enforce the fugitive slave provision of the Constitution. That provision was merely an article of agreement, enjoining the state in these particulars, but conferring no power on any government or officer, state or national. Congress thus acted without constitutional authority; but more than that, it transcended specific constitutional limitations. It blanketed in all justices of the peace and other magistrates thus violating Article II, section 2; it conferred federal judicial power on state officers, which cannot be done constitutionally;[9] it transgressed the Fourth and Fifth amendments.

The act... provides that persons may be deprived of their liberty without due process of law.[10] ... It provides no process for their apprehension; none for their detention; none for the final delivery of the escaping servant. Everything is to be done by the claimant. He is to arrest the fugitive, or the person whom he may take to be a fugitive;

---

[9] See also Lysander Spooner, *A Defense for Fugitive Slaves against the Acts of February 12, 1793, and September 18, 1850* (Boston, 1850); "Defence of Fugitive Slaves," *Chronotype*, December 4, 1850.

[10] Similarly, James G. Birney, in a letter to Joshua Leavitt and others, January 10, 1842 (Dwight L. Dumond, *Birney Letters* [1938], pp. 646–647), argues: "We forbid the free states from treating as free, men, women, children, flying from bonds, and seeking refuge within their limits; we enjoin the authorities to deliver them up afresh to their pursuers; we authorize any one claiming another as his slave to haul him before a Justice of the Peace; it may be one of his own choosing, and to have the case decided on affidavits, and on ex parte testimony of his own procuring. This we do, and our fellow creatures, dwelling among us in peace, fearing no harm, are precipitated—often within the compass of a few minutes—from their fire-sides and families, into the horrible gulf of slavery. This we do, without the intervention of a jury, although the Constitution provides that, 'in suits at common law, where the value in controversy shall exceed twenty dollars, the trial by jury shall be preserved,' and 'that no persons shall be deprived of life, liberty, or property, without due process of law.'—All this we do converting the free States into hunting grounds for human prey, and attempt to cover it from the world and even from ourselves, by calling the slave, a 'person held to service under laws,' and the slave catcher, 'the party to whom such service is due.'"
See also Horace Mann, "Letter to Editors of Boston *Atlas*, June 6, 1850," in his *Slavery: Letters and Speeches* (Boston, 1851), p. 307; "Speech in House of Representatives, February 28, 1851, on Fugitive Slave Law," *Cong. Globe*, 31st Cong., 2d sess., Appendix X96, pp. 237–249; "Resolution Passed by a Meeting in Faneuil Hall, October 15, 1850," published in *Chronotype*, October 15, 1850; "Speech of the Honorable Charles Allen at City Hall, Worcester, Massachusetts, November 5, 1850," *Chronotype*, November 9, 1850; Editorial, *Chronotype*, November 26, 1850; Letter from Joshua Quincy to J. Ingersoll, Esq., October 15, 1850.

the Fourteenth Amendment

he is to bring him before the magistrate; he is to keep him in custody while the magistrate examines the evidence of his claims; he is to remove him when the certificate is granted. From beginning to end of the proceeding, there is nothing like legal process ... the act then is palpably repugnant to the very letter, as well as the whole spirit of the Constitution.... [The act,] exposing, as it does, every member of the community to arrest, confinement and forcible transportation without process of law, by every other man who may claim him as a fugitive from service, is repugnant to the first principles of civil liberty and subversive of the very ends of society.... There is such a thing as natural rights, derived, not from any constitution or civil code, but from the constitution of human nature and the code of Heaven, ... the same in all ages, ... and destined to no change, proclaimed by our fathers in the Declaration of Independence to be self-evident, and reiterated in our state constitution as its fundamental axiom, that all men are born equally free.[11]

James covered the same range of constitutional argument even more explicitly and succinctly. After adverting to the federal division of powers and then to the Fourth Amendment, he says:

It [the act of 1793] is contrary to the principles of the compact—contrary to the rights reserved to the states—contrary to the whole Constitution both in letter and spirit. Shall it be said, that, in this great charter of our liberties, which throws its protecting shield over him who stands charged with having violated the laws of his country in the commission of crime, there cannot be found at least equal protection for the man who is acknowledgedly free from moral guilt, and to whom moral wrong is not imputed ...

The issue between the claimant and the claimed, is of a mixed character. On the part of the person claimed, his natural rights are involved in the issue; whilst on the part of the party claimant, the question involved is one of property alone. The liberty of the party claimed being on his part the matter in issue, the Constitution comes directly to his aid, in his application for a jury trial: for it declares, in the Fifth Article of Amendments that "no person shall be deprived of life, liberty, or property without due process of law."

[11] See also Chase's argument in *James G. Birney* v. *State of Ohio* (December term, 1837), 8 Ohio Reps. 231, another phase of the Matilda case.

Now, will any man, having due respect for the reputation of his own opinions, venture to affirm, that the unceremonious mode pointed out by the act of Congress, of settling the question between the parties in issue . . . can be denominated "due process of law," in the sense intended by the Amendment? There is no way known to the law of this state, whereby a man can be ultimately deprived of life, liberty, or property, but by the verdict of a jury; and no process to deprive him of either, without the intervention of a jury, can be denominated "due process of law," within the meaning of the Constitution.[12]

To imaginative abolitionist thinkers like Alvan Stewart, as we shall see, the due process clause was a grant of power. It extended the legislative and judicial protection of the nation to those who had been deprived of their liberty within and by the states contrary to its requirements. But while the clause bestowed with one hand, it took away with the other. It was at the same time a grant of federal power and a limitation upon that power. When Congress legislated in the interests of slaveholders under the fugitive slave clause of the Constitution, the abolitionists insisted on the doctrines in other respects claimed by the South: namely, that Congress transcended both the ban of the Fifth Amendment and the constitutional division of powers in the federal system. It was not the business of Congress to enforce the constitutional restraints on state action; and even if it were, Congress could do so only in conformance with the limitations on its own power embodied in the amendments.

States' rights was now the cry of abolitionism. When Congress legislated in defiance of procedural requirements of the due process clause, it remained for the states either to withhold compliance or to supply the deficiencies of the federal policy. Jury trial was the most prominent of those requirements, and no arrest without war-

---

[12] For other arguments on the jury trial denial of the Fugitive Slave Act see Spooner, *op. cit.;* "Speech of the Honorable Charles Allen at City Hall, Worcester, Massachusetts, November 5, 1850," *Chronotype,* November 9, 1850; "Speech of Mr. Farley at Faneuil Hall," *Chronotype,* November 15, 1850; Editorial, *Chronotype,* November 26, 1850; Letter from Joshua Quincy to J. Ingersoll, Esq., October 15, 1850; Manchester meeting, November 6, reported in *Chronotype* November 12, 1850.

the Fourteenth Amendment

rant only less so.[13] These the states must institute if the equal protection of the laws was to be provided. The equal protection to all which is the assurance of effectual protection to any was to be provided, and the practice of kidnaping free Negroes and selling them into slavery was to be reduced by supplying to the alleged fugitive the jury trial of the issue of his slavery guaranteed by the due process clause. So, once again, the ideas of equal protection and due process of law, together with man's natural and inalienable rights, are found in combination, supplementing and amplifying each other, providing between them the source and duty of affirmative authority and prescribing the character of its exercise, serving in the hands of the abolitionists the cause of free men marked out by the community for separate treatment.

---

[13] New Jersey passed a law authorizing the justices of inferior courts to issue warrants for the arrest of fugitive slaves on application of the owner. Chase reports in his speech in the Matilda case that the question of the constitutionality of this act came before the Supreme Court of New Jersey and that "the Chief Justice and Justice Ryerson a majority of the court, expressed strong inclination to view the federal act as unconstitutional." The case was apparently argued in behalf of the Negro by F. T. Freylinghuysen of New Jersey. Before the decision of *Prigg* v. *Pennsylvania* in 1842, Connecticut, Massachusetts, New York, Vermont, and Pennsylvania attempted to prevent kidnapping by requiring the claimant to obtain a warrant for the arrest of the fugitive or by requiring jury trial. Dwight L. Dumond, *Anti-Slavery Origins of the Civil War* (1939).

CHAPTER III

The Power and Duty of Congress

IT WAS hardly conceivable that so dynamic a movement led by men who breasted the wrath of the mob and put at hazard life and fortune in a humanitarian crusade would easily or long be confined by iron curtains or universally accepted constitutional dogmas. The rights of abolitionists in the North must be vindicated. The free Negroes must be elevated legally, morally, educationally. The appendages of slavery that reached out into the North must be amputated. The hated institution must be uprooted in the national capital. But abolitionists would not be satisfied with these peripheral and symbolic attacks. They would never be satisfied until abolitionism should "burst in thunders over the whole South, pouring forth a flood of light, truth . . . conviction"—and *compulsive legislation*. They would not rest until they had wiped out slavery where it lived and flourished, until the institution itself was everywhere dead.

Fourteenth Amendment

This could be done, the Constitution could be brought into complete adjustment with the politically reoriented approach, the inescapable nationalistic implications of the movement could be fully realized only if the final step were taken: only if the national power to achieve the objective everywhere in the country was avowed and established over the barrier of states' rights and the federal system.

It was the special contribution of Alvan Stewart—leader of the New York State Anti-Slavery Society, early antislavery recruit from the temperance cause, successful Utica lawyer, yet a radical and an innovator—to assert and give plausibility to this very proposition: that the federal courts and the federal Congress possessed constitutional power and were under a constitutional duty to move against slavery everywhere in the nation, not only in the District of Columbia and the federal territories but in the states as well. In an argument characterized, on the one hand, by bold imagination and, on the other hand, by an illuminating disregard for historical fact, Stewart built his constitutional case for this radical proposition solely on the due process clause of the Fifth Amendment, converting that apparent prohibition on power into a source of authority.

Stewart marked out the constitutional logic of the new alternative in a speech before the New York Anti-Slavery Society in September, 1837. It was published in October of that year in *The Friend of Man* and widely discussed throughout the movement. It was too radical a departure to be adopted officially, but its influence on the whole crusade was remarkable. From that time forward, though they did not endorse Stewart's method, abolitionists ceased to doubt that the power of the national government could constitutionally be used, in one way or another, to bring an end to slavery throughout the land. The revolution in federalism was thus launched.

The principal propositions of Stewart's original and provocative work were these:

1. The word "person" in the Fifth Amendment "covers the whole

ground of our humanity, and means everybody," "every human being in the Union, black or white, bond or free...." The word "person" is used to designate slaves elsewhere in the Constitution: "No Person held to Service" (fugitive slave clause); "three fifths of all other persons" (apportionment of representatives clause). The same word in the amendment, used without qualification or exception, must certainly include the slaves whom elsewhere it was designed to reach exclusively.

2. "The true and only meaning of the phrase 'due process of law,' "—"almost an extract, in words and spirit, from Magna Charta"—"is an indictment or presentment by a grand jury, of not less than twelve, nor more than twenty-three men; a trial by a petit jury of twelve men, and a judgment pronounced on the findings of that jury, by a court" (citing Story and Coke.)

3. "Man was not a slave justly, when made so by all the forms of our national Constitution. Rank injustice lies at the bottom of the principle, even when [the] slave had had the benefit of all the forms prepared by that Constitution for his defense."

4. The due process clause was placed in the Constitution by the convention which framed it as the indispensable concession of the South in the great compromise upon slavery. The North agreed "to kidnap the escaped slave for the benefit of the slaveholder by the fugitive slave clause," "to share the legislative power over the District of Columbia and territories with the South where slaves might be," and "to go and pour [its] blood out in suppression of a slave insurrection." The *quid pro quo* of the South was that the Constitution should establish the terms upon which slavery might exist, namely, only after full satisfaction of the formal requirements of indictment, trial, and judgment. These were the "great constitutional earmarks," "the infallible tests" which would constitute and identify a man a slave, and their absence was "proof positive, at least a constitutional presumption," that slavery did not exist. "Thus the great and difficult question was arranged in the formation of the Constitution."

the Fourteenth Amendment

5. "There is not a slave at this moment in the United States upon the terms mutually agreed upon by the people of this country, at the formation of the Constitution." Consequently, "any judge in the United States, who is clothed with sufficient authority, to grant a writ of habeas corpus, and decide upon a return made upon such a writ; on the master and slave being brought before said judge, to inquire by what authority, he, the master, held the slave; if the master could not produce a record of conviction, by which the particular slave had been deprived of his liberty, by indictment, trial, and judgment at court, the judge would be obliged under the oath which he must have taken, to obey the constitution of his country, to discharge the slave and give his full liberty."

6. Moreover, Congress has power to abolish slavery throughout the nation. It could do so simply by passing a declaratory statute carrying into effect the spirit and intention of the Fifth Amendment.

Story is quoted for the proposition that:

If there be any general principle which is inherent in the very definition of Government, and essential to every step of the progress to be made by that of the United States, it is, that every power vested in the Government, is in its nature sovereign, and included by the force of the term, a right to employ all the means requisite and forcibly applicable to the attainment of the end of such power, unless they are excepted in the Constitution, or are immoral, or are contrary to the essential objects of political society.

Stewart then continues on his own:

The Constitution, having taken up, staked out and defined the great landmarks of personal liberty; and having placed each individual, or "person" of this Republic in a condition to enjoy the full benefit of a Jury trial before a Court—proceeding upon the principles of the common law, before liberty can be taken away, can it be tolerated, that States and individuals of slave States by the boldest tyranny, shall seize upon and defraud 2,500,000 of American citizens of their liberty, and convert them into abject slaves, in the face of their own high and solemn constitutional barriers, which was made paramount to all State Constitutions, laws, usages, judicial or legislative?

Stewart's speech is at once thoroughly characteristic and very exceptional. It portrays at its typical best and worst the inventive process (interpretation is far too dull a word) by which the leaders of abolitionism read a revolution into the Constitution. The whole system of power relations between the states and the federal government was to be rearranged and redistributed by a simple declaratory statement of what always had been true, as if no change were being made. An institution, deep-rooted in the economic, social, and political fabric of a large segment of the nation and of the national government itself, recognized, tolerated, given a place in the Constitution by the Founding Fathers of the Republic, was to be uprooted, struck out of constitutional existence, "not as a new principle, but as an old one..."

The "supporting" historical data were striking: the Fifth Amendment assumed to have been drafted in the Constitutional Convention; the due process clause specifically introduced as the most important element in the compromise over slavery! Not a case cited or a Father quoted—the whole argument *a priori*, hypothetical, suppositional. True, Madison's *Notes* had not yet been published.[1] Knowledge of the Constitutional Convention depended upon such meager sources as the *Journal*, published in 1819, and such fragments as Luther Martin's Report. The basic historical facts, however, were known. They were simply irrelevant. The abolitionists were not concerned with historic meanings or precedents in the sense that scholars are, even if they were aware of them, which they generally were not. What matter that the Fifth Amendment was added later as a part of the Bill of Rights, that, just four years before the Supreme Court had declared it binding

---

[1] In his argument before the Supreme Court of New Jersey in the cases of *State* v. *VanBeuren* and *State* v. *Post* (1845), 20 N.J. Law 368, several years after the publication of Madison's *Notes*, Alvan Stewart showed that he had read them with care, but this did not in any way change his due process argument.

the Fourteenth Amendment 47

only on the federal government, that slaveholders could hardly have been expected to have shown enthusiasm in 1787 for a rule or standard which prescribed a sort of inquest in office found or an elaborate judicial certification system for every slave in the country? These were mere facts, hardly to be regarded as refutations of the great moral, political, constitutional truths being asserted.

Once all this is understood, the argument is hearty fare indeed. Parts of it are hurriedly and loosely written, but the summary paragraphs, both in the argument itself and in the resolutions, are well done, the more so because of the spareness of constitutional interpretation up to this time. The emphasis on the inclusiveness of "person" is strongly laid; the values to be derived from invoking purely procedural safeguards are clearly shown; the case for freedom by judicial decision and congressional action, using due process in combination with the "necessary and proper" and supremacy clauses, are ably articulated, though the leap from prohibition in the amendment to power in the "necessary and proper" clause was too easily made. Once slaves are regarded as persons, the rights traditionally associated with due process may easily be employed to expose the wrong and even the unconstitutionality of slavery, for the legal provisions and presumptions that established and bolstered the slave status unquestionably denied and foreclosed procedural rights. Slaves were persons; persons were entitled to due process; due process required judicial proceedings as a prerequisite to deprivation of liberty; slaves had had no such proceedings; ergo, they had been deprived of their liberty without due process of law. Being constitutionally free, it naturally was the business of the courts to declare them so whenever the question was properly raised. Since the instances were numerous and of a nature not easily remediable by individual action, and Congress as well as the courts were under a duty to carry out the provisions of the Constitution, Congress should pass a declaratory statute "imparting the blessings contained within its [the Constitution's] mighty folds."

To sum up, Stewart (1) built his argument entirely on the due process clause of the Fifth Amendment—this is unique; (2) demonstrated the antagonism between the historic elements of due process and the slave status as such; (3) consequently, showed the great advantages of exploiting the constitutional reference to slaves as persons rather than as property; and (4) openly avowed the power and duty of the federal courts and of Congress to move against slavery everywhere in the nation. In the Revolutionary period and again soon after the adoption of the Constitution, early abolitionists had claimed this power for Congress.[2] In the present movement, N. P. Rogers and others had vaguely implied or silently assumed it. But Alvan Stewart distinctly and expressly asserted it and produced a constitutional argument for its existence.

In the years that followed, a small but important band of radical extremists of the abolitionist movement took up, elaborated, and expanded the constitutional doctrine of Stewart. This wing boasted such leaders as Gerrit Smith, William Goodell, George Mellen, Lysander Spooner, Joel Tiffany, and eventually James G. Birney. They produced a series of tracts and arguments which were widely distributed throughout the abolitionist movement and, it must be added, also widely controverted. In these works the central thesis of Stewart—that Congress possessed constitutional power and even was under a constitutional duty to abolish slavery in the states by

---

[2] Antislaveryism in America in the early period was directed to abolishing or minimizing the effects of slavery in the states by state rather than national action. Although, in 1776, the Continental Congress had suppressed the slave trade, the unrestrained power of revolutionary government was not at this time generally invoked in behalf of the slave. There were important exceptions, however, in which the direct intervention of the national government was advocated. See Samuel Hopkins, "Dialogue concerning Slavery," *Works* (1776), Vol. 2, p. 576; and "A Farmer," *Serious Address to the Rulers of America* (1783). After the adoption of the Constitution came two famous appeals for national action—that of the Pennsylvania Abolition Society in 1790, relying upon the Preamble for federal power, and that of Absalom Jones and other free Negroes of Philadelphia in 1799. The latter, too, relied upon the Preamble as the source of congressional power and asserted the claims of slaves as citizens to "equal and national liberties."

In 1806, the Quaker, John Parrish, published a book, *Remarks on the Slavery of the Black People,* asserting the power of Congress to abolish slavery and basing it on the Declaration of Independence and the Preamble to the Constitution. Parrish also contended that the slaves were set free by the Declaration of Independence and that the Declaration constitutes "the leading principles of the constitution."

the Fourteenth Amendment 49

direct action—was maintained intact.[3] The constitutional support, however, was not so rigorously confined to the Fifth Amendment.[4]

Spooner[5] and Tiffany,[6] besides the citizenship point discussed later, lodged their constitutional argument primarily in the "We the people" clause of the Preamble and the habeas corpus and republican form of government guarantees. Into these two guarantees, especially the latter, they loaded the whole array of natural rights, and of these the federal government was the guarantor.

In the theory of Tiffany and Spooner the constitutional prohibition against the suspension of the privilege of the writ of habeas corpus did not suffer from the limitations of the national citizenship argument. It was universal in sweep: the Constitution forbids the denial of the writ without discrimination of persons and hence "the privilege is not confined to citizens but extends to all human beings." The object of the writ was "to secure to all persons their natural right to personal liberty," and consequently by its very nature it denied the right of property in man, applied equally to restraint by private individuals and government officials, and "is of itself sufficient to make slavery impossible and illegal." While this provision was in form a procedural safeguard merely, it was in fact an unqualified guarantee of a substantive and absolute right, for "the writ itself is based upon the hypothesis that all men have a natural inherent right to liberty—and ... it was one of the professed objects of the Constitution to secure the blessings of liberty

---

[3] Gerrit Smith introduced a resolution to this effect for a minority of the business committee at the Buffalo convention of the Liberty party, October, 1847. S. P. Chase was mainly responsible for its failure to be adopted. This was the position taken by the Liberty League in 1847 and by various state conventions and mass meetings held between 1845 and 1847 in Illinois, Michigan, Ohio, and Massachusetts. See T. C. Smith, *Liberty and Free Soil Parties in the Northwest* (New York, 1897), chap. vi.

[4] Stewart himself in later years added to due process as a source of federal authority to abolish slavery throughout the states the common defense and general welfare clause, the war power, and the republican form of government guarantee. Letter from Alvan Stewart to Gamaliel Bailey, *Albany Patriot*, Vol. 7, No. 26 (May 10, 1847).

[5] Lysander Spooner, *The Unconstitutionality of Slavery* (Boston, 1845).

[6] Joel Tiffany, *A Treatise on the Unconstitutionality of American Slavery: Together with the Powers and Duties of the Federal Government in Relation to That Subject* (Cleveland, Ohio, 1849).

to the people, and for that purpose only, this provision was inserted...."

In Spooner's view the habeas corpus provision emphasized judicial rather than legislative power. Tiffany, however, maintained that the guarantee was unrestricted not only in its application to any human being but also in its application to any suspender; and the privilege of the writ accordingly was placed above the authority of both state and national legislation. Moreover, though the clause is negative and prohibitory in character, the end of maintaining the privilege of the writ being required, Congress was invested with the means of enforcement "and a positive duty enjoined upon them to do so."

With respect to the republican form of government clause, Spooner and Tiffany argued that slavery was flatly incompatible with such a government; that in order to have a republic "the public, the mass of the people, if not the entire people," must "participate in the grant of powers to the government, and in the protection afforded by the government." The guarantee, according to Tiffany, did not run to the states but to every citizen in the state "to secure him, not only from governmental, but also from individual oppression." "And if there be a single citizen who is, or has been robbed of full and ample protection in the enjoyment of his natural and inherent rights, by the authority, or permission of the state in which he lives," this guarantee was violated and the national government was under obligation to redress the wrong.

Spooner, too, elaborated this natural rights conception of the guarantee. He argued that republicanism is more than a form. It is a system based upon beliefs and interests held in common, and these beliefs and interests must harmonize with the principles of each of the state governments. In our system the interests are not economic and the beliefs are not ephemeral. "The great bond of union agreed upon in the general government, was 'the rights of man'—expressed in the national Constitution by the terms 'liberty and justice.'"

the Fourteenth Amendment 51

Gerrit Smith thought that the Constitution "on the face of it, and by every rational and just construction of it, gives power [to Congress] to abolish every part of American slavery." He argued that the Preamble itself made certain that

the Constitution is not a den of slavery; but a temple of liberty. A temple of liberty ... for the Goddess herself stands in its vestibule, [for] one of the objects of ordaining and establishing the Constitution was "to secure the blessings of liberty." Passing on, we find, that the Constitution harmonizes with the Preamble—the temple with the vestibule. For instance, the Constitution provides, that "the right of the people to be secure" in their persons, etc., against "unreasonable searches and seizures shall not be violated;" and that "no person shall be deprived of life, liberty, or property, without due process of law;" and that "the United States shall guarantee to every state in this Union a republican form of government."[7]

Goodell developed his theory of federal authority by three easy steps.[8] He first pointed to the Preamble and then annexed to it the "necessary and proper" clause, which invested Congress with power to carry out the purposes of the Preamble, and the supremacy clause, which made laws doing so superior to any conflicting state enactments. He also relied upon the republican form of government guarantee.

The well-known principles of a republic are that all men are created equal and have certain inalienable rights especially liberty. The very pith and essence of a republican form of government is the protection and security of those rights. The United States have therefore guaranteed to every state in this Union a government founded—based upon the equal rights of every citizen, in his person, and property, and in their management ... an unequivocal guarantee ... of the abolition, by the United States, of all the slavery in every state in this Union.[9]

---
[7] Letter of Gerrit Smith to Salmon P. Chase, *Albany Patriot*, Vol. 6, No. 52 (November 10, 1847), p. 206.
[8] William Goodell, *Views of American Constitutional Law in Its Bearing upon American Slavery* (Utica, N.Y., 1844). See also his many articles in the Liberty press, especially Volumes 6 and 7 of the *Albany Patriot;* and his *Slavery and Anti-Slavery; A History of the Great Struggle in Both Hemispheres; with a View of the Slavery Question in the United States* (1852).
[9] Goodell further pointed to the bill of attainder, ex post facto, title of nobility, and impairment of contracts clauses as specific limitations "looking directly to the security of individual rights, the preservation of republican equality among the people."

In his treatment of due process, Goodell followed closely Alvan Stewart's procedural argument. However, by defining liberty in the due process clause as "the power of acting as one thinks fit, without restraint or control except from the laws of nature," Goodell plainly imports into the clause substantive and natural rights conceptions.[10]

Mellen[11] found federal power,[12] judicial[13] and legislative,[14] in the Preamble[15] and the amendments, especially the Fourth, Fifth, and Eighth, which ensure "that the rights of no person, or of any of the people, should be violated in their persons, their property, their liberty, or their life." In fact, Mellen argued,

---

[10] Goodell makes use of the comity clause of Article IV. He contends that that clause is violated by the slave states in the treatment they accord to colored sojourners who are free citizens under the laws of other states. The slave states also violate the rights, under this clause, of white citizens of the free states who are rendered liable to legal punishment and lynch law in the South for speaking or writing against slavery in the North.

[11] George Mellen, *An Argument on the Unconstitutionality of Slavery, Embracing an Abstract of Proceedings of the National and State Conventions on This Subject* (1841).

[12] Mellen argued that the self-evident truths and inalienable human rights, proclaimed to the world in the Declaration of Independence, are embodied in the Preamble and amendments of the Constitution—those truths and rights especially which say that "all men are created equal, that they are endowed, by their Creator, with certain unalienable rights... [to] life, liberty, and the pursuit of happiness." Accordingly, the life and liberty which are guaranteed by the Fifth Amendment are safeguarded absolutely, and may not be taken away by any process or any action whether governmental or private. Consequently, the amendments are not only prohibitions on Congress but also upon the states and even upon individuals, for, "Can a neighbor of mine have a greater command over my liberty than the acknowledged government of the country? The idea... is preposterous." The Preamble is of like prohibitory effect and lays a like restraint upon all. But the Preamble and amendments are not alone declarations of objective and of rights with universal coverage; they are also delegations of power to the federal government and of a kind of power which carries with it an affirmative obligation and duty to go about the business of securing the objectives and inalienable human rights by bringing them into existence if they are denied and protecting them against all comers. This power and duty reach not only the federal territories but the states as well, not only governmental denial but individual invasion made possible by the failure of the state to carry out its primary duty of protection.

[13] "It would be in the power of the slave," Mellen argued, "or any of his friends, to bring his case before the Supreme Court of the United States, to ascertain whether he can be held in bondage consistently with 'law' or with 'equity' [Constitution, Art. III], or consistently with our present Constitution; whether it acknowledges in terms, or by language, in its ordinary acceptation, that could be construed as to give one citizen or one person of the United States the right over the liberty of another; whether, in the view of this Constitution, all of the people of the United States do not stand on an equal footing, and that it does not acknowledge, by that clause in

the Fourteenth Amendment 53

in order to effect these objects, it was found necessary [in the Constitution] for the states to surrender, in the last resort, the liberty of the individual to the care of the general government, that, when the states could not or would not protect him, then the general government, with its ample abilities and powers, could step in and do it; ... the result was and is that each and every individual in the country could, and can, look to the general government of the United States for the preservation of his inalienable rights, instead of ... to the state governments; and ... this constitutes the distinctive character between the Union and the Confederacy—the states, as was alleged, being incompetent, or unwilling, in their confederate capacity, to shield the individual in the different states either from external or internal foes.[16]

---

the Fourth Article of the Amendments, 'the right of the people to be secure in their persons, houses, papers and effects, against unreasonable searches and seizures, shall not be violated'; and also in the Fifth Article of the amendments, 'no person shall be deprived of his life, liberty, and property without due process of law,' and also in the Eighth Article of amendments, '... no cruel and unusual punishments inflicted'—the great truth put forth in the Declaration of Independence that 'all men are created equal, that they are endowed, by their Creator, with certain unalienable rights, that among these are life, liberty, and the pursuit of happiness,' ... and that this is the principle on which they found their judgment as to the 'law and equity' that should be awarded to every individual embraced within the limits of the United States...."

[14] Mellen relied upon Article I, section 8, clause 1, which invests Congress with power to provide for the common defense and the general welfare. Having the power, he argued, "it is their duty ... to interfere with the internal policy of the states," whether it is done as "we the people" or "we the states," if that policy is detrimental to either objective. And slavery is such a policy. It is "an obstruction to the common defense, and requires constant care and vigilance of our army, and consequently is an expense to the country; and ... the general welfare suffers by its continuance.... It injures the morals, the peace, and the harmony of the communities in which it exists, and the advancement of civilization, and the general cause of peace, of virtue, of science."

[15] Mellen argued: "Justice" cannot be "established" or "domestic tranquility" secured so long as the injustice of slavery exists; the "common defense" cannot be safely provided for when troops are needed to keep the Negro in subjugation, when "slavery lays the country open to the facility of external attacks" and constitutes a possible fifth column; "the general welfare" is not being promoted by maintaining within our borders this moral and political evil; and the "blessings of liberty," "made the keystone of the arch that was to bear the weight of the Republic," are certainly being denied to the blacks.

[16] This power also is vested in Congress by Article I, section 8: "to ... provide for the common Defence and general Welfare." It also springs from the federal guarantee of a republican form of government to the states. Mellen makes no use of the comity clause. Nor does he refer to or show awareness of *Barron v. Baltimore*, though he devotes a chapter to the discussion of United States Supreme Court cases having a bearing on the slavery issue, citing such cases as *Marbury v. Madison, McCullough v. Maryland, Gibbons v. Ogden, Cohens v. Virginia, Sturgis v. Crowninshield*. He relies heavily on Alvan Stewart's constitutional argument especially, but not alone for the due process point.

Significant of the doctrinal progress often made by active partisans of an intense struggle, James G. Birney, too, eventually joined the radical extremists who were making a direct attack upon the principles of federalism. Posing the question, "Can Congress, under the Constitution, abolish slavery in the states?"[17] he answered in a series of four unsigned articles published in the *Albany Patriot*

[17] A sweeping act of legislation might do away with slavery; so might a sweeping decision of the judiciary. Betokening the radical reform and essentially lay character of the antislavery movement, the courts were not an important forum of abolitionism—not, at least, until it became the dominant national issue and all institutions of government were swept resistlessly into the maelstrom. In the earlier stages, the main arenas were elsewhere—in revival meetings, in benevolent societies, on the hustings, in Congress. The Constitution itself, with its inescapable compromises on slavery and its federal principles, constituted a major obstacle to an American Somerset case.
Yet in general treatise and specific case, abolitionists persistently appealed for just such a decision. Hardly a likely institution to "volunteer in comprehensive and radical reforms" or to "proceed, self-moved, to a very self-denying duty," the judiciary proved unresponsive. Quite the contrary: the federal courts, particularly the Supreme Court, accepted the philosophy of slavery. In *Prigg v. Pennsylvania* (1842), 16 Peters 539, a case of the greatest historical importance, they sustained the Fugitive Slave Act of 1793, and, by insisting upon the exclusiveness of congressional power over fugitive slaves, invalidated the efforts of the northern states to protect the civil rights and liberties of free Negroes. They intimated a doubt whether Congress could constitutionally exclude slaves from interstate commerce. Repudiating an exercise of congressional power, and using the very argument of Pickens and Pinckney, they finally opened the territories to slavery in *Dred Scott v. Sandford* (1857), 19 Howard 393.
For the abolitionists, three remedies were possible: to change the judges, to change the Constitution, and to find something higher than the Constitution on which to rely. The first of these remedies was contemplated as an objective of political action on the eve of the Civil War. The second was the remedy achieved when secession, war, and victory opened the way to constitutional amendment. Either of the first two depended upon control of the machinery of government. Accordingly, the third, namely, the higher law doctrine, was the principal reliance of abolitionism. Long before Seward, Spooner explicitly stated this doctrine for the abolitionists. Law, said he, is "simply the rule, principle, obligation, or requirement of natural justice." Natural law is paramount law. "It follows that government can have no powers but such as individuals may rightfully delegate to it: that no law, inconsistent with men's natural rights, can arise out of any contract or compact of government; that constitutional law, under any form of government, consists only of those principles of the written constitution that are consistent with natural law and man's natural rights: that any other principles, that may be expressed by the letter of the constitution, are void and not law, and all judicial tribunals are bound to declare them so."
In scattered cases not squarely involving the issue of abolition, counsel and sometimes dissenting judges invoked the doctrines and constitutional clauses of the movement. Counsel called upon due process in *Prigg v. Pennsylvania* (see argument of Hanley, p. 576) and in *Jones v. VanZandt*. In his brief in the VanZandt case, Chase repeated the argument which he had worked out nearly ten years earlier in the Matilda case. See Salmon P. Chase, *An Argument for the Defendant, Submitted to the Supreme Court of the United States, at the December Term, 1846, in the Case of Wharton Jones v. John VanZandt* (Cincinnati, 1847). In an Ohio fugitive slave case,

the Fourteenth Amendment 55

for May and June, 1847. Since these articles are a high-water mark of Birney's constitutionalism, and represent in many ways the farthest doctrinal advance of the radical extremists, they deserve special attention.

Birney built his thesis that "full power to abolish slavery in the states was given" to Congress in the Constitution along three main

---

counsel and a dissenting judge asserted the power of Congress to enforce the due process and comity clauses. *Ex parte Simeon Bushnell* (1859), 9 Ohio 77. Before the Supreme Judicial Court of Massachusetts, Sumner contended for a concrete application of the statement in the Massachusetts bill of rights that "all men are born free and equal," not to abolish slavery, but to terminate some of its badges and indicia. The argument was delivered December 4, 1849. Charles Sumner, *Works* (Boston, 1874), Vol. 2, pp. 326–376. Foreshadowing the future problems of freedom, the case involved discrimination against Negro children in attendance at the common schools. *Sarah C. Roberts* v. *City of Boston* (1849), 5 Cushing (Mass.) 198. Chief Justice Shaw rejected Sumner's argument. But the Massachusetts legislature in 1855 expressly forbade discrimination and "distinctions on account of race, color, or religious opinions." Sumner maintained that the constitutional phrase meant "equality before the law"; that it effaced all political or civil distinctions as well as institutions founded on birth; and that it condemned the inequality inherent in segregation, though the facilities be "equivalent." Out of various French constitutions, Sumner developed the idea that, to conform to the notion declared in the Bill of Rights, the law must be equal to all "whether it recompense or punish . . . protect or repress," and thus showed an awareness of distinctions emphasized later in the congressional debates on the adoption of the Fourteenth Amendment.

Five years before the Dred Scott case, a California judge maintained that the due process and just compensation clauses of the Fifth Amendment prevented a state or territory from depriving slaveholders of their slave property if they brought their property into the state or territory when it was free. *In re Perkins* (1852), 2 Cal. 424.

One clear-cut situation, however, squarely presented the basic issues, excepting the power of Congress. *State* v. *Post* and *State* v. *VanBeuren* (1845), 20 N.J. Law 368. It reached the Supreme Court of New Jersey in 1845 and the judges were directly but unsuccessfully challenged to avail themselves of the opportunity to follow the example of Mansfield. The question before the court was whether New Jersey's slaves, held in limited servitude under the earlier statutes of that state, were freed by the state constitution of 1844 which declared: "All men are by nature free and independent, and have certain natural and inalienable rights, among which are those of enjoying and defending life and liberty, acquiring, possessing and protecting property, and of pursuing and obtaining safety and happiness."

Counsel in the case were J. P. Bradley and, opposing him, Alvan Stewart, the eminent abolitionist lawyer and leader of the New York Anti-Slavery Society. In his elaborate argument, Stewart maintained that the rights embodied in the New Jersey constitution and declared by the paramount natural law to be inalienable required immediate liberation of the slaves in New Jersey, as similar provisions had judicially been held to do in Massachusetts. His principal reliance, however, was on the natural rights conception and the due process clause of the Constitution of the United States. Stewart referred briefly to the attainder, republican form of government, and privileges and immunities clauses. The latter meant that southern states could not enslave free northern Negroes (pp. 37–38). The Constitution springs from "our weakness and need of protection" and consequently "is a covenant of the whole people with lines. He first pointed to the jailing, without charge of crime, of free colored seamen in southern ports. These cases, he asserted, "evolve a central principle."

In the free states, these [seamen] are "citizens," and under the Constitution of the United States, entitled, without molestation, not only to go and come at their pleasure, through the slave states, but to settle down there and utter any sentiment contained in the Declaration of 1776, or elsewhere, where and when they choose. Freedom of speech is secured to everyone by the Constitution, and none of our institutions are supposed to be incompatible with its most unlimited exercise. If a condition of things exists, in or out of the states, and wherever the United States has jurisdiction; if it depends for its continued existence and growth on nothing being said or written about it anywhere, then must that condition of things require that freedom of speech and of the press be sacrificed to it—that our rights under the Constitution declared to be "the supreme law of the land," be relinquished, in its favor. If Congress proceed, not at once, after fully ascertaining the fact, to remove the condition of things, which cannot exist without the nullification of a divine

---

each person, and of each person with the whole people, for the protection and defense of our natural rights, of life, liberty, and the pursuit of happiness." Due process, as in his earlier historic argument, was a procedural requirement of an adjudication by a court. But a "person" within the meaning of the Fifth Amendment is "a human being possessed of natural rights of life, liberty, and the pursuit of happiness." Slaves are persons and hence to deprive them of these natural rights is to violate the amendment. The due process clause is thus read in a mixed technical and substantive sense. There being no record of judicial conviction, the clause automatically frees the slaves. Though there is some confusion on the point arising out of Stewart's reference to the due process argument he would make at Westminster, there can be little doubt that he was either unaware of, or heedlessly disregarded, *Barron* v. *Baltimore*. He says flatly: "I demand that these persons be delivered up to enjoy their liberty, on the ground of the declaration in the Constitution of the United States declaring that 'no person shall be deprived of life, liberty, or property without due process of law.' There is not a slave or servant, so held, of the four thousand of both sorts in New Jersey but what are entitled to their liberty by the Constitution of the United States" (p. 42).

Most of the incidents of slavery cannot be justified by any process. "Will any man contend that plantation and cart whip discipline is due process of law? Will any pretend that being deprived of the right to learn to read, or write, . . . is due process of law? . . . The pursuing of fugitives with bloodhounds, cannot be the due process of law of the Constitution.

"The separation by sale of husband from wife, and wife from husband, and children from both, to suit the convenience of the master, cannot be due process of law. The being born of slave mothers, on a slaveholder's plantation, cannot be due process of law? The being torn away from home, kindred and friends, and sent by the middle passage to a slave auction in South Carolina, and sold on the boards into hopeless bondage, cannot be due process of law?" (pp. 34-35).

right, sought to be secured to us, then are Congress slaves themselves—poor unworthy cowards, unequal to what they have voluntarily undertaken—fit only to grace the triumph of those who show them before the world, and who glory, that they have overthrown the Constitution of their country.

Presumably the part of the Constitution referred to in the first sentence of the quotation—"under the Constitution of the United States, entitled..."—was the comity clause, guaranteeing to the citizens of each state "all Privileges and Immunities of Citizens in the several States." This clause by 1847 was widely invoked in connection with the free colored mariner problem; and Birney's earlier phrase, "in the free states, these seamen are 'citizens,'" makes plain that he had in mind the comity clause.

But Birney's next statement suggests national not state citizenship, or, at least, national privileges and immunities. The right to travel and settle down in any of the states and the right to speak where and when one chooses are referred to as guarantees of the United States Constitution, not dependent on the provisions of the states, either the state of origin or the state of sojourn. In effect, then, Birney is here reading into the comity clause a United States citizenship, having at least the privilege or immunity of unhindered travel and residence, but he does so without specific allusion to the comity clause and without the slightest explanation of the means or justification for the interpolation.

The other important idea in the quoted passage is formulated with similar vagueness and imprecision—at least in regard to the reasoning on which the conclusion is based. The statement of the conclusion itself is not wanting in clarity. Congress is obligated to remove any practice, institution, or condition which is incompatible with the existence or full exercise of a right secured to everyone by the Constitution. But how is this conclusion derived? Adverting to the supremacy clause, as Birney does, is not helpful. That clause merely says that the Constitution and two other types of law are the supreme law of the land. The Constitution, besides mentioning some rights, allocates powers among the branches of the national government. The supremacy clause says nothing about this allocation of powers, except that only laws made in pursuance of the Constitution are part of the supreme law of the land, suggestive of limited rather than unlimited congressional power.

Then there is the question of what rights are secured by the Constitution and to whom they are guaranteed. Freedom of speech, says Birney, is secured "to everyone by the Constitution," not just citizens, as his comity clause talk had earlier implied. If so, it is not immediately apparent from the language of the First Amendment which begins with the words "Congress shall make no law." In fact, from this point of view, Birney is here undertaking a more difficult task than Stewart did in his due process argument. In the latter case, at least, the constitutional words are: "No person shall be . . . deprived." If, however, it can be shown or agreed that "freedom of speech is secured to everyone by the Constitution," and if it can be shown or granted that Congress is empowered or directed to execute the guarantee, then the rest of the conclusion follows easily. Congress must obliterate whatever tends to nullify the right.[18]

Birney turns next to the situation of the territories and the new states carved out of the territories. Admit, he says, that slavery is unconstitutional in the territories and that Congress by virtue of the "needful Rules and Regulations" clause must abolish it,

it follows, as day follows night, that the general government has the power to protect its citizens—not in the states, but in the territories only, and this although the same Constitution extends over both states and

---

[18] Birney thereafter proceeds to make use of due process ideas: "Why are those seamen imprisoned? For fear of communication with the slaves. Let us mitigate it—excuse it, if we can, by the execution of their 'inspection' laws. But what man ever dreamed that the inspection laws of any state would so interfere with the constitutional liberty of the citizen, as to cast him into jail, even uncharged with crime?

"If anything is needed to fill up the measure of this outrage, it is, that the state of South Carolina adopted her constitution after the adoption of the Constitution of the United States, and that it contains a provision, that no free man shall be deseized of his liberties, or privileges, or outlawed, or exiled, but by the judgment of his peers, or by the law of the land."

territories, and that it is the same everywhere, so far as personal rights are concerned. To be more plain—a citizen of the United States may be arrested, imprisoned and enslaved, say in South Carolina, and Congress would have no power in any way to interfere, because "slavery is a state institution," whilst in a territory the aegis of the Constitution is spread over him and protects all his rights. If this be the true conclusion of the Constitution ... the rights of citizens, even on paper, are not so well guarded as they supposed they were.

... Now suppose this territory, wishing to be admitted into the Union, duly holds its convention—makes a state constitution, providing for slavery—submits it to Congress, and that it is approved by that body:— can Congress sanction that part of it which provides for slavery, when it had itself no power in any way to establish slavery? Can Congress confer power which it does not itself possess? Indeed, so far from possessing it, the only power that it does possess in the premises is to see that everyone is free and not enslaved. Now I want a candid and impartial answer to the above question. If it be in the affirmative, Congress cannot part with the power that it has of protecting every individual, whether in territory or state. To exercise it is an inalienable duty. Wherever slavery is practiced in our limits, there the power of Congress penetrates for the relief of the victim. If the answer be in the negative, then are the rights of anyone—of everyone—at the mercy of the first that can prevail on Congress to give to a state a power which we never gave them, and do by another what we said they should not do.

How much more consistent with itself—how much more according with all our notions of government—how much more lovely and venerable without at all adding to the powers of Congress, is our Constitution thus interpreted, for the protection of all, than when interpreted to give to a state its own creation a power which it does not possess itself; and this the power of enslaving, one, too, with which it can never again interfere.

In the first paragraph of this passage, Birney speaks only of the rights of citizens; and, since he is in part concerned with the territories, he could only be speaking of United States citizens. Indeed, Birney was explicit: "The general government has the power to protect *its* citizens"; "a citizen of the United States may ..." Substantially, the argument is that the general government has the power to protect the rights of the citizen in the states because it has the power in the territories, and the parts of the Constitution dealing with the rights of citizens make no distinction between the territories and the states. "The same Constitution extends over both... and... is the same everywhere, so far as personal rights are concerned." This again presupposes that the rights of citizens are binding on, and perhaps in, the states, and that Congress is to safeguard them. But, letting that pass, what rights? In one sentence, Birney's answer is "all" the rights of the citizen; in another, "personal rights"; in a third, by way of example, the right not to be "arrested, imprisoned and enslaved." Are "personal rights" the rights of the amendments? Certainly many of the rights mentioned in the amendments are, but are they all, and are personal rights to be found nowhere else in the Constitution? Birney does not say. His earlier reference to the rights of unrestricted travel and residence, free speech, and immunity to arbitrary seizure indicates that some of the rights are in the amendments and some are not.

In the second paragraph the terminology changes. The desired protection must now be extended, not just to citizens, but to "all," "everyone," "every individual." The rights apparently are the same. And a theory of another source of congressional power over the states is propounded. Being under a duty to protect the freedom of everyone in the territories, and possessing no power to enslave anyone, and the duty being inalienable and the power, by the law of nature, unconferrable, Congress cannot transfer either the duty or the power to a state upon its admission to the Union. Certainly Congress cannot eliminate inalienable duties or confer unconferrable powers. But does a state upon admission acquire no constitutional status? Is it in exactly the same position as a territorial government, possessing only such powers as Congress chooses to give it? Later history has clarified the answers to these questions; but even at that time it was conceded that a new state derived its

the Fourteenth Amendment

powers from the Constitution and that, in general, they were the same as those possessed by the original states. Birney's theory of congressional power receives little strength from this source.

Finally, Birney takes up and applies "the foregoing principles" to the hardest case, "the case of the slave in one of the original states."

One so held, say in South Carolina, petitions, by writ of habeas corpus, a judge of the United States, or indeed a judge of the state of South Carolina, who is bound in the same manner to make the Constitution of the United States paramount to the Constitution and laws of South Carolina, if they should come in conflict—to be set at liberty. The only facts that can be proved against him are, that his parents and ancestors ever since they were captured in Africa, as they were escaping by the blaze of their burning village, had been slaves—that they had uninterruptedly borne the sorrows of that miserable and almost hopeless condition; that the petitioner himself, by the law of the state, was a slave, and that he was black, or that he had, in his veins, a drop of African blood.

The above is all that can be proved against the slave... Now let us see what, on the other hand, he can prove.

In the first place, he proves that allegiance and protection are inseparable. This doctrine is so well established, so generally, may I not say almost universally acknowledged,—that the abundant proof of it contained in the best writers on public law is unnecessary. A slave, for instance, may be tried before a court for robbing the United States Mails, or for piracy. We try him, because we demand from him allegiance. There is, on his part, a tacit condition that he will be subject to the laws. For this allegiance we own him, what we refuse to pay, protection—"entire security." Without this protection—this security—we have no right to try him for the violation of the laws of a country which deprives him of both.[10] For his allegiance, what do we render to him?

He would prove that the United States entered into the family of nations with this declaration in her mouth—that all men are created free, and endowed by their Creator with a right to liberty that never can

---

[10] Note the use of the word "deprives." The government deprives a man of protection when it withholds or fails to supply the protection. In this sense, a state deprives a person of life, liberty, or property without due process of law when it fails to supply the due process of law without which life, liberty, and property cannot be taken.

be alienated;[20] "that true sovereignty is unalienable in its nature;" that, uncharged with crime, he was debarred from pursuing his happiness as he wished to do, without interfering in any improper manner, with the happiness of others; and that governments were instituted among men to secure their rights, not to destroy them.

He would prove that the slavery in which he was held was a condition of force—of unlawful force,—and that the Constitution under which we live was made and ratified under the firm expectation that slavery would, in a reasonable time, be extinguished in all the land; but so far from this being the present tendency of things, the slaveholders have contrived to usurp and direct the government, with the design, by its means, to render slavery perpetual.

He would also prove that the strength of slavery was an unerring index of the strength of barbarism with any people—that no nation could permanently advance in civilization who authorized and practiced this, the most palpable form of oppression.

He would prove that slavery was inconsistent with all the objects of the Constitution; that so far from establishing "justice" it had always been regarded as the strongest manifestation of injustice; that instead of insuring "domestic tranquility," it weakened it, and often broke in upon it in the most horrible manner, and in ways not to be mentioned; that

---

[20] The Declaration of Independence played a large, frequently a dominant, role in the constitutional theory of the abolitionists. It was one of the routes by which abolitionists got men's natural rights into the constitutional law of the nation. In Mellen's development, any link between the Declaration and the Constitution was implicit and rudimentary. Both expressly embodied the natural and inalienable human rights which were part of the law of the land anyway. Tiffany was more explicit and legalistic. The Declaration was a "solemn deed of acquittance of all rightful power to violate the natural and inalienable rights of man." By the affirmation in it of "the existence of certain great fundamental principles," the people "estopped themselves" from ever "rightfully" trampling upon them. Spooner's view was even more precisely worked out. He concluded that the Declaration was "the constitutional law of the country ... for the purpose of recognizing and establishing, as law, the natural and inalienable right of individuals to life, liberty, and the pursuit of happiness."

Goodell carried forward and elaborated these notions and introduced a new element which touched upon the character of the federal relationship. To him, the Declaration of Independence was "the first and fundamental constitution of the United States," which had never been "repealed or repudiated." It was the Declaration of Independence—not the Articles of Confederation nor even the Constitution of 1789—that established a national government for the United States. To believe that "there were thirteen separate dis-united states wholly independent of each other, and that this condition of things continued until the adoption of the Federal Constitution ... when for the first time, they became the United States and under the authority of a general government" is to hold a theory which is "at war with incontrovertible historical fact, and stubborn chronological dates.... Before the Declara-

the Fourteenth Amendment

instead of providing for the "common defence," there was nothing that more certainly and permanently impaired it; that, instead of promoting the "general welfare," he need only refer to the unhappy and unprosperous condition of the slave states, when compared, in every way, with that of the free; that instead of securing the "blessings of liberty" to themselves and their posterity, it entailed on them evils too numerous to be counted—evils which never fail to follow the wilful violation of one of God's commands, whether it be by nations or individuals.

He would prove that slavery was not only sinful before God, but incompatible with the Constitution of the United States; and that individuals, whether they constitute a nation or not, will be held responsible for persisting in error; that the slaveholders are the enemies of the slaves, as they must be, having deprived them of their rights, and compelled them to work without wages; that the non-slaveholders of the free states act as their sentinels, returning the slaves who are attempting to escape; and that the constitutional provision for their re-delivery is immoral, and therefore void.

That the Constitution of the United States, and the laws made in pursuance of it are the "supreme law of the land,"—obligatory everywhere, in a state as well as in a territory—and that wherever a condition of things exists in opposition to them, they must put it down, or it will put them down.

---

tion of Independence, there were no independent sovereign states; and the declaration which asserted their independence, asserted likewise their union, as United States of America, affirming moreover the object of their assumed independence to be the institution of a new government (not governments) upon the basis of the self-evident principles then recognized. There has been no state sovereignty that has not been connected with the union of the states and modified by it." Thus was the national government established; thus, too, was its character defined: says Goodell, relying heavily on an earlier speech by John Quincy Adams, " 'The elements and principles for the formation of a new government were all contained in the Declaration of Independence, but the adjustment of them to the condition of parties to the compact was a work of time, of reflection, of experience, of calm deliberation or moral and intellectual exertion.'

"In other words, the Declaration of Independence comprises and embodies the fundamental elements and principles of American constitutional law. The adoption of the Articles of Confederation first, and of the Constitution afterwards, are to be regarded in the light of 'exertions' for the adjustment and proper application of these great principles of constitutional law. These principles, asserted in the original Declaration of 1776 when the nation came into existence, continue to constitute now . . . the vital essence, the pith, the marrow, and the substance, of our constitutional law. The mere outward form, the minutely detailed provisions of the subsequently written constitution, these are but the instruments, of which those principles are the living spirit and substance." J. Q. Adams, *An Oration Addressed to the Citizens of the Town of Quincy, July 4, 1831; An Oration Delivered before the Inhabitants of the Town of Newburyport, at Their Request, July 4, 1837;* "Seventy-six," *The Emancipator,* January 4, 1838.

[These reasons] make out, so clearly, the right of the slave to his liberty, that an upright and fearless judge could not hesitate to declare him free.

Here, then, with typical eloquence and absence of technical constitutional argument, Birney presents his summation. Petitioning a judge, on behalf of a slave, for a writ of habeas corpus, he puts forward on an equal footing, with fine impartiality, the Declaration of Independence and slavery as an index to barbarism, the Preamble to the Constitution and the sinfulness of slavery in the eye of God, reciprocal allegiance and protection, and the supremacy clause of the Constitution. Yet these apparently diverse elements are pulled together into one loosely knit entity, a single pattern with a constitutional design. The Declaration, the Preamble, the barbaric oppression and systematic denial of the rights of slaves, divine and moral laws—all are adduced simply as defining the realm of protection which is the governmental *quid pro quo* for allegiance and to supply which "to every individual," "whether in territory or state," is "an inalienable duty" of Congress. It is this idea of the reciprocal character of protection and allegiance that dominates the thesis and gives a rough unity to the whole. The allegiance exacted was not the complicated modern kind that turns on loyalty. It was simply subjection to the laws, obedience. The protection was to be "entire security." Of what rights, Birney nowhere carefully itemizes. He does not particularly refer to the Bill of Rights. He makes it clear, however, by his allusion to rights not there mentioned, that he is not confining himself to them. They are neither his primary concern nor his limitation. The rights to be protected are mainly, though perhaps not exclusively, natural rights, which "individuals, whether they constitute a nation or not," cannot deny or destroy. The rights especially identified by Birney are the right to liberty, the right to pursue happiness as one wishes without improperly interfering with the happiness of others, the right to the wages of one's labor, the right not to be arrested, imprisoned, and enslaved unless for crime duly charged

the Fourteenth Amendment 65

and regularly established, the right to free speech and press, and the right to travel and settle where one pleases. Protection was to be extended to "all," to "everyone." Protection was an indispensable part of sovereignty, an "inalienable duty" in the presence of allegiance. And allegiance, in Birney's sense, was not confined to citizens. Consequently, despite Birney's frequent reference to the rights of citizens, he is not here enunciating a doctrine of national citizenship with attendant privileges and immunities. In the end, the rights of citizens turn out also to be the rights of everyone, the natural rights of men.

The doctrine of reciprocal allegiance and protection presents a simple and unsophisticated view of government. Birney's work is more diffuse and general than that of Stewart. But the basic weaknesses and strengths of the one are the basic weaknesses and strengths of the other. In a consolidated, unitary form of government, in a government uncomplicated by notions of constitutional limitations on power and by federalism, all this would be easy enough. But Birney and Stewart both fail to come to grips with federalism; and Birney, even more than Stewart, fails to come to grips with the specific constitutional language imposing limitations and allocating powers. Even when Birney comes closest to these issues, his argument is curiously unresponsive and beside the point. No one would doubt, to take one example, the proposition that Birney repeats often and impressively, that "the Constitution of the United States, and the laws made in pursuance of it are 'the supreme law of the land'—obligatory everywhere, in a state as well as in a territory—and that wherever a condition of things exists in opposition to them, they must put it down or it will put them down." The Constitution of the United States and laws made in pursuance *are* the supreme law of the land; and they *are* obligatory in both territories and states. Moreover, opposing conditions must be put down.

But all this tells us nothing about what the Constitution, admittedly obligatory everywhere within the jurisdiction, provides—

especially whether it provides different things for the territories and for the states—and who is responsible for putting down opposing conditions. Without knowing this, how can it be discovered that slavery is such a condition and that Congress is the agency duty bound to abolish it in the territories and in the states?

Our concern with these theories, however, is not limited to their logical strength or infirmity. The existence of the theories and the elements that compose them are the crucial matters for the antislavery origins of the Fourteenth Amendment.

Here again, in the doctrines of this band of radical extremists of the antislavery movement, is to be seen the main body of the constitutional concepts and clauses that later appeared in the Fourteenth Amendment. The element that received unvarying emphasis by these writers, that served as the common foundation for somewhat different superstructures, was once more the protection of the laws and the duty of the government to supply it. They all linked this idea to the Lockeian premise as to the origin and purpose of government. With the exception of Mellen, they all tied it specifically to the Declaration of Independence as part of the constituent and binding law of the United States. They all connected it directly with the Preamble, which rendered it explicit and made it part of the Constitution. They all carried it further into various implementing portions of the Constitution. They all defined the area of protection as men's natural rights. Among the rights to be protected, those mentioned in the First and the Fourth amendments, the due process clause of the Fifth Amendment, and the Eighth Amendment were commonly specified. The contexts suggest, however, that it was the character of the rights rather than their location in amendments which was regarded as giving them importance. With the qualifications later to be noted in the cases of Tiffany and Gerrit Smith, it was not asserted that the entire Bill of Rights was binding on the state or subject to federal legislative protection. Neither was this proposition denied.

All these writers, except Spooner, relied upon due process ideas.

the Fourteenth Amendment 67

Some gave the clause a substantive meaning, some a mixed substantive and procedural meaning, and most of them merely a procedural meaning.

So far, these are the basic and recurrent elements in all abolitionist constitutional theory. The distinctive feature of the doctrines of the radical extremists was of course their obliteration of the federal system. Once the duty of government to supply protection and the area to be protected were set forth, the radical extremists established their extreme radicalism by applying these doctrines to the national government. It was as simple as that. In reality, they did not so much obliterate the federal system as disregard or ignore it. Governments had a duty to protect men in their natural rights. The national government was a government. Let it then proceed to protect men's natural rights.

Beyond this point, the radical extremists rummaged among many parts of the Constitution. They did not confine themselves to the Preamble and certain of the amendments, though these were their primary reliance. They lingered over the republican form of government guarantee, the habeas corpus provision, the common defense and general welfare grant, the bill of attainder, ex post facto, titles of nobility, and impairment of contracts limitations on the states, and even the judicial article. But their primary object was to find constitutional references to the rights to be protected, not an allocation of central government authority. Once a mention of the rights was found, the rest was easy. Governmental authority was presumed to accompany governmental duty; and the governmental duty was implicit in the existence of government. This explains why the radical extremists were little bothered by the distinction between congressional limitations on power and constitutional grants of power—why, that is, the amendments could be used as a source of authority. The amendments, or at least those with which the abolitionists were most concerned, were declaratory constitutional safeguards of natural rights. As such, they were merely a method of emphasizing what would have been true without them—they mentioned rights which the government was under a duty to protect by laws. This also explains why the radical extremists did little more than toy with the "necessary and proper" clause; it, too, was at best confirmatory.

Though many of the adherents and proponents of these sweeping and revolutionary doctrines about the national power were distinguished leaders of the abolitionist movement, the doctrines, however great their effect, remained a lesser and tributary stream. The main body of the movement, although it accepted the idea that the due process and other clauses of the amendments were grants of power as well as restrictions, never deviated from the position that Congress could not, by *direct* legislation, constitutionally abolish slavery in the southern states. On purely theoretical grounds, this difference of point of view among the abolitionists on whether federalism constituted a limitation on national power was of some importance. It gives point to the question: Were the Thirteenth and Fourteenth amendments in abolitionist eyes altogether declaratory; or, on the contrary, was the function of the Thirteenth Amendment and later of the Fourteenth Amendment to bridge the gap between the radical extremists and the more moderate main body, to make constitutionally explicit the view of the minority and to overturn the federal system as the majority had acknowledged it to be?

Though the split in abolitionist constitutional theory had theoretical consequences, it was of little immediate practical significance. So far as the main body was concerned, the federal limitation on the national power, while a principle never to be denied or doubted, was to be understood as not diminishing the granted powers of Congress.[21] They thereby rejected almost from the outset the ram-

---

[21] Among the abolitionist leaders, H. B. Stanton was the first to espouse and develop this proposition. In the American Anti-Slavery Convention of 1839 he offered and supported in an able speech the following resolution: "Resolved, That the political power of the free states is sufficient, if properly exercised, to ultimately exterminate slavery in the nation." "The doctrine of this resolution," Stanton asserted, "is almost new—contrary to the generally received opinion even among abolitionists." *Sixth Annual Report,* American Anti-Slavery Society, 1839.

the Fourteenth Amendment

ifying principle which the Supreme Court used thirty years later to frustrate the constitutional culmination of their great reform: that all the powers vested in the national government, and especially those vested in Congress, must be interpreted in the light of our federal system. By an exercise of these powers, the moderate abolitionists thought, slavery could be abolished throughout the nation.

Emancipation in the District of Columbia, desired for its own sake, was even more sought after because discussion and action in the national capital would "make Congress the channel through which the healing truths of immediatism will flow to the deliverance of the masters from prejudice, and the slaves from chains." The District of Columbia was the "bridge over the moat leading to the whole South." Emancipation in the national territories would, by preventing spread, accomplish a relative attrition. A prohibitory law, applied to interstate commerce, would sever the connection between the slave-breeding and the slave-consuming states, thus cutting off the supply of slaves to the Deep South and the profitableness of slavery in the northern slave states. If this "great jugular vein," were cut, said H. B. Stanton, "the monster would die—starvation would slowly but surely consume him in his southern, and apoplexy in his northern abode."

In this manner the gap was closed, in all but a remote theoretical sense, between the far from orthodox federalist majority and the consolidated central government minority among the abolitionists. Congressional votes and congressional authority—national political action and national constitutional power—were to be the instruments of both groups.

The antislavery response to the so-called gag resolutions introduced in Congress in 1838 shows how early and how wittingly the moderates in the movement embraced the notion of universal emancipation indirectly achieved by congressional power. The official annual report of the American Anti-Slavery Society for 1839 freely confesses to the charge in one of the resolutions "that the petitions for the abolition of slavery in the District of Columbia and the Territories of the United States, and against the removal of the slaves from one state to another, are a part of the plan of operations set on foot to affect the institution of slavery in the several states, and thus indirectly to destroy that institution within their limits." The basis of the distinction was thus the difference between direct and indirect action. Congress could abolish slavery in the states if the abolition resulted from the exercise of a power given to Congress or if it were necessary and proper for carrying into execution a power given to Congress. Consequently, the abolitionists emphatically denied a resolve "that, by the constitution of the United States, Congress has no jurisdiction whatever over the institution of slavery in the several states of the Confederacy." Congress had the power "to regulate, or abolish the slave trade ... part and parcel of the institution of slavery." It owed "protection to the slave against foreign aggression." It could "punish the slave for treason or other crime against the United States" independently of any slave state or slaveowner. Having these powers, Congress could exert them to the full and, indeed, for the very purpose of destroying slavery in the states.

The abolitionists repudiated with equal vigor two other resolutions, one declaring "that Congress has no right to do that indirectly which it cannot do directly," the other asserting that all attempts by Congress to abolish slavery in the District of Columbia, in the territories, and in interstate commerce, done with a view to the overthrow of slavery in the states, "are a violation of the Constitution, destructive of the fundamental principles on which the Union of these States rests and beyond the jurisdiction of Congress. . . ." Far from conceding these positions, the abolitionists maintained that it was both the "right and duty" of Congress "to exercise in a moral way every power conferred by the Constitution which may indirectly overthrow slavery."[22]

[22] See also *Report,* Ohio Anti-Slavery Society, fourth anniversary meeting, Putnam, Muskingum County, May 29, 1839.

CHAPTER IV

Paramount National Citizenship

IN SOME WAYS doctrinally and perhaps historically the most significant contribution made by the abolitionists in the constitutional development of the United States was their conception of paramount national citizenship. The refinement and constitutionalization of the Lockeian and Jeffersonian heritage of equality and governmental protection, the imaginative and skillful exploitation of the substantive and affirmative potential of due process were, in one sense, only intermediate steps in the achievement of this larger end. Embodying in the Constitution and implementing with congressional power political ideals the application of which would undermine what were widely believed to be compromises of the Constitution and which would both safeguard men's rights and do so regardless of color, these equal protection and due process elements were, in and of themselves, constitutional landmarks as well as monuments to the creative minds leading the movement.

But powerful though they were as abolitionist weapons, their range was limited to the federal jurisdiction.

The greatest of the constitutional barriers to abolitionism—the hampering, pervasive, and all but universally acknowledged restrictions of federalism—though they had been pierced and undermined, had not yet been successfully demolished. Until that was done, abolitionists might sweep the national territories clean, might contain and prevent the spread of slavery, might even cripple slavery by cutting away its appendages, but men would not believe that these or other measures could be pressed to the point of abolishing slavery without subversion of our political system and a breach of the Constitution. A latitudinarian reading of the powers of Congress as in no way limited by the federal principle could never be made to look like anything other than a willingness to destroy that principle in fact while paying it homage in name.

On the other hand, the method proposed by Stewart and elaborated by Goodell and Birney was equally inadequate, but for a different reason. Preoccupied with demonstrating the conflict between slavery and the amendments, straining to show that what appeared to be merely a prohibition on power or at best an assertion of a right was in reality a grant of authority, Stewart, Goodell, and Birney simply ignored *Barron* v. *Baltimore* (1833), 7 Peters 243, and never squarely faced the problem of federalism. What was needed and what paramount national citizenship was designed to supply was a theory—not so eccentric and extreme as to revolt the constitutional predilections of the day while overturning one of them—which would fit and encompass the basic nationalistic implications of the abolitionist movement.

The conception of national citizenship and of certain privileges and immunities attaching to it, though vague, rudimentary, and ill defined, was yet basically present in abolitionist constitutional theory as early as 1834-1835. Appearing as a part of the undifferentiated mass of the total religious, ethical, natural rights argument, the expression "American citizen"—sometimes "citizens of the United States"—was roughly interchanged with "human beings" or "persons having inalienable rights." Alvan Stewart, in his due process argument, interchanged "person" and "citizen" in this undeliberative offhand way, and Elizur Wright, in his fourth annual report, casually spoke of slaves as citizens. H. B. Stanton's reference to "citizenship with the dignities and immunities of manhood" shows the interlocking and undifferentiated character of the two ideas. The emphasis was on citizens possessing the "dignities and immunities" of human beings rather than on human beings with the privileges and immunities of citizens.

When, as happened by 1834, these "dignities and immunities" of men, these natural inalienable rights of persons, were read into the amendments of the Constitution, not only was progress made in shifting from citizens as human beings to human beings as citizens, but a foundation stone of national citizenship as distinguished from state citizenship was laid. Thereafter, the protection of these rights was increasingly claimed by men as "free American citizens" and it began to be claimed from the national government.

Up to this point, however, the doctrine of a national citizenship superior to state citizenship and possessing attributes of its own remained unformulated. The first tentative efforts at its articulation derived from another source, from concern with the rights, not of abolitionists, but of free Negroes in the northern states. That was the work of the Ellsworth-Goddard argument before the Supreme Court of Connecticut in the *Prudence Crandall* case[1] and of Charles Olcott in the report on the laws of Ohio[2] made to an antislavery gathering at Putnam, Ohio, in 1835.[3] In both the brief and the report, reliance was placed on the comity clause of the United States Constitution and, because of that reliance, the

---

[1] *Prudence Crandall* v. *State of Connecticut* (1836), 10 Conn. 339.
[2] These two documents and episodes are fully analyzed by Howard Jay Graham in *Wisconsin Law Review*, Vol. 1950, No. 4 (May, 1950).
[3] At one other focal point—lynching—the abolitionists attacked the abrogation of the rights of free persons of color. Here, of course, the problem was not one of unequal laws: laws supplying benefit or protection to others but withholding them from Negroes and mulattoes, as in the Ohio code and constitutional provisions; or the failure to supply protection of the fundamental rights of free Negroes and mulattoes when the invasion of them is facilitated by legislation intended to benefit others, as in the Fugitive Slave Act. Failure or refusal of officials to enforce existing law,

question of the meaning of citizenship was directly faced. Taken together and read as a single argument, the brief and the report asserted that there is a citizenship created by and existing under the United States Constitution, even that it is an "American citizenship," that all free persons born in and residents of the United States occupy that status, that they have the privilege of unrestricted ingress into and egress from the states of the Union and that the state of sojourn must accord them, by virtue of the comity clause, all the privileges and immunities granted other citizens, at least of the same class.

The Ellsworth-Olcott argument thus took the first indispensable step of turning to the United States Constitution for a definition

---

if not their passive or active participation in its breach, was now the dominant factor.

The case of the "deluded McIntosh"—a mulatto who had killed an officer, was forcibly taken from a St. Louis jail by an angry crowd and burned to death—provided a particularly shocking instance of mob violence and interruption of the ordinary processes of the law. The abolitionists claimed that "some of the aldermen of the city and many distinguished persons" actively participated, that "the feeble remonstrances of the sheriff and a few others, were treated with contempt," and that "there was not the least show of resistance on the part of the civil authorities." To cap this "horrid piece of savagism," the courts apparently gave it their tolerance if not their sanction. A judge, whose name actually was Lawless, instructed the grand jury called to indict the leading actors, that no indictment was to be returned if the perpetrators were "the many, the multitude . . . not the act of numerable and ascertainable malefactors," the few.

Elizur Wright utilized the occasion to make, among other things, a constitutional argument. "Legal protection" was his keynote and his central theme. "When our fathers entered into Union, it was on the express condition that the rights of the citizens should be everywhere under the shield of law. The citizens of each state were to be entitled to all the privileges and immunities of citizens in the several states. No person was to be deprived of life, liberty, or property without due process of law. No person was to be punished for any crime, without a fair trial before an impartial jury, without having full information of the charge brought against him, nor without being confronted with the witnesses against him, and having compulsory process for obtaining witnesses in his favor. The people were to be secure against unreasonable searches and seizures, and against excessive, cruel, and unusual punishments. Above all, every citizen was to enjoy that noblest privilege of republicanism, freedom of speech and of the press. . . . These conditions have . . . every one of them. . . ." been trampled under foot.

Thus Wright invoked in this typical mob lynching situation the three constitutional notions of the guarantee of the protection of the law, privileges and immunities of citizens, and due process. Moreover, the privileges and immunities of citizens under the comity clause and the due process rights of persons under the Fifth Amendment, together with other guarantees and rights specified in the first eight amendments, were identified as "the rights of the citizen" which were to be "everywhere under the shield of law." They accordingly were closely tied up with citizenship and the obligation of legal protection.

of "citizen." This was a step which precluded freedom on the part of the states to do so. Limitations were then found in the comity clause on state power with respect to the privileges and immunities of citizens. Finally, it was suggested, by a reference to "the laws of Congress in the supremacy clause," that there was some undefined degree of federal legislative power in the premises.

It must be recognized at once that, while the Ellsworth-Olcott argument began to articulate what before had been unformulated, it was far from a statement of a full-blown doctrine of national citizenship, founded in the Constitution, and possessing unimpairable attributes. It either left entirely unanswered or failed to answer satisfactorily some crucial questions:

1. Is there a national citizenship independent of state citizenship?

2. If so, are there privileges and immunities which attach to it and which the states absolutely may not impair or destroy no matter how uniform or equal the deprivation or denial?

3. Aside from the desirable consequences of such citizenship, what are the constitutional evidences of it?

4. Does the federal government, does Congress possess the power to define the class of national citizen and to identify or create the privileges and immunities? The urgent need of the abolitionists for a constitutional doctrine which would generate federal power and at the same time limit state power in the absence of federal action had clearly not yet been met.

Whether the Ellsworth-Olcott argument supplied the elements out of which such a doctrine could be elaborated was a question fought out by the abolitionists in the decade 1836–1846. The episodes, during this period, through which the elements of the argument and the argument itself were tested and culled suggested, if they did not assure, a negative answer.[4] They were so limited in their fact situations as to involve only a small and separable part

---

[4] The history of the comity clause in this context goes back to the Missouri controversy of 1820, thirteen years before the organization of the American Anti-Slavery Society. At that time colonization was regarded by the South as a method of getting rid of the disquieting influence of free Negroes and by the North as a method of removing a class regarded with contempt and as permanently and biologically

of the total problem of abolitionism. Of these, the Crandall case and the Putnam report on the laws of Ohio dealt with the legal devices used by free states to exclude free Negroes or discriminate against them once admitted. Other incidents involved the vengeance wreaked by slaveholders upon abolitionists caught in the South for acts and words in the North;[5] and the attempted interference by the southern states with the civil liberties of abolitionists in the North.

The episodes, however, which were best known and which most completely tested the Ellsworth-Olcott argument as an abolitionist tool arose, on the one hand, out of the infamous laws on free colored seamen of the southern coastal states[6] and, on the other

---

inferior. The comity clause was invoked against a provision in the constitution of Missouri excluding free Negroes and mulattoes from the states.

In a "Memorial to the Congress of the United States on the Subject of Restraining the Increase of Slavery in New States to Be Admitted to the Union" (1819), Daniel Webster, George Blake, Josiah Quincy, James T. Austin, and John Geallison concluded that the comity clause "obviously applies to the case of the removal of the citizen of one state to another state; and in such a case it secures to the migrating citizen all the privileges and immunities of the citizens in the state to which he removed." The conclusion on the meaning of the comity clause was precisely the opposite of that later taken by Massachusetts in the Negro seamen controversy when it was contended that citizens of Massachusetts took their Massachusetts' rights with them to South Carolina.

For other supporters of the point of view taken by the committee see the remarks in Congress of Tallmadge, Fuller, and Blake. 16th Cong., 1821.

William Jay used the comity clause to attack the restrictions in the Ohio laws on the admission of free persons of color discussed in the Olcott report. Jay, *Miscellaneous Writings on Slavery* (Boston, 1853), pp. 371–394.

[5] Lewis Tappan, *Address to the Non-Slaveholders of the South on the Social and Political Evils of Slavery* (1843); William Goodell, *Views of American Constitutional Law in Its Bearing upon American Slavery* (Utica, N.Y., 1844); Horace Mann, Speech on the Fugitive Slave Law, February 28, 1851, published in *Slavery: Letters and Speeches* (Boston, 1851).

[6] The main targets of attack were laws, such as that passed by South Carolina in and after 1822, forbidding the entrance of free colored seamen to any of the state's ports and enforcing the ban by search of vessels, imprisonment, whipping, and sale into slavery of the offending seamen.

In 1823, Amos Daly, a Rhode Island Indian, was tried under the foregoing laws by a summary court consisting of a magistrate and three freeholders. Judge William Johnson of the United States Supreme Court, to whom an appeal was made to intervene, felt that he was without power to act, though he apparently thought there was merit in the comity clause point which had been raised. Report of Committee on Commerce, 27th Cong., 3d sess., January 20, 1843.

See also the argument of William Jay in the case of Gilbert Horton. Bayard Tuckerman, "William Jay and the Constitutional Movement for the Abolition of Slavery" (1893), pp. 31–33; Resolve and Declaration of a Joint Special Committee of the Legislature of Massachusetts, February 3, 1845; John Palfrey, "Papers on the Slave Power," first published in the *Boston Whig*, 1847.

hand, out of efforts in the North to liberate slaves whose masters voluntarily brought them into free states for a temporary stay or whose masters sought to pass through free states with them.[7] Neither the nullification of the seamen laws nor the freeing of slaves temporarily brought into free states would greatly shake the hated institution; and the constitutional argument which would achieve these purposes was more likely to be a partial cure applicable to particular and limited fact situations than a sweeping remedy for slavery or a culmination to the great reform.

As the winnowing process proceeded through these episodes, the defects of the Ellsworth-Olcott argument gradually emerged. We can see now that the argument basically did not possess the potentiality of development into a full-fledged doctrine of national citizenship. The reason also is now apparent: the dominant role played by the comity clause. The difficulties and weaknesses of the comity clause, which provides (Art. IV, sec. 2) that "the Citizens of each State shall be entitled to all Privileges and Immunities of Citizens in the several States," might be stated somewhat as follows:

1. The immediate and obvious impression created by the clause is that it deals with persons who migrate, with the citizen of one state who moves to another. As such, it leaves untouched the broad masses of the people, stationary in their original states or settled down and stabilized in the ones to which they have gone. It applies only to travelers, visitors, sojourners, or persons in process of moving. Once they have come to rest and taken up new residences, once they have lost citizenship in their old states and acquired it in the new, they no longer can claim whatever protection the clause has to offer.

2. The benefit of the clause extends only to those who are citizens of a state. "The Citizens of each State shall be entitled. . . ." What-

---
[7] *Commonwealth* v. *Aves* (1836), 18 Pickens (Mass.) 193; *Willard* v. *Illinois* (1843), 4 Scammon (Ill.) 461; *People of the State of New York* v. *Lemmon* (N.Y.C. Sup.Ct. 1852; N.Y. Sup.Ct. 1857; N.Y.Ct. Appeals 1860); *In re Perkins* (1852), 2 Cal. 424.

ever those benefits are or may be, they are not conferred on persons who are not citizens of a state. And the language in no way tends to restrict the right of the states themselves to determine who are their citizens or to define the class with rigorous exclusiveness. Thus the clause does not serve to restrain a state from drawing a citizenship line between classes of its own inhabitants; nor does it appear to lay any restraints upon a state in dealing with its own citizens either by forbidding some actions altogether or by requiring uniform and nondiscriminatory treatment.

3. The clause therefore seems dominantly to be a provision for nondiscrimination against outsiders, a guarantee of equal protection for those entering the state. Its only reasonable interpretation is that migrating citizens must receive in the state to which they remove the same rights as the citizens of that state—not the rights of citizens in the state which they have left, not the rights of citizens in any of the several states.[8] Such persons may not be discriminated against because they are outsiders. They may not be treated as aliens or foreigners. They are entitled, under the clause, to the same treatment as the natives of the same class receive. The clause gives them no rights which cannot be taken away by the state if, at the same time, the rights are taken away from the natives.

4. The inherent weakness of the clause arising from its double-edged character lay just below the surface and soon became apparent to abolitionists and proslaveryites alike. If the rights guaranteed to travelers or migrants were those of the state of sojourn, a southern slave brought to a free state would be free; but a free colored citizen of Massachusetts would be subjected in South Carolina to

---

[8] In the 1819 memorial to Congress (see note 4 *supra*) this possible construction was laid at rest. "It would be impossible," the committee argued, "that all the rights, advantages, and immunities of citizens of the different states could be at the same time enjoyed by the same persons. These rights are different in different states; a right exists in one state, which is denied in others, or is repugnant to other rights enjoyed in others. In some of the states, a freeholder alone is entitled to vote in elections; in some, a qualification of personal property is sufficient; and in others, age and freedom are the sole qualifications of electors. In some states, no citizen is permitted to hold slaves; in others, he possesses that power absolutely; in others, it is limited."

the Fourteenth Amendment 79

the Draconian laws of that state governing free persons of color. Conversely, if the traveler or migrant took with him the rights of his home state, South Carolina would be forced to recognize the privileges and immunities of colored citizens of Massachusetts; but the southerner could take slavery with him into the free states. Obviously, a constitutional clause with this potential of inversion permitting it to be turned against the user no matter which alternative starting point he selected had a limited future.

5. The language of the clause does not yield easily to the idea that national citizenship is referred to. In any event, if the ellipsis is supplied and the words "of the United States" are read following the word "Citizens" the second time it occurs in the clause,[9] still

---

[9] This was precisely the doctrine developed by the South and invoked in its behalf with respect to all the fact situations enumerated above which involved Negroes. In a congressional speech urging the admission of Missouri as called for by the compromise made in 1821, Pinckney of South Carolina claimed authorship of the comity clause and explained its meaning: "At the time I drew that constitution, I perfectly knew that there did not then exist such a thing in the Union as a black or colored citizen, nor could I then have conceived it possible such a thing could ever have existed; nor notwithstanding all that is said on the subject, do I now believe one does exist in it; and in order to prove this, the only question for consideration is, what is a citizen of the United States? And I now answer, as we consider one in the state to which I belong.

"In South Carolina, we consider all white persons born in the same, or adopted according to law, to be citizens, and entitled as such, to all the privileges of a citizen, where not disabled by something personal to themselves. Their privileges vary according to their sex and situation.

"Thus, this alone is called a citizen there; and nothing less than this can in my opinion constitute a citizen of the United States." *Annals* 16th Cong., 1st sess., February 13, 1821, pp. 1132–1134.

South Carolina legislative resolution, December 6, 1844: "That free negroes and persons of color are not citizens of the United States within the meaning of the Constitution, which confers upon citizens of one state the privileges and immunities of citizens in the several states."

Charles O'Connor, arguing in behalf of the slaveholder in the famous Lemmon case, maintained that a citizen of a state, when he departed from it, leaves behind him all the political rights and all the "special and peculiar rights and privileges conferred upon him" by the state as a citizen thereof. He does not acquire political rights or rights of citizenship from the state to which he has gone until he has lost his earlier citizenship. Therefore, the traveler, having neither the rights of his original state nor of the state of sojourn, is protected in nothing by the comity clause unless there are rights appertaining to national citizenship distinct from those which may belong to an individual by virtue of his citizenship in a particular state and these rights are the ones secured by the clause. O'Connor argued that there were such rights and that this was implied by the fact that the comity clause spoke of the privileges and immunities of "citizens" simply, without reference to the state of their domicile or travel.

the subject of the clause is not such citizens but citizens of the states. It is the "Citizens of each State" who are the beneficiaries of the clause. They are by this reading said to be "entitled to all Privileges and Immunities of Citizens" of the United States "in the several States." Therefore, even assuming citizens of the United States are referred to, there is no guarantee to them. They are simply put forward as a standard. Their existence is presupposed. By this reading of the clause, citizens of each state may not be accorded fewer privileges and immunities, in any of the states, than belong to, or are the right of, United States citizens. But what is a United States citizen? What are his privileges and immunities? About this, even when we accept the reading suggested, the clause has nothing whatever to say. From it we merely know that there are United States citizens and that they have privileges and immunities.

6. Finally, the comity clause as a source of federal power presents peculiar difficulties. It is, to begin with, not stated as a grant of power or even as a limitation on power. Like the clauses pertaining to the fugitive slave and fugitives from justice, in the same article, it is much more plausibly an article of compact between the states, a provision as to interstate relations. It does not even have the advantage, suggested by but not explicitly included in the fugitive slave clause, of being a flat prohibition on state action. In effect it seems to be a requirement of affirmative state action. It commands that each state shall guarantee and supply to the citizens of other states certain privileges and immunities. The one circumstance that suggested the possibility of federal and even congressional enforcement of this clause was the very powerful one arising from congressional enforcement of the companion fugitive slave clause. Abolitionists occasionally pointed to that fact but always with hesitancy; for they had been steadfastly insisting not only that the Fugitive Slave Act transcended the limitations on congressional power found in the amendments, particularly the Fifth, but also that power to carry out the fugitive slave clause was not to be found

the Fourteenth Amendment

among the grants to Congress, and hence Congress, by so acting, was violating the Tenth Amendment and the principles of the federal system.

These points were illustrated and the weaknesses of the comity clause for either proslavery or antislavery purposes were fully revealed in 1843 in the famous episode involving free colored seamen. Remonstrance and all other methods prosecuted on a state level having failed to procure relief from southern laws imprisoning colored crewmen on coastal vessels, it was decided to seek the intervention of the national government. One hundred and fifty Bostonians appealed directly to Congress, urging it to "render effectual . . . the privileges of citizenship, secured by the Constitution of the United States." They thus made the comity clause the explicit basis both of the rights they claimed and of the authority of Congress to protect those rights. In the House, the petition was referred to the Committee on Commerce, which eventually made a divided report.[10] The majority opinion was submitted by Robert C. Winthrop of Massachusetts; the minority, by Kenneth Rayner of North Carolina. Between them, these two opinions cover the whole range of the limitations of the comity clause.

The majority, in adopting and refining the constitutional position of the petitioners, dealt first with the meaning of state citizenship under the comity clause. They argued that some of the states recognized no distinction of color in relation to citizenship, that the colored man of Massachusetts had "enjoyed the full and equal privileges of citizenship since the last remnant of slavery was abolished . . . by the Constitution of 1780"; and that therefore "the Constitution of the United States . . . at its adoption [in 1789] found the colored man of Massachusetts a citizen of Massachusetts." As such, he was entitled to all the privileges and immunities "of a citizen in the several states." However extended or limited those privileges and immunities might be, "the citizens of each state" were "entitled to them equally, without discrimination of color or

---

[10] 27th Cong., 3d sess., January 20, 1843.

condition." So the Negro citizen of Massachusetts was entitled to the same privileges and immunities in southern states as white citizens of Massachusetts were, and the seamen's laws which imprisoned them without charge or trial constituted "a plain and palpable violation" of the comity clause of the United States Constitution.

The Winthrop report next analyzed the doctrine of the Prigg case for its bearing on the relation between the comity clause and the reserved powers of the state. "If the police power of the state," said the majority of the Committee on Commerce, "cannot be permitted to divest a master of his constitutional right over his slave," as secured by one of the provisions of Article IV (the fugitive slave clause) "as little can it be suffered to divest a free citizen of his constitutional right over himself, his own actions, and his own motions," as guaranteed by another provision of Article IV (the comity clause). "If on the contrary this police power can make a citizen no citizen in one state, it is hard to perceive why it cannot make a slave no slave in another state."

The minority made a categorical attack upon each of the constitutional points of the majority. The comity clause, argued Rayner, cannot mean that a citizen of Massachusetts, on going to South Carolina, is entitled to all the privileges and immunities respecting taxation, jury service, release under insolvency laws, and suffrage which he possesses in Massachusetts, despite the fact that such privileges and immunities are not conferred by South Carolina on its own citizens. It can only mean that South Carolina "is bound to extend to the citizens of each and every state the same privileges and immunities she extends to her own 'under like circumstances.' " The privileges and immunities to be accorded are nowhere defined in the Constitution. They are left entirely to state regulation. It was in consideration of this very fact, "in view of the variant regulations the several states might adopt," that the comity clause was incorporated in the Constitution. "Therefore, the term citizens, as used in the Constitution, has no specific or definite meaning, only so far as qualified by the regulations which the respective states may have adopted in defining their privileges and immunities." But if the construction of the majority be accepted as correct and the meaning of state citizenship for the purposes of the comity clause is not left to state determination, free Negroes are not citizens within the meaning of the clause.

The terms, privileges and immunities which are expressive of the object intended to be secured to the citizens of each state in every other, plainly import, ... something more than those ordinary rights of personal security and property, which, by the courtesy of all civilized nations, are extended to the citizens or subjects of other countries while they reside among them. None can, therefore, in the correct sense of the term, be a citizen of the state who is not entitled, upon the terms prescribed by the institutions of the state, to all the rights and privileges conferred by those institutions upon the highest class of society.

In no state, not even Massachusetts, does the Negro occupy that position.

Finally, Rayner fixed his attention on the power of Congress under the comity clause. He was less concerned to deny it, however, though he did that too, than he was to show that, if conceded, it might be used against the abolitionists themselves. This he did by inverting the line of reasoning supplied by the majority.

The Memorialists ask Congress to enforce the same relations in regard to the white and colored man in South Carolina, which prevail in Massachusetts.... do not the Memorialists see ... that if Congress has the power to enforce, in the slaveholding states, the same relations between a white and colored man, that exist in the non-slaveholding states, it must have the right to enforce in the non-slaveholding the same which exist in the slaveholding.

In view of the difficulties and weaknesses in the comity clause—its double-edged and reversible character, its textual ambiguities, its failure to yield easily any universal, federally enforceable standards or a theory of national citizenship, above all its whole tendency to make everything dependent upon state-determined state citizenship and state-determined privileges and immunities—in view of all this, it is no wonder that the attempt of the abolitionists to make the comity clause a useful constitutional weapon proved abortive. And, to the extent that the comity clause was a central element in the Ellsworth-Olcott argument, that argument, too, was not capable of sustaining the ultimate development of a theory of national citizenship.

The comity clause did, however, make a significant though an indirect contribution to paramount national citizenship as that doctrine finally evolved. The national government would naturally be the primary guardian of national citizenship. The federal courts certainly, and perhaps the federal Congress, would determine the conditions under which such citizenship existed and the scope of its privileges and immunities. But, while the doctrine of paramount national citizenship would strip the states of any power in these respects, yet by reading national citizenship, once created, into the comity clause, the states were placed under a constitutional obligation, not simply to refrain from impairing that citizenship or destroying those privileges and immunities, but by legislative, executive, and judicial action to secure and maintain them. The protection of the laws for citizens of the United States—national laws by virtue of national citizenship, state laws by virtue of the comity clause—was thus guaranteed.

In addition, during the argument over the comity clause, and especially by applying it to particular fact situations, the abolitionists had identified and laid claim to a list of rights, on behalf of themselves, free Negroes, and slaves, not simply as rights natural or civil, but as privileges and immunities incident to citizenship. For slaves, they had claimed a right of freedom in free states. For free Negroes and Mulattoes, they had claimed the rights freely to move about the country, to pursue a lawful calling without legal discrimination, to be immune from "seizing, imprisoning, whipping, and selling as slaves for life . . . without cause assigned, hearing, and trial," and to be protected in their rights to themselves,

the Fourteenth Amendment 85

their own actions, and their own motions. For themselves, abolitionists had claimed freedom of speech, press, assemblage, and the protection of the laws. Though the citizenship to which they were attached changed from state to national, these basic rights continued to be claimed as privileges and immunities incident to it.

By the middle 1840's paramount national citizenship, the distinctive doctrine of abolitionism, had been brought to this stage of development: the abolitionists had claimed the protection of the United States Constitution against local proscription and suppression. They had claimed it, moreover, as "American citizens." In doing so, they had loosely interchanged "citizens of the United States" with persons having inalienable natural rights, on the one hand, and with persons having the rights guaranteed by the constitutional amendments, on the other. An idea of state citizenship fixed and circumscribed by the United States Constitution had been called into service to stay the course of state and local discriminations against free Negroes and Mulattoes and to free the slaves and safeguard the rights of whites. Occasionally, the United States citizenship of free Negroes had been asserted. In scattered instances, the citizenship even of slaves had been vaguely suggested. The comity clause had been fully explored and, though discarded as a primary instrument, its indirect contributions and its value as a secondary support were recognized. The reciprocity of allegiance and protection had been applied particularly to the rights of citizens. These were beginnings. They were little more. They presented ideas and doctrines which could be, but had not yet been, synthesized and focused.

National citizenship as a constitutional doctrine, separated from the undifferentiated mass of the total religious, ethical, natural rights argument, and distinguished from a mere demand for constitutional protection based on a claim of right, had yet to be propounded. At best, emphasis had been on the desirable consequences for abolitionist purposes of such citizenship rather than on its constitutional evidences. There had been no clear avowal or sustained development of a national citizenship either prior to or independent of state citizenship, the existence and privileges and immunities of which were fixed by the United States Constitution or to be fixed and enforced under it by the federal government. National citizenship had not been invoked as a source of national government authority throughout the nation unlimited by state lines and federal principles.

The principal spokesmen and most articulate exponents of the theory of paramount national citizenship, the men who built on these beginnings and supplied these deficiencies, were Lysander Spooner and Joel Tiffany, especially the latter.[11] Spooner and Tiffany sought to establish a citizenship of the United States existing independently of state citizenship by the Preamble of the Constitution and by the Lockeian and Jeffersonian premise as to the origin of government. Those by whose authority the Constitution of the United States was established, argued Spooner, "must of course be presumed to have been made citizens under it." According to the Preamble, the constituent authority derived from "the people of the United States." This class was not limited to the persons who voted or were entitled to vote upon the ratification. Women and children did not have the suffrage, but they were certainly citizens. Those who participated in the adoption acted in behalf of all others. By "the people of the United States," the Constitution meant "all the people then permanently inhabiting the United States." No exceptions were made or authorized. Thereafter, by the same token, all persons born within the jurisdiction of the United States became citizens by birth. Resident foreigners might be added to these two groups through the naturalization power of Congress.

---

[11] Lysander Spooner, *The Unconstitutionality of Slavery* (Boston, 1845); Joel Tiffany, *A Treatise on the Unconstitutionality of American Slavery: Together with the Powers and Duties of the Federal Government in Relation to that Subject* (Cleveland, Ohio, 1849).

the Fourteenth Amendment

But, aside from the specific language of the Preamble, United States citizenship followed from the purpose for which the national government was created. The "great paramount object," said Tiffany, of the institution of the national government, no less than of other governments, was the protection of the citizen in the enjoyment of his natural and inalienable rights. At the time of the adoption, it was the universally received doctrine of the American people that all men had an equal right to life, liberty, and property and that governments were instituted by them for the protection of those rights. Possessing the rights equally and equally needing protection, "all men" were "equally entitled to participate in the formation of the government" and to its "equal protection" once formed. "We the people" of the Preamble were thus the same as "all men" of the Declaration of Independence and both were citizens of the United States.

Thus, out of the Preamble to the Constitution, which had the binding force of any of the specific provisions of the Constitution (binding, moreover, not only on the federal government but on the states as well), out of its declaration of the sources of ultimate constitutional authority and the unqualified description of the class granting it—all "We the people of the United States"—out of these and the unlimited character of the naturalization power of Congress taken together with the supremacy clause, these two abolitionist lawyers compounded their basic proposition: that there is a United States citizenship created or recognized by the Constitution and that it belongs to all inhabitants permanently resident in the United States at the time of the adoption of the Constitution, to all persons born in the United States and subject to its jurisdiction, and to all persons in whose favor Congress has exercised its unlimited power of naturalization.

Having said that there were United States citizens and who they were, two steps remained to be taken: first, to say what it meant to be a United States citizen, what were the rights attached to the status; and second, to determine the nature and location of the federal power to supply the requisite protection, and especially whether it was limited by the principles of federalism. Spooner and Tiffany took both steps in their stride.

What then are the privileges and immunities which the American citizen has a right to demand of the federal government? The answer is, he has a right to demand, and have full and ample protection in the enjoyment of his personal security, personal liberty, and private property,"[12] . . . protection against the oppression of individuals, communities and nations, foreign nations and domestic states: against lawless violence exercised under the forms of governmental authority.

These are the privileges and immunities of United States citizens. They are to be distinguished from the various constitutional guarantees designed to secure those privileges and immunities. These guarantees are to be found in the amendments which are not themselves confined to citizens of the United States. In order "to secure to each citizen the blessings of personal liberty," said Tiffany, certain rights were guaranteed to "all persons under the jurisdiction of the federal government." These were the right to petition, the right to keep and bear arms, the right to be free from unreasonable searches and seizures, the right not to be held answerable for infamous crimes without indictment or presentment, the right to a speedy public jury trial and to confrontation of witnesses; immunity from double jeopardy, compulsory self-incrimination, and deprivation of "life or liberty, etc., without due, legal process."[13]

---

[12] Spooner was less comprehensive on this subject. He thought that one attribute of such citizenship was the natural right to personal liberty. Moreover, he argued that the Constitution contained positive provisions designed to enforce and secure the natural right to liberty. "The positive provisions of the Constitution in favor of liberty" which must "of themselves, have necessarily extinguished slavery if it had had any constitutional existence to be extinguished" are twelve in number. They range through the various powers of Congress and touch upon the contracts clause, qualifications for president, and jury trial provisions.

[13] Spooner made no mention of the due process clause. Tiffany has a short chapter on due process, using it in its mixed substantive and procedural sense. He begins his discussion by characterizing it as a "fresh and imperative . . . guarantee for freedom . . . which cannot be realized while slavery is permitted in the Union." He then gives it its technical meaning as the "legal process" required to be followed in arresting and detaining criminals, the "process" required to be constantly in the hands of the officer "from the beginning of the arrest to the end of execution."

the Fourteenth Amendment

In a similar way, the framers of the Constitution made provision for the "protection of the property of the citizen, so far as it was necessary, beyond the state governments, by providing against forfeitures; and that private property should not be taken for public use without adequate, and just compensation—that courts should be open for the redress of grievances—that in all cases at common law, when the amount in dispute exceeded $20, the right of trial by jury should be maintained."

The importance of this distinction between privileges and immunities of citizens of the United States and the constitutional rights provided to secure them becomes apparent when federal enforcement is discussed. Both the privileges and immunities and the constitutional rights were to be enforced by the federal courts in appropriate cases. Both carried with them an incident of federal legislative power. But federal legislative and judicial activity was limited by a doctrine of state action in regard to privileges and immunities but not in the case of the amendments. Referring to the former, Tiffany said: "We do not hold that the federal government is bound to enact laws to see that those rights are observed between citizen and citizen in the same state. It is peculiarly the province of the state governments to do that; and they will be presumed to have performed that duty, except in those cases where, by positive enactments, they have authorized a violation of these rights." As between citizens in the same state, therefore, the power of Congress with respect to the privileges and immunities of citizens of the United States was merely corrective, precisely in the way the Court later declared it to be in connection with the Fourteenth Amendment. Not so, however, with the guarantees of the amendments. They were, to begin with, binding on the states[14] as well as on the national government. And, more than that, they were in any event subject to federal legislative enforcement. "Congress," said Tiffany, "have full and ample power to put an end to

---

[14] Again Spooner is less sweeping than Tiffany. He emphasized the word "Congress" in the First Amendment, but he thought that the Second Amendment at least applied to the states as well as the nation.

slavery throughout the Union, by enacting such laws as may be necessary to enforce those guarantees."[15]

Thus, in these works of Spooner and Tiffany, all the principal elements of the abolitionist constitutional doctrine of paramount national citizenship had now been supplied and the major pattern of their interrelationship established.[16] United States citizenship was created by or evidenced in the Constitution. It included all persons born within the jurisdiction of the United States or naturalized by Congress. It was panoplied with indestructible privileges and immunities. These consisted of the natural and inalienable rights of men to "the enjoyment of personal security, personal liberty, and private property."

---

[15] Since his theory of the unconstitutionality of slavery was based primarily on natural law, natural rights concepts which, though already binding, were given expression as the law of the land in the Declaration and Constitution, Spooner tended more or less unavoidably to talk in terms of the judiciary as the agency of enforcement. Slavery violated natural law and the Constitution; judges were the principal executors of these. Additional positive enactment was not necessary. Spooner took this view despite the fact that he used several pages showing the irreconcilability of slavery with the grant and exercise of many of the powers vested in Congress; and despite the fact that his emphasis on the guarantee by the United States of a republican form of government to the states tends to suggest legislative rather than judicial action.

Unlike Spooner, Tiffany laid stress throughout on the legislative power of the national government. In his view, that power arose as an incident of securing to citizens "full and ample protection in the enjoyment of their privileges and immunities." He invokes the federal legislative power, also, to execute the guarantee of a republican form of government. It is this power, too, says Tiffany in so many words, which must be exerted to maintain the privilege of the writ of habeas corpus, though the affirmative power to legislate for that purpose must be derived mysteriously from a constitutional negation of that very legislative power. When the federal legislative power flowed from this source, it did not extend to seeing that "those rights are observed between citizen and citizen in the same state, . . . except . . . where, by positive enactment" the states have authorized a violation of the right, and in the enforcement of prohibitions on federal and state power in the amendments.

[16] Gerrit Smith, in a speech in the New York state capitol in 1850, repeated in part in his congressional speech on the Kansas-Nebraska bill in 1854, argued: (1) Slavery being a denial of man's natural and inalienable right, and law existing for the protection not the destruction of rights, "no paper however authoritative" and even though a constitution "can legalize" slavery "or sanction its legality, or protect its existence." (2) If before 1776 there had been "legal and constitutional slavery in this land," the Declaration of Independence, "for some purposes the highest constitutional authority in the nation," brought it abruptly to an end throughout the land. (3) Contrary to the law of nature, abolished by the Declaration of Independence, slavery is also condemned everywhere in the nation by the Constitution of the United States. The Preamble, by the use of the phrase "We the people,"

In Tiffany but not in Spooner they also either consisted of the rights of the first eight amendments or those rights were guaranteed to all persons in order to secure to citizens their privileges and immunities. The privileges and immunities of citizens of the United States and the guarantees of the amendments were all binding both on the states and on the national government. They were to be protected or supplied by state laws according to a standard of equality. But Congress, too, had legislative power in the premises. At the very minimum, it was empowered to nullify state laws which violated the rights of citizens or the guarantees of the amendments and itself to supply "full," "ample," "equal protection" of these rights and guarantees if the states failed to act or to act properly.

---

designates the citizens of the United States. That phrase "necessarily means all and not a part—every kind and not one kind—of the people, who were, at that time, permanent inhabitants of the country. . . . It follows that, if there were slaves in this country, at the time the Constitution was adopted, that instrument made them all citizens, and, therefore, made them all free." (4) By many of its other provisions, including the amendments and particularly the due process clause, the Constitution forbids slavery. The due process provision is "an organic and fundamental law . . . paramount to every other law"—a proposition for which *Taylor* v. *Porter* is cited—overriding the claim that the slaves are held by law and therefore by "due process of law." (5) Finally, Smith concocted an elaborate argument out of history, context, and grammar to strike at the basis of *Barron* v. *Baltimore* and show that the amendments were not only applicable to the federal government, but operated as a restraint upon state power as well.

During the Civil War, and five years after the Dred Scott decision, Attorney General Edward Bates rendered an opinion that freemen of color born in the United States are citizens of the United States. The salient features of the opinion are these: (1) The Constitution uses the word "citizen" to express "the political quality of the individual in his relation to the nation"; it means "a member of the nation." (2) Suffrage and the right to hold office are not incidents, privileges, or immunities of citizenship; these consist solely of the duty of allegiance and the right of protection. (3) These political rights and obligations attaching to birth in a country are "common to all nations," "as old as political society," "preëxistent and natural." Consequently the Constitution does not make or create natural-born citizens—"it is in fact made by them"—it only recognizes them. (4) Citizens are all "politically and legally equal." (5) Every citizen of a state is necessarily a citizen of the United States; and every citizen of the United States is a citizen of the state in which he is domiciled. (6) There is no class of persons intermediate between citizens and aliens. (7) Though logically the theory of citizenship by birth, preëxistent to the Constitution and natural, which the Constitution therefore recognizes but does not create, and by which all persons born in the country are equally under a duty of allegiance and equally have a right to protection, quite regardless of color or race, would apply to persons who were slaves, yet Bates declines to say so because that question was not before him. (8) Dred Scott was distinguished on technical grounds. (November 29, 1862) 10 Ops. A.G. 382.

Like much of abolitionist constitutional theory, this doctrine was a slow and evolutionary development, a gradual and almost organic growth. But, as with the rest of abolitionist constitutional theory, imaginative and able minds not only catalyzed the process but added a touch of creation. Spooner and Tiffany cannot be dismissed as simple compilers. The reduction or accommodation of all these elements—equality of protection, personal security, personal liberty, and private property, and privileges and immunities of citizens—to and within an interlocking, triple-reinforced theory of paramount national citizenship was an act of constructive originality.

The doctrines of the two minority groups—the Stewart contingent and the paramount national citizenship theorists,—interesting in themselves as a study in the history of constitutional growth and creation, are very suggestive with respect to the meaning of the Civil War amendments. Could it be that so far as those amendments did anything more than declare and ratify what events had already confirmed, they enacted into the Constitution the doctrines of the two minority groups? These groups accepted the basic tenets of the main body of abolitionism about the natural and constitutional meaning of due process, equality, and protection. They agreed with the majority in turning to the United States Constitution and the national government as the sources of right and power which would liberate the slave, emancipate the free Negro, and protect the whites. They diverged from the majority over the degree of deference to be paid to the dogma of federalism. They would pay it no deference. They differed over the specific constitutional sources of the national authority: one holding that it derived primarily from the ideas of equal protection and due process; the other, that it derived primarily from national citizenship.

The Civil War amendments, *if the doctrines of these two minority groups are their origins,* first, incorporated both equality, due process, and national citizenship as sources of national au-

the Fourteenth Amendment

thority, and second, confirmed the central government in its direct power to protect men in these rights. With respect to the views of the minority, the amendments were therefore declaratory. With respect to the views of the majority, they were amendatory on the subject of federalism. They empowered Congress to do directly what the majority, since 1838, had maintained Congress could do indirectly through an unlimited and purposeful exercise of the powers already given it. In this sense, and to the degree that abolitionist history and doctrine were epitomized by the Civil War amendments, the high purpose of those amendments—so far as the main body of abolitionism is concerned—was to put at rest an abstraction, to mark the end of a ritual.

CHAPTER V

Conclusions; the Antislavery Origin

~~~~~~

THE THREE much-discussed clauses of section 1 of the Fourteenth Amendment were the product of and perhaps took their meaning, application, and significance from a popular and primarily lay movement, which was moral, ethical, religious, revivalist rather than legal in character. The movement was comprised of people who knew little and cared less about the erudition and ancient usages of the law, who came to the reading of the Constitution as dogmatic, even fanatical reformers. To these abolitionists, centering in the Western Reserve of Ohio, the clauses of the document were, for the most part, without a significant past, and were to be filled with a present content only by the goals of their crusade. It was as a culmination of this movement and usage that the clauses of section 1 of the Fourteenth Amendment were made a part of the Constitution; and their accepted meaning was the meaning which these reformers gave them on the hustings, in revival meetings, in pamphlets, and in the thousand other outlets to their ardor.

The epochal period.—The antislavery origins of the Fourteenth Amendment go back to the period 1835–1838. Parts of them, it is true, had an earlier abolitionist usage. Nor can later contributions be ignored. But during this period an all-important reorientation of the movement from that of private conversion to public action took place. The shift entailed a change from a program which used equality and liberty as aids to attack the ethical and moral evils of slavery to a program which employed liberty and equality, now joined by other constitutional concepts, as primary arguments and levers to overturn slavery. The early legal and constitutional argument had been subordinate, and had been presented simply as an adjunct or reinforcement of ethical and moral arguments. The expediency of abolition, rather than the power to abolish, was the central theme. The later constitutional and legal argument was increasingly independent and primary, with the accent on power rather than upon mere expediency. Slavery was still a sin, and an ethical, moral, and political evil, but its abolition was not to wait upon individual conversion; it was to be rooted out by political action.

This period of shift, bringing the abolitionists face to face with the necessity of utilizing and resolving constitutional issues, forcing them to adjust the constituent instrument to the greatest social reform and power reallocation in our history, was a period of remarkable fertility in our constitutional development, an epochal formative period, a period of constitutional creation.

By the end of this period, when the American Anti-Slavery Society fell to pieces, and some of the leaders and members had begun to think in terms of political action, the abolitionists had come forward with a nationalistic constitutional theory. All the elements were present, but in varying degrees of maturity. The twenty years between 1840 and 1860, however, were not years of doctrinal stagnation. Many steps remained to be taken by way of doctrinal development, adjustment, and shift in emphasis.

The equal protection of the laws.—By all odds the most important of the elements of abolitionist constitutional theory, the one constantly emphasized by all abolitionists, was the double-barreled concept of the equal protection of the laws. Based on a state of nature in which all men were conceived to be equal, supplemented by laws of nature and of God which endowed all men equally with certain indivestible rights, strengthened and carried forward by the doctrine of the social compact, sanctioned by the starting point of their political philosophy, namely Locke, abolitionists accepted as an unshakable axiom of political faith, a *pons asinorum* of social salvation, the notion that governments were instituted to protect man in his inalienable rights to life, liberty, and property and that the standard by which this protection was to be meted out was that of equality.

Besides being the premise of the function and purpose of all government, this concept was the basic element of American government in particular. It was unchallenged as an essential part of the theory of the revolution and of the early Republic. It was recognized by and read into many of the state constitutions. It was made explicit in the Declaration of Independence, asserting that "all men are created equal," that they are entitled to "life, liberty, and the pursuit of hapiness," and the treating these rights as the gift of the Creator to man as man—therefore "unalienable," and proclaiming the right of the people to throw off any government which failed to carry out the primary duty of protecting men in these inalienable rights. It is the method and the measure by which justice, specified in the Preamble of the Constitution as a fundamental object of the organization of government, is to be established and tested. It is the universal correlative of the allegiance and obligation of obedience which the constitutional system exacts.

Humanitarian, ethical, and religious sentiments and principles

the Fourteenth Amendment 97

all reinforced these theories of government. Just as the great objection to slavery was its lack of legal protection for slaves, as well as the concomitant, invidious, and discriminatory treatment of free Negroes and the wholesale public and private invasion of the rights of abolitionists, so the first object of the abolitionists was to gain legal protection for the basic rights of members of all three classes. Because the curse and evil of slavery was the chattelization of man, the annihilation of personality, and the degradation of character, the remedy must be an affirmative protection of human beings as such, regardless of color, condition, or belief. Philosophic humanitarianism thus combined with political theory in general, and with American political theory in particular, in behalf of a basic proposition. The proposition was nothing more nor less than this: because every person living in a social state needs, desires, and has a right to the protection of the law—for which governments are instituted among men, and to which human beings are entitled by their humanity—slaves and free Negroes, together with the friends of both, must receive legal protection in their fundamental rights along with all other human beings.

Thus, it is this idea of the equal protection of the laws, omnipresent in abolitionist usage, the first approach of which drove slavery from the land, which secured to colored freeman all the political, economic, and governmental privileges, benefits, and safeguards dispensed to others, and which blanketed the white friends of both of these classes, indeed, of every human being in the land, with the civil rights and safety for person and property vouchsafed by the United States Constitution and the idea of society.

The equal protection of the laws is violated fully as much, perhaps even more, by private invasions made possible through failure of government to act as by discriminatory laws and officials. In the system of human bondage, characterized by limitations on the movements, residence, and economic opportunity of free colored persons, and of the exception from laws and agencies designed to confer the protection and bounty of government; in the system of freedom, marred and violated by the grossest outrages, mainly at the hands of private persons, to the indispensable conditions of freedom of free men, white and black—in both systems the dominant factor is the absence, in varying degrees, of the protection of the laws and officials of men in their fundamental rights. The fact that such protection is supplied to others makes the failure to supply it to the victims an abrogation of the standard of equality in the provision of legal protection.

The two parts of the phrase are thus inseparable. Every violation entails both an absence of protection and a denial of equality, at least whenever fundamental rights are at stake. When this is realized, modern doubts that the equal protection and congressional enforcement provisions of the Fourteenth Amendment were intended to reach situations of state inaction are at once dissipated. If the abolitionist origins of the Fourteenth Amendment are accepted, they were. The states are forbidden to fail to carry out their primary duty of protection; and, when carrying it out, are forbidden to fail to adhere to the standard of equality. Congress is authorized to enforce this provision, that is to say, is authorized to supply the protection of the laws when the states do not, and to correct deviations by the states from the prescribed standard of equality.

Due process of law.—In comparison with the concept of the equal protection of the laws, the due process clause was of secondary importance to the abolitionists. It did, however, reach a full development and, by virtue of its emphasis in the party platforms, a widespread usage and popular understanding.

The due process clause, like the equal protection concept, was used by the abolitionists as an instrument for the threefold and intermingled purpose of freeing the slaves and securing for free Negroes and the abolitionists the use and protection of the laws and the courts. In all three connections, its employment in the early stages was primarily procedural. It was not, however, either exclusively or basically negative. Stewart's shrewd exploitation of the antagonism between the procedural requirements of due process and the slave status was an express demand that the protection of the courts be supplied. The same affirmative element runs throughout the earliest due process usage in connection with the rights of abolitionists. Here it was not just a matter of preventing the legal actions of governments by interposing the formal due process requirement. It was a demand that due process be supplied as the means or requirement of protecting abolitionists from mobs and individual violence.

In 1834, Goodell wrote:

Neighbor, suppose someone hated you so violently that he wished to have you mobbed, and should get up a false report about you, pretending that you had done this thing and that thing and the other, that you never even thought of—and suppose by this means, one hundred men should be persuaded to surround your house, and pelt it with stones, and drag out your furniture and burn it, without once stopping to find out whether or no the man who accused you could prove the truth of his charges against you: what would you think of it and what kind of a "land of liberty" would you think you lived in, where your enemies had only to accuse you in order to get you punished—whether guilty or not—whether the offense charged upon you were any breach of the law or not—and all this without any court, or judge, or jury! And yet, this is the way in which abolitionists have been treated.[1]

From the very beginning of its abolitionist usage and while reliance was still placed entirely on its procedural connotations, due process was viewed not merely as a restraint on governmental power but as an obligation imposed upon government to supply protection against private action. Not to supply such protection was regarded as a denial or deprivation of due process of law. Thus a power of legislative enforcement or, more exactly, an obligation of the legislature to guarantee it, was very early coupled to the due process clause, though that clause appears to be nega-

---

[1] William Goodell, *An Appeal in Behalf of the American Anti-Slavery Society Addressed to the People of the City of New York Aug. 1834* (New York, 1834).

tively stated in the Constitution, and while accepting it as a simple procedural requirement. Once the clause became a substantive guarantee, once the natural rights to life, liberty, and property were read into it, together with certain auxiliary natural rights, the legislative power and obligation became even more clear and apparent.

The substantive development of due process also came very early. Indeed, almost from the inception of its application to slavery, it was put forward to safeguard property in slaves and liberty in men absolutely. This began when it was asserted by the South as a qualification upon "the right to legislate" designed to keep that power consistent with the "principles of natural justice ... the social compact," and "the inalienable rights of American citizens." It was thereafter immediately utilized by the abolitionists to attack the laws sustaining slavery on the identical ground that they conflicted with those principles and rights.

Over the next thirty years due process as a substantive conception became a part of the constitutional stock in trade of abolitionism. Some distinguished partisans were conspicuous exceptions. Spooner deliberately and continuously refused to rely upon due process, either procedural or substantive. Tiffany thought of it almost entirely as a formal requirement. But its firmly substantive character and the affirmative obligation of Congress in connection with it were, as we shall see, proclaimed and widely broadcast by the party platforms. In this respect, most abolitionists followed the party line. Even Alvan Stewart, who came to it slowly, before long was to be counted among the rest.

The meaning of the due process clause was never really a subject of controversy between proslavery and antislavery forces. The protagonists were in virtual agreement on substance, procedure, and legislative obligation. Their difference was as to whether slaves were persons or property. In all else pertaining to the meaning of the clause, they were at one. Accordingly, when the phrase ultimately was placed in the Fourteenth Amendment, there was no problem of selecting between conflicting lines of usage by pro-

the Fourteenth Amendment 101

slavery and antislavery forces or of overruling Chief Justice Taney's opinion in *Dred Scott* v. *Sandford* on this point. There was only one line of usage and it was common to both camps.

Privileges and immunities of citizens.—The core of the notion of citizenship is the protection of the laws. From whatever source derived—whether from a reciprocal and correlative duty of allegiance or more generally from the Lockeian premise on the purpose of government and the participants in its formation—this element is basic and indispensable. When United States citizenship began to be discussed, it was hence almost unavoidably in these terms. Goodell's statements in 1834, after the New York riots, is very much in point.

> We are generously offered protection on condition that we shall renounce our principles and cease to disseminate them.... We are to be protected, not in the enjoyment of our civil and religious liberties as free citizens; but if we will relinquish those rights, then we are to be unmolested in our persons and our property.... The protection we ask is a protection different from this; and it is a protection we supposed we had a right to claim, as free American citizens.... We ask them [our opponents] to remember that all the protection we need is needed by them, and is due to every citizen.[2]

The particular difficulties experienced in the development of the doctrine of United States citizenship, consequently, did not arise over differences about the essential nature or meaning of citizenship. The area of disagreement even about its privileges and immunities was not large, since their natural rights foundation was generally accepted. The difficulties arose almost exclusively from our federal system. United States citizenship had to be disentangled from state citizenship. Though both state and national citizenship might reside in one person, the independent and paramount character of the latter had to be established. Once this was done, the transition from right to power had to be made. The obligation to supply the protection had to be located in the national government and especially in the national legislature. In order that this

---
[2] *The Emancipator*, July 22, 1834.

national obligation might be discharged without contradictory interference by state authority, a negative limitation had to be placed on the states prohibiting them from abridging the privileges and immunities of citizens of the United States.

Since this superstructure of paramount national citizenship was the work of a minority and never became accepted by the large body of the abolitionist movement—it was never incorporated in the party platforms, for instance—it could not simply be read into the Constitution; it had to be written into it. If viewed as a culmination of the historic abolitionist movement, that is what the Thirteenth and Fourteenth amendments did.

The rights secured.—The history of the antislavery origins of the privileges and immunities, equal protection, and due process clauses of the Fourteenth Amendment makes clear their overlapping and duplicatory character. Each had a sweeping substantive meaning. In that sense, each was identical with the other two. Singly and collectively, they were intended to guarantee national constitutional and legislative protection to all men (citizens and persons) in their natural, inalienable rights. According to the antislavery origins and history, what were those natural, inalienable rights? Were these clauses, because of their natural rights content, a formula of imprecision, a charter of limitless discretion?

The abolitionists did not content themselves with the "life, liberty, or property" of the Fifth Amendment, or the "life, liberty, and the pursuit of happiness" of the Declaration, or the "personal security, personal liberty, and private property" of Blackstone, though these phrases were on everyone's lips. The detailed catalogue of specific rights which the abolitionists collected under the broad heading of natural rights and under these three clauses can be gathered rather easily from the goals of their crusade and the contexts of battles fought to attain them. One might say, with Justice Washington, that to supply the catalogue is "more tedious than difficult."

the Fourteenth Amendment 103

As the abolitionists saw it, slavery destroyed "a man's inalienable right to his own body," his ownership of himself. The slave was stripped of the "essentials of his moral nature"; he was changed from a man into a thing. And all the natural rights of manhood went with the change to thinghood. The slave was denied the right to contract or to acquire and hold property. His labor was coerced. No bargain was made, no wages given. He had no right to his earnings. His "provender and covering" were at the will of his owner. His right to personal security was demolished. He was given no protection for life or limb.[3] His personality, character, reputation were subject to defamation without redress. His family state and domestic relations were distorted and subject to disruption. His authority and responsibility to rear his children, to cherish, maintain, and defend his wife were obliterated. The members of his family might be torn from him and scattered. "His bed might be polluted with safety, his fireside invaded, his daughter dragged from him by the avaricious or the licentious as pleasure or profit might dictate." His rights of religion, reason, communication were all systematically abolished. He was forbidden "to assemble peaceably on the Sabbath for the worship of his Creator." He could not teach or be taught the Gospel. His "immortal mind was famished." Books were withheld from him. He was forbidden to read and write.

[3] According to the abolitionists, the slave codes authorized assault, battery, and many forms of violence to be committed upon the person of the slave by the master. They cited, as typical of such laws, the South Carolina provision permitting the owner, "in discharge of his responsibilities for the care and government of slaves," to impose cruel punishment almost without restraint "by whipping, or beating with a horse whip, cow skin, or putting irons on, or confining or imprisoning." The slave received some protection from injury by others. If his value was thereby diminished, the owner might bring suit for damages just as with damage to any property. The slave codes fell short of allowing willful murder. They also subjected to fine (in South Carolina the deterrent sum was 100 pounds) any person who did "willfully cut out the tongue, put out the eye, castrate or cruelly scald, burn or deprive any slave, of any limb or member." But the abolitionists were quick to point out that this merely meant that "the shadow of legal protection for life and limb" was extended to the slave. The substance, however, was not. The slave could not maintain an action at law no matter how grievous the injury done him. The master might "murder by system," or mistreat by design, "with complete impunity" if he did so only in the presence of Negroes or in course of administering correction.

All these rights, according to the abolitionists, were invaded, destroyed, or denied by slavery. So was one other: the right to be protected and protected equally in these various rights; the right, in the words of Weld, to have government "throw around the person, character, conscience, liberty, and domestic relations of the one, the same law that secures and blesses the other; in other words, to prevent by legal restraints one class of men from seizing upon another class, and robbing them at pleasure of their earnings, their time, their liberty, their kindred, and the very use and ownership of their own persons." Access to the courts, the rights to sue and be a witness, were indispensable to the establishment of this right.

The rights which abolitionists held were denied or abrogated by the treatment accorded free Negroes were these: the right to civil and religious equality, that is, the right to equal protection of their natural and religious rights; the right to be secure in their persons, houses, and property, that is, to receive the protection of the laws, courts, and public officials against lynch mobs, private violence, fraud, and calumny; the right to move about the country and take up residence where they pleased; the right to compete, without legal let or hindrance, for the ordinary sources of livelihood and economic opportunity, especially, the right to enter the common callings and occupations of the community and to be protected against private outrage in so doing; the right to avail themselves of the bounty of government as others do, particularly in the free use of the common schools.

Theodore Dwight Weld, in a sharp yet poetic passage, listed the rights denied to the abolitionists themselves:

the right of petition ravished and trampled by its constitutional guardians, and insult and defiance hurled in the faces of the sovereign people while calmly remonstrating with their servants for violence committed on the nation's charter and their own dearest rights!..."the right of peaceably assembling" violently wrested—the rights of minorities, rights no longer—free speech struck dumb—free men outlawed and murdered—free presses cast into the streets and their fragments strewed with

the Fourteenth Amendment 105

shoutings, or flourished in triumph before the gaze of approving crowds as proud mementoes of prostrate law.

The spirit and the power of our Fathers, where are they? Their deep homage always and everywhere rendered to free thought, with its inseparable signs—free speech and a free press—their reverence for justice, liberty, rights and all pervading law, where are they?

These were the specific rights of which slaves, free Negroes, and abolitionists were deprived. They constitute the spelling out in detail of the broad goals of the antislavery movement. They express the meaning of abolitionism. Read as the outcome of the abolitionist crusade, the object of the Civil War amendments, at least of the Thirteenth and Fourteenth, was to guarantee and safeguard these rights. To deprive men of them now or to allow men to be deprived of them now is a frustration of these historic purposes and a breach of those amendments. They are the basic, the irreducible minimum content of the amendments. Whether the amendments should, by some process of analogy or selective incorporation, be expanded to include additional rights is another and an unrelated question.

The first eight amendments.—The abolitionists saw slavery, the discriminations against free Negroes, and the mistreatment of the abolitionists themselves as violations of rights and guarantees imposed in the first eight amendments to the United States Constitution. These systems and breaches were above all else deprivations of life, liberty, and property without due process of law, conceived both substantively and procedurally. They were also denials of free speech and press, of the rights of peaceable assembly and petition. They were unreasonable searches and seizures. They were transgressions of the criminal safeguards of the Fifth, Sixth, and Eighth amendments. They were even at times and to some extent a violation of the right to bear arms, assured in the Second Amendment, and of the right to a jury trial in common-law suits, stated in the Seventh Amendment.

This is not to say that *all* abolitionists put forward *all* the first eight amendments to combat *all* phases of slavery, free Negro discrimination, and abolitionist mistreatment. They certainly did not. Charles Olcott in his two lectures published in 1838 maintained that "all the amendments to the Constitution are wholly incompatible with the substance of slavery. By them, the rights of conscience, speech, press, trial by jury, etc., are guaranteed in words, in the most solemn and ample manner to the 'people' generally, without any proviso, restriction, exception, or qualification whatever.... All slaves (who are 'people' also) are totally deprived of every one of the rights guaranteed by the express words of these amendments." Joel Tiffany, in his *Treatise on the Unconstitutionality of Slavery*, explicitly asserted that all the amendments were violated by slavery and, moreover, that they were all binding on the states. But these are extreme statements and even they do not include all the abuses of free Negroes and abolitionists in the coverage of the amendments.

Certain of the rights in the first eight amendments received well-nigh universal abolitionist attention. They were the rights mentioned in the due process clause of the Fifth Amendment and in the First and Fourth amendments. The rights in the other amendments received only casual, incidental, and infrequent reference. The criminal safeguards and limitations in the Fifth, Sixth, and Eighth amendments were not extolled as monuments in human liberty or as particularly valuable in themselves. Men who were enslaved, lynched, or mobbed, however, were subject to cruel punishments without judicial process, including those particular safeguards and limitations. It is an overstatement to say that an integral part of the abolitionist movement was the application of all the first eight amendments to the states.

The significant thing about the abolitionist appeal to the amendments was that it was much more an appeal to certain rights mentioned in the amendments than to the amendments themselves as constitutionally binding on anybody. The rights particularly claimed and which were mentioned in the amendments were also "the rights of citizens which our Fathers placed everywhere under the shield of law as the express condition upon which they entered the Union." They were required by justice. They were indispensable to liberty. They were what governments were instituted to protect and to protect equally by laws. They were the privileges and immunities of citizens of the United States. They were the natural and inherent rights of all men. This was the character of the substantive guarantee of life, liberty, and property in the due process clause and its procedural guarantee of judicial process and jury trial. It was also the character of the right to personal security safeguarded by the Fourth Amendment.

So, too, with the rights of the First Amendment. Freedom of discussion, especially, was regarded as falling among man's inherent rights, given to him for the development and promulgation of the law of nature and required to be exercised in his function as the chosen instrument for the salvation of the world. "When, therefore, this right is called in question," wrote one abolitionist, "then is the invasion, not of something obtained from human convention and human concession, but the invasion of a birthright—of that which is as old as our being, and a part of the original man."

This circumstance—that the amendments were a meeting ground of constitutional and natural rights—explains what otherwise would be a bewildering source of confusion. Despite *Barron* v. *Baltimore,* and despite their awareness of it, the abolitionists continued to talk as if they regarded the amendments as binding on the states. A few of them, such as Joel Tiffany and Gerrit Smith, simply thought that the Supreme Court was wrong. Most, however, perceived no contradiction. The "immortal Bill of Rights," that is, men's natural rights, was obligatory upon the states—obligatory, indeed, upon all governments. The duty of the states to protect these rights was obligatory in the absence of the Bill of Rights. Marshall did not and could not hold otherwise without denying the foundation of all government. That the federal courts were not necessarily the agency for the enforcement of these obligations upon the states was a different matter and a conclusion within the competence of the Supreme Court to reach. *Barron* v. *Baltimore* was therefore an irrelevancy, properly to be ignored when the duty of the states to safeguard the rights mentioned in the amendments was under consideration.

Federalism.—In the early stages little serious thought was given to the problem of integrating the abolitionist creed or reconciling it with the American federal system. The constitution of the American Anti-Slavery Society and most of its auxiliaries disavowed any intention of interfering with slavery in the states, making it plain that there was no claim of national authority to do so. Since the original motivation of the movement was individualistic—to convert slaveholders as individuals—and since the abolitionists had great faith in the pamphlet revival campaign as the instrument for accomplishing this purpose (thus bringing about the reform on a local level), the absence of serious concern about federalism as a limitation on the powers of the central government was natural. The Supreme Court opinion handed down in 1834 in *Barron* v. *Baltimore,* which precluded abolitionist use of the amendments as restraints on state power, was therefore not only not a disturbing factor; it was completely ignored.

While it was not articulated in these early stages, congressional power was implicit in some of the constitutional doctrines of the movement. Principal among these carriers or conductors of federal legislative power was the idea of the protection of the laws. Constituting the reason for the existence for government, placed at the base of the American system by the Declaration of Independence, state constitutions, and the Preamble to the United States Constitution, the obligation to protect and protect by laws was the highest purpose and duty of government. Moreover, by its very nature such protection could not be achieved by inaction; it demanded an affirmative exercise of power. When abolitionists connected this obligation of government with national citizenship,

the Fourteenth Amendment

due process of law, habeas corpus, the republican form of government guarantees, and even with the general welfare clause, the doctrine of national power was strengthened, not created.

Once the possibility of individual conversion was cut off by southern isolationism, once abolitionists were forced to reorient their movement into channels of political action and issues of constitutional power were thereby pushed into the foreground, the cause could succeed only if the barrier of federalism were breached. The leading minds of the movement reached this conclusion almost immediately. The more forthright among them resorted to a direct attack upon federalism. They read the congressional obligation to protect men in their natural and inalienable rights into national citizenship and the due process and other clauses of the Constitution. Moreover, Congress was to protect men's rights fully, equally, and regardless of state lines.

The more moderate and politic abolitionists resorted to an indirect attack upon federalism. They read the granted powers of Congress over the District of Columbia, over the federal territories, over the admission of new states, over interstate commerce as in no way limited by the effect their exercise might have upon institutions and practices sanctioned by state laws which Congress did not have the power to annul. The granted powers of Congress might thus purposefully be exerted to do indirectly what Congress was not authorized to do directly. To this extent, there was a cleavage in abolitionist constitutionalism; but it was a cleavage as to method, not as to result. Federalism was destroyed in either case. To the extent that abolitionism was consummated in the Thirteenth Amendment and reconsummated in the Fourteenth Amendment, therefore, a fundamental and revolutionary reallocation of the powers of government between the states and the nation was sanctified by the organic law of the land.

The theory of the South.—On many of these points the constitutional theory of the South, also well articulated before 1840, agreed with that of organized abolitionism. The proslavery forces, too, laid their basis in Locke, the social compact, the natural inalienable rights of men, and the protective purpose of government. They even talked about equality of protection and especially applied it as a requirement of the federal government. The guarantees of man's inalienable rights were embodied in the Preamble, the due process clause of the Fifth Amendment, and other provisions of the amendments. Anti- and proslaveryites united to assert that there were extraconstitutional and substantive limitations on the power of government, that Congress could not impair or destroy man's inalienable rights and, indeed, was under a duty affirmatively to sustain and promote them. Both factions talked about the rights of citizens of the United States.

The unbridged gulf between them separated the natural rights involved and the beneficiaries of the status of men and/or citizens. To the southerner, the natural right involved was property; to the abolitionist, liberty. And to the southerner the men who were to be protected in their inalienable rights were a selected class, not all human beings. So the difference between them was far narrower than the apparent range of the arguments and turned on none of the bases of the doubts that arose after the passage of the Fourteenth Amendment—not on the character of the rights secured or the duty of government to secure them by affirmative action, but on the question of whether slaves were persons (settled by the end of slavery), who were citizens of the United States (put at rest by the first sentence of the amendment), and the power of Congress over the states (removed from controversy by section 5 of the Fourteenth Amendment when taken together with the nature of the guarantees in section 1).

Part Two

THE DISSEMINATION OF THE CONSTITUTIONAL DOCTRINE

Introduction to Part Two

WHILE THESE doctrinal developments were under way, the processes of propaganda and political action were incessant. It was one task to create constitutional doctrines suited to the purposes of abolitionism. It was another and equally indispensable task to get them generally accepted, first among organized abolitionists, then among politicians and the people at large. In the performance of this task, active antislavery men were continuously engaged. Weld and Leavitt, in the years 1841-1842, undertook the management of the congressional bloc of abolitionists. Birney, Smith, Stewart, Chase, Goodell, Leavitt, diverted a portion of abolitionist political action into independent political parties. The lawyers of the movement made their voices heard in the courts. The unstilled presses of the movement ground out their weekly, monthly, and yearly grist.

Through convention resolutions and party platforms, through congressional debates, proceedings, and reports, through actions at law and arguments before courts, and, of course, through the continuing work of journals, pamphlets, and public lectures, the constitutional doctrines of abolitionism were publicized.

CHAPTER VI

Party Platforms and Resolutions

~~~~~~~~~~~~~~~~~~~~~~~~~~~~~~~~

THE MOVEMENT for the abolition of slavery and the concomitant protection of the rights of free Negroes and whites operated in the years 1840–1860 through three successive political parties: Liberty, Free Soil, and Republican. The first was the creation of the politically minded leaders of the virtually defunct American Anti-Slavery Society. It was a party organized around one idea only—abolition. In the Free Soil party, new men and measures were added; the old ones were not eliminated. The shift from liberty to free soil merely defined the new ground of the battle—the extension or nonextension of slavery into the new territories. The Republican party carried the issue to its fulfillment. These three parties and the introduction and full capitalization of this issue mark the successive steps by which slavery became the most pressing political question in the nation. They mark, too, the stages by which abolitionism was lifted from the creed of a much-vilified band of proselytizers to the officially espoused doctrine of the party and side that won the Civil War. Through these parties and on this issue the political, natural law, and constitutional principles of Weld and Stanton, Wright and Stewart, Birney and Chase were broadcast throughout the country—the very words and concepts that were laid down as the explicit bases for local, state, and national political campaigns. Thus they came to constitute the common property and understanding of the prewar generation.

The continuity of the abolitionist movement, leadership, and principles through the three political organizations is reflected in the content and authorship of their platforms. Those of the Liberty party in 1843, the Free Soil party in 1848, the Free Soil Democrats in 1852, and the Republicans in 1856 and 1860 contained virtually identical declarations on the constitutional position of slavery and the power of Congress respecting it. That Salmon P. Chase was responsible for the first three[1] and Joshua Giddings had a large

---

[1] Salmon P. Chase's special interest in the due process clause may be seen not only from his argument in the Matilda case but from a note which he enclosed to Birney on March 30, 1844, along with a formal invitation for a public expression of views on annexation: "May I suggest that your answer, which we desire to have be so brief that it may be generally read, should nevertheless state clearly our grand constitutional doctrine that slavery never has lawfully existed in any territory of the United States since the adoption of that Amendment which declares that no person shall be deprived of liberty without due process of law and never can exist. I go further and maintain that since then it has not lawfully existed in any state of the Union." Dwight L. Dumond, *Birney's Letters* (1938), pp. 804–806.

Chase, in a letter to J. M. Ray, Esq., secretary of the Loyal National Repeal Association of Ireland, November 30, 1843, refers first to the Declaration of Independence and the Ordinance of 1787. He then says: "The convention, therefore, did not think fit to confer any express power on the National Congress to abolish slavery in the states by direct legislation. They recognized the fact that slavery existed in some of the states, in several constitutional provisions; but they were careful to exclude all recognition of its rightfulness, and to vest in Congress no power to establish or continue it anywhere. Slavery, therefore, under the Constitution, is strictly a creature of state legislation. No person, under any act of Congress, can be constitutionally reduced to slavery. No person, under any act of Congress, can be constitutionally held as a slave for a single moment anywhere within the range of exclusive national jurisdiction.

"Some enlightened jurists in this country even go further and maintain that the national Constitution as it now stands does of its own force absolutely abolish slavery throughout all the states. They reason thus: The Constitution, as originally framed, did indeed recognize by implication the existence of slavery under state legislation as a matter of fact and perhaps of legal right. But the Constitution was afterwards amended in the mode prescribed by itself. Among the amendments thus incorporated into it was one which provided that 'no person shall be deprived of liberty without

the Fourteenth Amendment

hand in the other two establishes the direct connection between the constitutional pronouncements of these parties and principal figures of abolitionism.

Grant that other men differently motivated could conceivably have seen in the constitutional doctrines thus enunciated different and less reforming applications, grant that New England shipping men had an interest in the movement not unmixed with personal gain, that within the movement groups like the Liberty League were deeply concerned with such problems as the tariff and land monopoly,[2] that outside the movement there was a long-continued effort of business interests to exploit some of these constitutional concepts; grant even that some men who supported the party, and hence the language used, did so without hope of personal gain but from a mistake as to its abolitionist meaning—yet at best these groups would have been minorities, and at worst conspirators whose case rests upon the weight to be given to a secret and un-

---

due process of law.' Now every slave is deprived of liberty without any legal process. Slavery, therefore, is repugnant to the Constitution. This reasoning, if we regard only the terms of the instrument, is certainly unanswerable. If we look at the circumstances of the country at the time, however, it does not seem likely that the amendment was designed to have the effect attributed to it."

Chase makes it plain that he simply meant that the due process clause of the Fifth Amendment did not apply to the states—not that it was not of such a character as to prohibit slavery. (He thus recognized, without naming it, *Barron* v. *Baltimore*.)

"Be this as it may, we apprehend that no intelligent and disinterested person examining the provisions of the Constitution and the amendments, and comparing them with the facts of history, can withhold his assent from the conclusion that there has been no time since the organization of the existing government of the United States when slavery could be established or continued by national legislation."

When the laws of Maryland were continued in the District, "it was a flagrant violation of the implied contract at the formation of the Government, that slavery should never exist under the legislation of Congress. It was also a plain transgression of the letter and spirit of the Constitution, which not only did not confer on Congress any power to establish or continue slavery by law, but expressly declared that no person should be deprived of liberty without due legal process."

[2] The call for the Macedon Convention (1847) made tariff and land reforms a necessary product of man's inalienable rights: "4. No civil government can either authorize or permit one individual, or class of men to infringe the natural and equal rights of another individual or class of men, nor may the government itself under any pretext, infringe the natural right.

"5. All monopolies, class legislations, and exclusive privileges are unequal, unjust, morally wrong, and subversive of the ends of civil government.

"6. The primary and essential rights of humanity are, the right to occupy a portion of the earth's surface, with its free atmosphere, the right of self-ownership, the right to possess and to wield, at discretion, the powers conferred by the Creator, for the revealed purpose in so public a matter as a constitutional amendment. The dominance of the antislavery issue, the source, relation to abolitionism, and publicly avowed intent of the constitutional formulas used were flung far and wide to all who could hear the din of a national political campaign.

Equality, protection, due process, congressional power are the constitutional elements recurrently emphasized in the five party platforms. And the interrelationship of these elements is significant. "The fundamental truth," resolves the Liberty party platform of 1843, "of the Declaration of Independence, that all men are endowed by their Creator with certain unalienable rights, among

original ends of their bestowment in the well being of the possessor, in any manner not inconsistent with the exercise of the same rights in others.

"7. The right of each individual to occupy a portion of the earth's surface, implies the right and the duty of the Community, through the action of government, to restrict, within proper bounds, the accumulation of landed property by individuals, to the exclusion of others 'till they are left alone, in the midst of the earth.'

"8. The right of self-ownership inherent in all men, can never be alienated, by the government or by individuals, and consequently the custom of chattel enslavement can never be made legal.

"9. The right of self-ownership includes, of necessity, the right of each individual to the direction and to the products of his own skill and industry, and the disposal of those products, by barter or sale, in any portion of the earth where a purchaser can be found. These original and natural rights, civil government may neither infringe or impair and all commercial restrictions therefore (except the wise and needful prohibition of immoral and criminal traffic, which no man has a natural right to engage in) are unjust and oppressive.

"10. A tariff for the protection of one particular branch of industry, so far as it reaches its end, is an unjust tax upon one portion of the community for the benefit of another...."

"Honeoye Liberty Mass Meeting, held on the Twenty-Nine December, and the three succeeding days (1846). [The following Declaration of Sentiments was maturely considered and unanimously adopted.]

"7. That the rights of every man to self-ownership, includes, of necessity, his right to the products of his own industry, and his consequent right to dispose of those products, by barter or sale, in any portion of the globe where a purchaser can be found and 'the true foundation of republican government is the equal rights of every citizen, in his person and property, and in their management.'

"8. That, to claim for man, *as* man, the inalienable right of self-ownership, and yet deny to him the inalienable right of unrestricted free trade, is, therefore, equivalent to the affirmation and denial of the same proposition, in the same breath, and those who undertake the overthrow of chattel slavery, and yet plead for commercial restrictions, involve themselves in absurdity and inconsistency, and thus invite disgrace and defeat."

A national reform meeting, at Seneca Falls, March 22, 1847, added a resolution for "Laws restricting the hours of labor to ten per day, in all chartered manufacturing corporations and on all public works."

the Fourteenth Amendment 119

which are life, liberty, and pursuit of happiness, was made the fundamental law of our National Government by that amendment of the Constitution which declares that no person shall be deprived of life, liberty, or property without due process of law."

This early, succinct, and popular statement thus makes the principles of the Declaration of Independence a part of the Constitution, having the binding force of that instrument. It does so, moreover, explicitly through the due process clause of the Fifth Amendment, which is used in an unmistakably substantive sense: Congress is not only not granted powers in the Constitution, it is forbidden to deprive men of their inalienable rights; and it is forbidden to do so absolutely, no matter by what procedure. There is a plain implication that the Fifth Amendment imposes on Congress not merely a negative restraint but an affirmative obligation to protect men against all invasions—not only its own but also those of private persons—of these inalienable rights. Men are endowed with these rights by their Creator—they are not grants of men, government, or society—and governments are established solely for the purpose of preserving and protecting them, continues the Declaration. If the truth of the inalienability is made a part of the Constitution through the Fifth Amendment, is not the proper function of government with respect to them—necessarily operative because of the nature of government even in the absence of specific constitutional directives—also a part of that amendment?

In the Free Soil platform of 1848, the denial to Congress of constitutional power to deprive "any person of life, liberty, or property without due legal process" is given a substantive cast by being linked, on the one hand, with the Preamble-conferred purpose to establish justice, provide for the general welfare, and secure the blessings of liberty, and, on the other hand, with the assertion that the Constitution confers on Congress no more power to make a slave than to make a king. Because of all three—the lack of grant, the specific prohibition, and the injunction of the Preamble—Congress was said to be under a duty to abolish slavery wherever it had jurisdiction and thus was responsible for slavery's existence.[3]

The Free Soil Democratic platform of 1852 tightens the link between these various elements. Since governments are instituted to secure men in their inalienable rights, no man can be deprived of them "by valid legislation except for crime." The absence of the power to make slaves and kings and the duty of Congress to abolish slavery within its jurisdiction are stated, by the use of the word "therefore," in the terms of a logical consequent of the due process clause.[4] What had been a plain implication was hence now made quite explicit. The due process clause not only imposed on the federal government a substantive restraint; it imposed on Congress an affirmative obligation to protect and enforce the inalienable rights which it identified—life, liberty, and property.

Finally, the Republican platforms of 1856[5] and 1860[6] are rededica-

---

[3] Free Soil party platform of 1848: "Resolved, That our fathers ordained the Constitution of the United States in order, among other great national objects, to establish justice, promote the general welfare, and secure the blessings of liberty, but expressly denied to the federal government, which they created, all constitutional power to deprive any person of life, liberty, or property without due legal process.

"Resolved, That in the judgment of the convention, Congress has no more power to make a slave than to make a king; no more power to institute or establish slavery than to institute or establish a monarchy. No such power can be found among those specifically conferred by the Constitution or derived by any just implication from them.

"Resolved, That it is the duty of the federal government to relieve itself from all responsibility for the existence or continuance of slavery wherever the government possesses constitutional authority to legislate on that subject, and is thus responsible for its existence."

[4] Free Soil Democratic platform of 1852: "1. That governments deriving their just powers from the consent of the governed are instituted among men to secure all those inalienable rights of life, liberty, and the pursuit of happiness with which they are endowed by their Creator and of which none can be deprived by valid legislation except for crime.

"4. That the Constitution of the United States, ordained to form a more perfect union, to establish justice, and secure the blessings of liberty, expressly denies to the general government all power to deprive any person of life, liberty, or property without due process of law; and, therefore, the government, having no more power to make a slave than to make a king, and no more power to establish slavery than to establish a monarchy, should at once proceed to relieve itself from all responsibility for the existence of slavery wherever it possesses constitutional power to legislate for its extinction."

[5] Republican platform of 1856: "Resolved, That with our republican fathers we hold it to be a self-evident truth, that all men are endowed with the inalienable rights to life, liberty, and the pursuit of happiness, and that the primary object and

the Fourteenth Amendment

tions to the identical constitutional formulas. The principles of the Declaration are reasserted and reëmbodied in the Constitution. Affirmed again is the duty to maintain the due process provision of the Constitution by "positive legislation" "whenever such legislation is necessary" against all attempts to violate it. Denied once more is the constitutional authority of Congress, a territorial legislature, or "any individual or association of individuals" to give "legal existence to slavery in any territory of the United States."

These five platforms[7] thus express fundamentally the same con-

---

ulterior designs of our federal government were to secure these rights to all persons within its exclusive jurisdiction; that, as our republican fathers, when they had abolished slavery, in all our national territory, ordained that no person should be deprived of life, liberty, or property without due process of law, it becomes our duty to maintain this provision of the Constitution against all attempts to violate it for the purpose of establishing slavery in any territory of the United States, by positive legislation prohibiting its existence or extension therein; that we deny the authority of Congress, of a territorial legislature, of any individual or association of individuals, to give legal existence to slavery in any territory of the United States, while the present Constitution shall be maintained."

[6] Republican platform of 1860: "2. That the maintenance of the principles promulgated in the Declaration of Independence and embodied in the federal Constitution—'that all men are created equal, that they are endowed, by their Creator, with certain unalienable rights, that among these are life, liberty, and the pursuit of happiness. That to secure these rights, governments are instituted among men, deriving their just powers from the consent of the governed'—is essential to the preservation of our republican institutions; and that the federal Constitution; the rights of the states, and the Union of the States must and shall be preserved.

"8. That the normal condition of all the territory of the United States is that of freedom; that as our republican fathers, when they had abolished slavery in all our national territory, ordained that no person should be deprived of life, liberty, or property without due process of law, it becomes our duty, by legislation whenever such legislation is necessary, to maintain this provision of the Constitution against all attempts to violate it; and we deny the authority of Congress, of a territorial legislature, or of any individual to give legal existence to slavery in any territory of the United States."

[7] Other party platforms embodied the same ideas. At the "Honeoye Liberty Mass Meeting, held on the Twenty-Nine December, and the three succeeding days (1846). [The following Declaration of Sentiments was maturely considered and unanimously adopted.]

"1. That Civil Government has its basis in the social nature of man, the necessities of his condition, and the will of his Creator.

"2. That all men are created equal, and are endowed by their Creator with certain inalienable rights, among which are life, liberty, and the pursuit of happiness.

"3. That for the security of these rights, governments are instituted among men, deriving, under God, their just powers from the consent of the governed.

"4. That 'the rightful power of all legislation is to declare and enforce our natural rights and duties, and take none of them from us.' That 'the idea is quite unfounded, that, on entering society, we give up any natural right.' . . .

"29. That the Constitution of the United States was based upon the fundamental stitutional notions and, in fact, are seen to be simply progressive reformulations and occasionally verbatim repetitions. They show the stability and persistence, betokening continuity of movement, of the ideas of: (1) the Constitution as the embodier and implementer of the principles of the Declaration of Independence; (2) the due process clause as the particular channel through which these principles as well as the prohibition of slavery in the Northwest Ordinance got into the Constitution; (3) the consequently absolute and substantive character of the Fifth Amendment; and (4) the affirmative obligation which it imposed on Congress not merely to refrain from creating, supporting, and enforcing slavery wherever it had jurisdiction, but by legislation to prohibit and extinguish it, whether established by governmental action, local custom, or private individual power.

Significantly, too, these five party platforms, while they invested the Fifth Amendment with a sweeping, substantive, and power-giving character, while they pointed to universal liberty through-

principles of common law already cited and upon the self-evident truths of the Declaration of American Independence—that in the light of those fundamental principles and self-evident truths, it is to be construed, as well as in the light of its declared objects, as set forth in its preamble, that it must accordingly be so construed as to render it capable of establishing justice, ensuring domestic tranquility, providing for the common defence, promoting the general welfare, and securing the blessings of liberty to ourselves and our posterity.

"30. That slavery is unconstitutional and illegal, throughout the United States, because inconsistent with the foundation principles and declared objects of the Constitution as derived from the Declaration of Independence and from the common law, and set forth in its preamble, —because, moreover, it was previously made illegal, by decision of the Court of King's Bench, in 1772—because the Constitution itself expressly provides that 'the States shall pass no bills of attainder, nor laws impairing the obligation of contracts,' —that 'no person shall be deprived of life, liberty, or property, without due process of law,' —and that 'the United States shall guarantee to every State in this Union a Republican Form of Government.' "

Call for the Macedon Convention, June 8, 9, 10, 1847:

"1. The true foundation of Civil government is the equal, natural, and inalienable rights of *all men*—and the moral obligation resting on the entire community to secure the free exercise of these rights, including life, liberty, and the pursuit of happiness, to each individual, in his person and his property, and in their management.

"2. The rightful authority, therefore, of Civil Government, under God, is vested not in a select few, but in the mass of the people, who are held responsible to the Supreme Judge and Providential Governor of all men, for the just administration of the same. The resident and permanent subjects of a government, being of mature

the Fourteenth Amendment

out the nation, while they espoused a course of conduct which would obliterate the reserve powers of the states—while they did these things, yet at the same time they were meticulously careful to reaffirm acceptance of the formal doctrine that "slavery in the several states . . . depends upon state laws alone, which cannot be repealed, or modified by the federal government." "No interference by Congress with slavery within the limits of any state" was therefore constitutionally possible. The general government had no power "to establish or continue slavery anywhere," but neither did it possess the power by direct action to abolish slavery everywhere. The powers it did possess, however, it was under a constitutional duty to exercise fully and completely for that purpose. It possessed the power and was under the duty to abolish slavery in the District of Columbia, to forbid its existence and prevent its spread in the national territories, to admit no new slave states. It possessed the power and was under the duty to see that United States ships and public works were free of slaves.

age, and unconvicted of crime, being thus responsible, are equally entitled to share in all the activities and offices of the government, and in the protection of its equal laws, irrespective of property, birth, nativity, avocation, color, or condition.

"3. The sole and indispensable business of civil government is to secure and preserve the natural and equal rights of all men, unimpaired, to prevent and redress, violations of original rights. And the benefits of government are not purchased by the giving up of any portion of our natural rights for the protection of the rest.

"13. At all events, the Federal Government is authorized and bound to carry out the grand and declared object of the Federal Constitution, to 'establish Justice . . . and secure the Blessings of Liberty to ourselves and our Posterity.' In other words, it is authorized and bound to abolish injustice and repress despotism and Slavery.

"Slavery in the United States, is illegal, unconstitutional, and anti-republican. The Federal Judiciary is bound, thus to decide, in the case of any slave claiming his freedom. It is the business of the Federal Government (and consequently of the voter) to provide such a Judiciary. And Congress is bound to guarantee to every State in this Union, a republican form of Government, which is incompatible with the tolerance of Slavery.

"14. The main business of civil government is to be performed by the Judiciary, and a reformation of that department, both in the State and Nation is imperiously demanded. The oath of the Judge and Juror to decide each case according to law and evidence is—(and should be legislatively defined to be) an oath to 'DO JUSTICE and execute judgment'—upon the maxims of Common Law—that 'no human laws have any validity if contrary to this' and that all enactments 'contrary to reason are void.' And Judicial proceedings and the expenses attending them should be such as to make the laws available for the poor as well as for the rich."

Above all, Congress was under a duty to withdraw the national support given to slavery by the Fugitive Slave Act. The constitutional clause on which that act was based was not intended to cover fugitive slaves and if applied to them was null as a violation of higher law.

By the exercise of these various conceded powers, according to the program of the platforms, Congress could "limit, localize, and discourage" slavery to the point of extinction. To acknowledge the doctrine that Congress could not constitutionally abolish slavery within the states, in these circumstances, was to perform a ritual to an abstraction.[8]

---

[8] The abolitionist constitutional argument in Congress echoed the party platforms with little development or deviation. The great debates that raged around petitions, slavery in the District of Columbia, the annexation of Texas, the California question and the compromises of 1850, the Fugitive Slave Act of 1850 and its repeal—all provided likely occasions and issues for abolitionist constitutional as well as other doctrines, in the late 1830's and thereafter. The presence of an abolitionist bloc in Congress, dedicated to the great crusade and seeking to exploit every issue in its behalf, made almost inevitable the appearance of such argument. Debate by debate, as the argument did appear, it followed the now familiar pattern of natural rights, the Declaration of Independence, the social compact purposes of government, the Preamble, the Bill of Rights, the meaning of "person," liberty, and due process.

These basic natural rights concepts, which in the hands of abolitionist publicists were constitutional imperatives, in the hands of the abolitionist legislators tended to be indiscriminately adduced as considerations of legislative policy and constitutional necessity. Thus, with them, the constitutional duty and/or power, on the one hand, and the grounds for congressional action or inaction, on the other, were largely at one. Joshua Giddings, the long-time leader of the congressional bloc, filled his many speeches on every phase of the slavery question with references to the equality of man in a state of nature, the inalienability of his natural rights, the self-evident truths of the Declaration of Independence, the institution of governments for the purpose of protecting man's natural rights, especially liberty. He did so, moreover, both as a method of settling the constitutional issue of power and as an argument of policy for or against a given congressional action. Joshua Giddings, *Speeches in Congress* (Boston, 1853). See, for example, pp. 335, 338, 346, 394, 398, 399, 431.

CHAPTER VII

John A. Bingham

THE ROLE of John A. Bingham in the formulation of the three clauses of section 1 of the Fourteenth Amendment may now be seen in proper perspective. The constitutional ideas which Bingham so forcibly expressed in his congressional speeches of 1856,[1] 1857,[2] and 1859,[3] far from being his spontaneous creation, worked out in response to the problems then before him and perhaps in adaptation of the Wynhammer and Hoboken rhetoric, were the constitutional heritage of a quarter of a century of abolitionism. Far from tracing their antecedents to business cases, they were the familiar instruments for the establishment and protection of the civil and personal rights of men.

Though his work in the 'fifties may thus be stripped of its supposed genetic character, its importance in the antislavery origins of the Fourteenth Amendment is not diminished. In the hands of the principal draftsman of section 1 of the Fourteenth Amend-

---
[1] *Cong. Globe*, 34th Cong., 1st sess. (1856), p. 124.
[2] *Ibid.*, 3d sess., January 13, 1857, Appendix, pp. 135–140.
[3] *Ibid.*, 35th Cong., 2d sess., 1858–1859, pp. 981–985.

ment, the various strands of abolitionist constitutional development were combined. The work of Bingham was the meeting ground, in a sense that the work of no other individual was, of the three concepts and clauses that came to constitute the first section of the amendment. He accepted the amalgamation of natural rights, due process, and equal protection which had become the prime constitutional adornment of the party platforms. Embodied in the Constitution, he argued, is

> the great democratic idea that all men, before the law, are equal in respect of those rights of person which God gives and no man or state may rightfully take away, except as a forfeiture for crime,... those rights, common to all men ... to protect which, not to confer, all good governments are instituted.... The absolute equality of all the equal protection of each [in] those sacred rights which are as universal and indestructible as the human race ... are by this Constitution guaranteed by the broad and comprehensive word "person" as contradistinguished from the limited word "citizen."

The particular article by which this was done, Bingham makes clear, is the Fifth Amendment, providing that "no person shall be deprived of life, liberty, or property but by due process of law; nor shall private property be taken without just compensation."

The "natural and inherent" rights of men were not confined to the generalities of life, liberty, and property; they were further itemized by Bingham. In his 1856 speech he maintained that a law of Congress making it a felony to agitate against slavery deprived "persons of liberty without due process of law, or any process but that of brute force." In his 1859 speech he attacked as a violation of the due process clause of the Northwest Ordinance and of the "law of nature" a provision in the Oregon Constitution that "no free Negro or mulatto, not residing in this state at the time of the adoption of this Constitution, shall ever come, reside, or be, within this state, or hold any real estate, or make any contract, or maintain any suit therein." In that speech he also proclaimed "the equality of all to the right to live; to the right to

the Fourteenth Amendment

know; to argue and to utter, according to conscience; to work and to enjoy the project of their toil."

To this main stream of abolitionist constitutionalism, Bingham added the basic features of the Spooner-Tiffany national citizenship argument. His definition of citizenship was not so comprehensive as to include the slave, but Bingham, like Spooner and Tiffany, found that there is a national citizenship distinct from state citizenship and that it is a product of the United States Constitution. "The people of the several states," who according to the Constitution are to choose the representatives in Congress, and to whom political power is reserved by the Tenth Amendment,

> are the same community, or body politic, called, by the Preamble of the Federal Constitution, "the people of the United States." ... They are the citizens of the United States.... [They] are those, and those only, who owe allegiance to the United States; not the base allegiance imposed upon the Saxon by the conqueror, which required him to meditate in solitude and darkness at the sound of the curfew; but the allegiance which requires the citizen not only to obey, but to support and defend, if need be with his life, the constitution of his country. [They are] all free persons born and domiciled within the jurisdiction of the United States,

and aliens naturalized under the laws of Congress.

The Constitution conferred certain "distinctive political rights" upon citizens of the United States, as well as the natural rights guaranteed to all "persons" by the Fifth Amendment; and the supremacy clause (Art. VI) stood in the way of state impairment of either of these "by constitutional or statute law."

Finally, Bingham bolstered this doubly reinforced system with a third support, the comity clause. He acknowledged that there was "an ellipsis in the language employed" in that clause, but thought it "self-evident" that the privileges and immunities guaranteed against state invasion were those of citizens of the United States; that the safeguard would be "senseless and a mockery" if it did not "restrain each and every state from closing its territory and its courts of justice against citizens of the United States," and if the privileges and immunities did not include "the rights of life and liberty and property, and ... due protection in the enjoyment thereof by law."

In Bingham's system, therefore, as stated in these three Congressional speeches before the Civil War, are integrated the various abolitionist constitutional methods for establishing the power and duty of government to protect men, and to protect them equally, in their natural and inalienable rights: first, because the Fifth Amendment guaranteed such rights to all persons; second, because they are rights of national citizenship created and safeguarded by the constitutional references to "the people"; third, because they are privileges and immunities of citizens of the United States protected by the comity clause.

CHAPTER VIII

The Victory of the Republican Party

THE REPUBLICAN VICTORY at the polls in 1860 brought the antislavery movement to power. Twenty years of political action, forced on the abolitionists by the isolationism of the South, had thus come to fruition. The hold of the Radicals on power was not immediately complete. The extent of Lincoln's antislavery principles was not free from doubt[1] and remained to be tested. Radical control of Congress hung in a precarious and fluctuating balance. Slavery was deeply entrenched in the courts. Above all, the Republican party was not devoted exclusively to "the one idea." It was a het-

---

[1] Complained the Garrisonian wing of abolitionists upon Lincoln's nomination: the record "proves him perhaps, a good enough Republican for the Party's purposes, but far from being the man for the country's need. It shows him as a sort of bland, respectable middle-man, between a very modest right and the most arrogant and exacting wrong; a convenient hook whereon to hang appeals at once to a moderate anti-slavery feeling and to a timid conservatism practically pro-slavery, half-way assertions of human rights, and whole-way concessions to a wicked prejudice against dark-colored manhood, arguments against slavery extension, and apologies for continued complicity with slaveholding." *Twenty-eighth Annual Report*, American Anti-Slavery Society, 1861.

erogeneous multitude," a conglomerate of diverse and in part conflicting interests, some of which were more concerned with southern investments, trade, and markets than with southern morals.

These factors presented obstacles to the consummation of abolitionism. They did not prevent it or change the revolutionary significance of Republican accession to power. They were countermanded by other factors of greater weight. The origins and make-up of the Republican party assured its eventual dedication to the ultimate objectives of the antislavery movement. The abolitionists were the crusaders in the party, at once the most dynamic and doctrinaire element in it. They were the veteran antislavery radicals who had fused the remnants of the Liberty and Free Soil parties into the new Republican organization. Without them, it is doubtful whether that organization could have survived or would have been brought into existence at all. They supplied its *raison d'être,* its driving force, its only common bond—opposition to slavery expansion.

That bond was expressed in a platform declaration full of the spirit of the antislavery movement and of the age. Its words were not the negatives of political reaction or the disintegrating separatism of states' rights. Its view was straight ahead, into the future with nationalism and manifest destiny. Positive national power, the dominance of humanity over property, the expansive tendencies and material enrichment of a society of free and equal men—these were the motivating ideals and the clear demand of the party.

Now that power had been attained, the aim of the abolitionists was to see that the Republican party platform was carried out—to see that the instrumentalities of the federal government were used, not simply to secure the national territories against the spread of slavery, but to achieve the abolition of slavery everywhere in the country; and to do so regardless of the Court, the so-called compromises of the Constitution, and the accepted dogmas of federalism.

"We are struggling," resolved the American Anti-Slavery Society, "not for the non-extension but for the non-existence of slavery—not to make it sectional, but to drive it out of the land—not to restore the Missouri Compromise, but to terminate all compromises—not to repel the aggressions of the slave power upon northern rights, but to secure freedom and equality to all who dwell upon the American soil."[2] By preserving the Union, S. S. Foster asserted, at a Worcester, Massachusetts, Anti-Slavery Society meeting in February, 1861, "and enforcing the anti-slavery construction of the Constitution, slavery could ere long be wiped out." Carl Schurz, speaking in St. Louis on August 1, 1860, contended that the Republican party meant "to adopt a policy which will work the peaceful and gradual extinction of slavery; for if we do not, we shall have to submit to a policy which will work the gradual extinction of liberty."[3] An antislavery convention held in Worcester, Massachusetts, in September, 1860, resolved: "It is the duty of the national government to protect all inhabitants of the country in the enjoyment of all their natural rights . . . The Constitution, fairly interpreted, prohibits the existence of slavery in the states and invests the federal government with ample powers for its overthrow."[4]

Once the secession crisis was on the country, the earlier tendency of antislavery men to seek absolution from the national sin by disunion rapidly disappeared. All shades of radical opinion soon agreed that slavery would not die out in an independent South, but would be strengthened and perpetuated. "I say the man cannot be truly anti-slavery," wrote J. W. Bliss to Sumner, "who cares little if the South goes. . . . We mean both emancipation and Union—the one for the sake of the other and both for the sake of the country."[5] Gerrit Smith, despite his earlier disunionist and pacifist leanings, thought that force ought to be used to prevent secession until the South had agreed to abolish slavery. "This out-

---
[2] *Twenty-sixth Annual Report,* American Anti-Slavery Society, 1856.
[3] *Twenty-eighth Annual Report,* American Anti-Slavery Society, 1861.
[4] *Ibid.*
[5] Kenneth Stampp, *And the War Came* (1950).

break of rebellion," said an antislavery resolution, "has devolved upon the general government not only a constitutional right but a constitutional obligation to regard slavery as illegal in all the states which have seceded, and to treat their heretofore enslaved inhabitants as free."[6]

As the war clouds gathered, antislavery voices were heard on all sides predicting that slavery would be the most certain casualty of the struggle.[7] Even the Garrisonians, nonpolitical sectarians who had with anarchical zeal spurned the Constitution which recognized slavery and the government which protected slavery, began to talk of southern treason and of purging the land of the hated institution through the agency of northern soldiers. Long before the slogan was uttered, the policy of the radicals was, "Tax and tax; fight and fight; emancipate and emancipate."[8]

That the hour was at hand for the destruction of slavery and its incidents throughout the nation by the exertion of the federal power and that antislavery men realized it can be seen further in the unyielding attitude of the radicals toward all efforts at compromise.[9] Their rejection alike of the peace conference and the Crittenden proposals showed their unwillingness to accept partial victory. By these plans, prohibiting slavery in all territories now held or "hereafter acquired" north of lat. 36° 30′, slaveholders would have surrendered the advantage of the Dred Scott decision and substantially conceded the literal demands of the Republican platform. The *quid pro quo*—constitutionally denying Congress authority to interfere with the interstate slave trade or to abolish slavery in places under its jurisdiction, including the District of Columbia, surrounded by a slave state or states—could only be regarded as high if there was an intention to repudiate the compromises of

---

[6] *Twenty-eighth Annual Report,* American Anti-Slavery Society, 1861.
[7] See the speeches of Representative Washburn of Wisconsin, *Cong. Globe,* 37th Cong., 2d sess., 1861–1862, p. 516; Daniel E. Somes of Maine, *ibid.,* p. 969; Sydney Edgerton of Ohio, *ibid.,* Appendix, pp. 127–129.
[8] For a discussion of abolitionism during the secession winter between Lincoln's election and inauguration, see Stampp, *op. cit.,* especially chap. xii, "The Components of a Crusade."
[9] *Ibid.,* chap. viii, "Compromise Debacle."

the Fourteenth Amendment 133

the Constitution and to use congressional power over interstate commerce and places subject to federal jurisdiction as entering wedges for universal abolition. Otherwise, these concessions to the South could only have been looked upon as minor. Yet the Republicans stood out against them almost to a man; and both plans failed of passage through Congress.

The radicals went even further. By refusing their assent to a constitutional amendment guaranteeing slavery in the states against congressional action, they served public and unmistakable notice that they would be satisfied with nothing less than nation-wide emancipation and that they intended to use the power of Congress to achieve it. The nationalistic revolution in federalism had come to its juncture with the question of slavery. It was thus not simply a myth invented for home consumption when southerners asserted: "The Black Republicans ... intend to use the Federal power ... to put down and extinguish the institution of slavery in the Southern states."[10] "It is idle for gentlemen to talk to us about this thing being done according to the forms of the Constitution. A majority even might begin a revolution in that way; you might totally change the whole character of the government in fact, without abolishing its forms."[11]

The abolitionist policy during the first three years of the war of cutting away the secondary appendages of slavery, pursued with vigor and system, only magnified their fundamental purpose to "redeem, regenerate, and disenthrall" the nation "by the genius of universal emancipation." Abolition in the District of Columbia and the national territories, accomplished in 1862, Trumbull's confiscation act declaring free the slaves of all persons thereafter found guilty of treason or who aided the rebellion, the Emancipation Proclamation itself—all were significant mainly for what they portended rather than for what they did. There were, of course, few slaves in the District and federal territories; and enforcement

---
[10] Senator Alfred Iverson of Georgia, *Cong. Globe*, 36th Cong., 2d sess., 1860–1861, p. 11.
[11] Senator Thomas L. Clingman of North Carolina, *ibid.*, p. 3.

of the confiscation act and Lincoln's edict, since they applied to persons and places then within the control of the rebel armies, awaited the progress of national arms.

Even the Wade-Davis bill, the most drastic of these measures, passed by Congress in 1864 and vetoed by the President because of a doubt about the constitutional authority of Congress, was not a final step. It emancipated and made forever free all slaves in the rebel states. But it was only as permanent as radical control of Congress and did not in any event bring freedom in the loyal border states.

All these measures, partial and opportunistic as they had to be, were steps toward the ultimate goal defined and envisioned thirty years before by Weld and Birney, Stanton and Wright, Olcott and Stewart.[12]

---

[12] T. Harry Williams, *Lincoln and the Radicals* (1941).

Part Three

THE CONSUMMATION OF
ABOLITIONISM—THE THIRTEENTH
AMENDMENT

Introduction to Part Three

SECTION 1. Neither slavery nor involuntary servitude, except as a punishment for crime whereof the party shall have been duly convicted, shall exist within the United States, or any place subject to their jurisdiction. SECTION 2. Congress shall have power to enforce this article by appropriate legislation.—*Thirteenth Amendment, United States Constitution*

THE THIRTEENTH AMENDMENT was the first effort at consummation by the use of the constituent power. The words employed in the amendment—"Neither slavery nor involuntary servitude, except as a punishment for crime..., shall exist within the United States"— were drawn directly from instruments perennially at the center of the slavery controversy: the Northwest Ordinance and the Wilmot Proviso. The Ordinance of 1787 had come to stand along with the Declaration of Independence in the political argument of abolitionism. It varied through the stages of an expression of urgent and proper policy, the fundamental though nonconstitutional determination of the Fathers, and, finally, virtually constitutional status, as binding as the document itself. In the form of the Wilmot

Proviso, the keystone of antiextensionism, it had collected a vast array of supporters in the North and become the object of bitter attack in the South. To this language of Jefferson's proviso in the Northwest Ordinance, freed of its territorial limitation and broadened to cover the whole country, the framers of the Thirteenth Amendment added an all-important grant of enforcement power to Congress.

Looking at the words of the amendment as they stand, a number of critical questions present themselves: Could this simple prohibition of slavery and involuntary servitude have been intended as a consummation of abolitionism broadly conceived? Could language thus limited, however deeply embedded in the history of the antislavery controversy, and though coupled with a power of legislative enforcement, possibly have been envisaged as achieving anything more than release from physical bondage? Was the Thirteenth Amendment not rather simply the first step in a comprehensive three-step plan designed, first, through the Thirteenth Amendment, to abolish chattel slavery; second, through the Fourteenth Amendment, to restore the freed Negro to a condition of civil equality; and third, through the Fifteenth Amendment, to safeguard him in his political rights?

The traditionally accepted answers to these questions, placing a restrictive and partial interpretation on the amendment, were founded on a misgauging of the revolution in federalism designed to be achieved or ratified by the amendment; and, in turn, have caused constitutional historians and judges almost completely to miss the open-sesame bearing of the Thirteenth Amendment on the Fourteenth.

The original proposition for a constitutional amendment abolishing slavery throughout the United States was introduced in the House by James M. Ashley of Ohio on December 14, 1863. Ashley managed the amendment in the House; Lyman Trumbull of Illinois, in the Senate. It was debated bitterly and at length in the spring of 1864. It rode to easy victory in the Senate, but failed to

the Fourteenth Amendment 139

secure the requisite two-thirds majority in the House. This failure made it an issue in the presidential campaign of that year. In December, released from the limitations of his border-state policy by Maryland's voluntary abolition of slavery and sustained by the popular decision at the polls, Lincoln threw his full weight behind the amendment. The earlier negative action of the House was reconsidered in January, 1865, and, after a long debate in which nearly one-third of the members participated, was finally reversed.

The discussions in the House and Senate in the spring of 1864 constitute the first debate over the Thirteenth Amendment; those in the House in January, 1865, the second. Since these were integrally a part of a single episode, we shall consider them together. A third important congressional debate on the Thirteenth Amendment occurred in December, 1865, and in the spring of 1866 in connection with the Freedmen's Bureau bill, the civil rights bill, and other implementing legislation. That debate will be examined separately.

CHAPTER IX

The First Two Congressional Debates

THE CONGRESSIONAL debates in the spring of 1864 and in January, 1865, make plain that the traditionally accepted limiting answers to the questions posed in the preceding chapter were not the answers originally intended by the sponsors of the amendment or contemplated by its opponents.

As might be imagined from the subject and the historic occasion of these debates, rambling discursions into history, morals, religion, and politics were the order of the day. But, though the debates were, in these respects, long and pedestrian, as concerns the meaning of the amendment, they were singularly illuminating. In fact, in one crucial phase they were unique: many of the consequences of the amendment forecast by the opponents, far from being denied or minimized by the sponsors, were espoused as the very objects desired and intended to be accomplished by the measure.

Fourteenth Amendment 141

With the South no longer present in the halls of Congress and the outcome of the Civil War more or less clearly discernible, the whole character of the slavery debate shifted. Slavery was defended as a positive good and the true condition of the African race only by such rare "vestigial remainders" of an earlier age as Fernando Wood of New York. Abolitionist barbs about inhumanity, immorality, irreligion, and sin now evoked little response. The Christianizing, civilizing, and humanitarian merits of slavery were conspicuously not presented. The economic and social argument that slavery was indispensable to the prosperity and cultural refinement of the South—central features of the positive good dogma—became subdued and peripheral. The argument for natural rights to property, always a constitutional bulwark to the slavery system from the time of the Pickens' speech and the Pinckney report in 1836, also had practically vanished; though abolition by constitutional amendment was the ultimate contingency which the natural rights argument was best adapted to meet. These positions, occupied for thirty years by proslavery forces, now were left unmanned. In short, the battle had ceased to be over slavery itself.

With the victory of northern arms, slavery as a legal institution was at an end except in a few border states where it could not hope long to survive surrounded by a free nation. Those who resisted the Thirteenth Amendment—spokesmen of the loyal slave states, Democrats, and a few conservative Republicans—were in small part fighting a rear-guard action for a proslavery cause they knew to be lost. Far more importantly, they were organizing all their forces for a last-ditch stand against the second of the two revolutions which had been in progress: the revolution in federalism.

The principal argument put forward by the congressional opponents of the Thirteenth Amendment, accordingly, was that the measure constituted an unwarrantable invasion of the rights of the states and a corresponding unwarrantable extension of the power of the central government. In fact, so unwarrantable was the invasion and the extension as to violate the basic conditions of the federal compact, destroy the federal character of the government, and subvert the whole constitutional system. According to Fernando Wood, Democrat of New York,

> Within the scope and reason of the Constitution, any amendment to it would be legitimate when ratified by the required three-fourths of the states; but for those three-fourths to attempt a revolution in social or religious rights by seizing upon what was never intended to be delegated by any of the parties to the compact would be a prodigy of injustice. Carried out under the forms of law, a wrong more fatally so because made by the very highest authority. If an amendment were now proposed to the Constitution declaring an establishment of religion or prohibiting the free exercise of it by the citizen, it would be parallel with the present and no more obnoxious than this is to merited condemnation... The local jurisdiction over slavery was one of the subjects peculiarly guarded and guaranteed to the states, and an amendment ratified by any number of states less than the whole, though within the letter of the article which provides for amendments, would be contrary to the spirit of the instrument, and so in reality an act of gross bad faith.[1]

It would therefore be unconstitutional. It would revolutionize rather than amend the Constitution.[2]

The opponents of the amendment did not stop with sweeping declamation. In one speech after another they itemized their apprehensions, the factors which made the measure revolutionary. "The slavery issue," said Anton Herrick of New York, "which this resolution seeks to finally settle... is legitimately merged in the higher issue of the right of the states to control their domestic affairs, and to fix each for itself the status, not only of the negro, but of all other people who dwell within their borders."[3] "...the amendment," added William S. Holman, of Indiana, "confers on Congress the power to invade any state to enforce the freedom of the African in war or peace. What is the meaning of all that? Is freedom the simple exemption from personal servitude? No, Sir, mere ex-

---

[1] *Cong. Globe*, 38th Cong., 1st sess., 1864, p. 2941.
[2] Saulsbury of Delaware, *ibid.*, p. 1364; Powell of Kentucky, *ibid.*, p. 1483; Davis of Kentucky, *ibid.*, Appendix, p. 104.
[3] *Ibid.*, p. 2615.

the Fourteenth Amendment 143

emption from servitude is a miserable idea of freedom. A pariah in the state, a subject but not a citizen, holding any right at the will of the governing power. What is this but slavery?"[4]

Concluded Robert Mallory of Kentucky: "You propose to leave them [the emancipated Negroes] where they are freed, and protect them in their right to remain there. You do not intend, however, to leave them to the tender mercies of those states. You propose by a most flagrant violation of their rights to hold the control of this large class in these various states in your own hands."[5]

That the object of the amendment was not only to free the Negroes but to "make them our equals before the law" was a constant source of complaint.[6] Elijah Ward of New York expressed his opposition to the Thirteenth Amendment: "We are now called upon to sanction a Joint Resolution to amend the Constitution so that all persons shall be equal under the law, without regard to color, and so that no person shall hereafter be held in bondage."[7]

Thus, the case of those who resisted the passage of the Thirteenth Amendment was built almost entirely on opposition to the expansion and consolidation of the national power. With slavery already dead, that expansion and consolidation would be neither great nor of continuing importance if the amendment effected only a "simple exemption from personal servitude." The thing that gave the revolution in federalism significance was the sweeping conception of what the amendment did. Beyond toppling over the corpse of slavery, most if not all elements of the congressional opposition asserted that the amendment would guarantee to the emancipated Negro a basic minimum of rights—equality before the law, protection in life and person, opportunity to live, work, and move about—and that Congress would be empowered to safeguard and protect these rights.

Outside this area of basic agreement, opinions varied. Some charged that the amendment was designed to bring about social

---

[4] *Ibid.*, p. 2692.
[5] *Ibid.*, pp. 2982–2983.
[6] *Ibid.*, 2d sess., pp. 179–180, 216.
[7] *Ibid.*, p. 177.

equality;[8] others, that miscegenation[9] was within its purview; still others, that the enfranchisement[10] of the Negro was intended. But these diversities do not obscure the hard core of common understanding among the opposition as to the meaning of the amendment and what it would do.

The case made out by the sponsors and supporters of the Thirteenth Amendment was no less explicit on this central issue. The amendment was presented not as one step in a series of steps yet to come, not as an act of partial fulfillment, not as the opportunistic achievement of a limited objective. It was exultantly heralded as "the final step," "the crowning act," "the capstone upon the sublime structure," the joyous "consummation of abolitionism." To the proponents of the amendment, though slavery was dead, the remote contingency of its resurrection had to be precluded; the incidents of slavery had yet to be obliterated; the emancipated Negro and his white friends had to be protected in the privileges and civil liberties of freemen; and the federal power as the instrument for achieving these purposes had to be permanently assured. Victory in both revolutions needed to be appropriately symbolized and made permanent.

Throughout the debates, these were the points which the abolitionists hammered home with ardor and relentlessness. As had been true of their constitutional attack from the time of its original formulation, two major ideas were combined and recombined into a single argument and purpose: first, the Lockeian presuppositions about natural rights and the protective function of government; second, slavery's denial of these rights and this protection not only to blacks, bond and free, but to whites as well.

The opening speech in the House debate, delivered by James F. Wilson of Iowa,[11] chairman of the Judiciary Committee and co-author of the amendment, emphasized both of these elements and their interrelationship with clearness and force. The system

[8] *Ibid.*, 1st sess., 1865, pp. 2944, 2987.
[9] *Ibid.*, pp. 1465, 2979.
[10] *Ibid.*, pp. 180, 216, 2962.
[11] *Ibid.*, p. 1199.

of slavery, Wilson argued, violated the clauses of the Preamble, disregarded the supremacy of the Constitution, and denied the privileges and immunities of citizens of the United States guaranteed by the comity clause. Among those privileges and immunities were the rights of the First Amendment—"freedom of religious opinion, freedom of speech and press, and the right of assemblage for the purpose of petition." These rights belonged "to every American citizen, high or low, rich or poor." Yet to what extent were they respected as the supreme law of the land "in states where slavery controlled legislation, presided in the courts, directed the executives, and commanded the mob"?

Twenty millions of free men in the free states were practically reduced to the condition of semi-citizens of the United States; for the enjoyment of their rights, privileges and immunities as citizens depended upon a perpetual residence north of Mason's and Dixon's line. South of that line the rights which I have mentioned, and many more which I might mention, could be enjoyed only when debased to the use of slavery.... It is quite time, Sir, for the people of the free states to look these facts squarely in the face and provide a remedy which shall make the future safe for the rights of each and every citizen.

That remedy, thus aimed at the broad objective of making "the future safe for the rights of ... every citizen," was the seemingly narrow prohibition on slavery and involuntary servitude contained in the Thirteenth Amendment.

The eloquent arraignment of slavery by Senator Henry Wilson of Massachusetts, veteran abolitionist, followed the same familiar pattern.[12] Slavery was the "prolific mother" of mobbings, beatings, violence, southern maltreatment of northern seamen and citizens. Wilson asserted,

If this amendment shall be incorporated by the will of the nation into the Constitution of the United States, it will obliterate the last lingering vestiges of the slave system; its chattelizing, degrading and bloody codes; its dark, malignant barbarizing spirit; all it was and is, everything connected with it or pertaining to it, ... when this amendment

---
[12] *Ibid.*, March 28, 1864, pp. 1319, 1321, 1324.

to the Constitution shall be consummated, the shackle will fall from the limbs of the hapless bondman ... the schoolhouse will rise to enlighten the darkened intellect of a race imbruted by long years of enforced ignorance. Then the sacred rights of human nature, the hallowed family relations of husband and wife, parent and child, will be protected by the guardian spirit of that law which makes sacred alike the proud homes and lowly cabins of freedom. Then the wronged victim of the slave system, the poor white man ... impoverished, debased, dishonored by the system that makes toil a badge of disgrace, and the instruction of the brain and soul of a man a crime, will ... begin to run the race of improvement, progress and elevation.

Senator James Harlan of Iowa elaborated on the necessary incidents of slavery which it was the object of the amendment to abolish. These were: "the breach of the conjugal relationship"; the abolition of the parental relation, robbing the offspring of the care and attention of his parents"; abolition "of the relation of person to property," "the destruction of the slaves' capacity to acquire and hold" (property), and the imposition of "this disability on their posterity forever"; denial to the slaves "of a status in court," especially "the right to testify"; "the suppression of the freedom of speech and press, not only among those downtrodden people themselves but among the white race"; "perpetuity of the ignorance of its victims."[13]

The Thirteenth Amendment, argued E. C. Ingersoll of Illinois, will mean

freedom of speech, ... the right to proclaim the eternal principles of liberty, truth and justice in Mobile, Savannah, or Charleston with the same freedom and security as ... at the foot of Bunker Hill Monument. ... [It] will secure to the oppressed slave his natural and God-given rights ... a right to live, and live in a state of freedom ... a right to breathe the free air, and to enjoy God's free sunshine. ... A right to till the soil, to earn his bread by the sweat of his brow, and to enjoy the rewards of his own labor. ... A right to the endearments and enjoyment of family ties. ... [It will mean] that the rights of mankind, without regard to color or race, are respected and protected.[14]

[13] *Ibid.*, pp. 1439, 1440.
[14] *Ibid.*, June, 1864, pp. 2989, 2990.

the Fourteenth Amendment 147

"This proposed Amendment is designed," argued William D. Kelley of Pennsylvania, "... to accomplish the very purpose with which they charged us in the beginning, namely, the abolition of slavery in the United States, and the political and social elevation of Negroes to all the rights of white men."[15] "The effect of such Amendment," said Godlove S. Orth, of Indiana, "will be to prohibit slavery in these United States, and be a practical application of that self-evident truth, 'that all men are created equal; that they are endowed by their Creator with certain unalienable rights; that among these are life, liberty, and the pursuit of happiness.'" What shall be done with the former slaves and their masters? "... giving to each equal protection under the law, bid them go forth with the Scriptural injunction, 'in the sweat of thy face shalt thou eat bread.'"[16]

James M. Ashley of Ohio[17] argued as follows:

[Slavery] has for many years defied the government and trampled upon the National Constitution, by kidnapping, imprisoning, mobbing, and murdering white citizens of the United States guilty of no offense except protesting against its terrible crimes. It has silenced every free pulpit within its terrible control, ... it has denied the masses of poor white children within its power the privilege of free schools and made free speech and a free press impossible within its domain; ... it so constituted its courts that the complaints and appeals of these people could not be heard by reason of the decision "that black men had no rights which white men were bound to respect."

Thus the congressional debates[18] in the spring of 1864 and in January, 1865, explode the traditionally accepted beliefs about the scope and meaning of the Thirteenth Amendment. They show

---
[15] *Ibid.,* p. 2987.
[16] *Ibid.,* 2d sess., 1865, Part 1, pp. 142–143.
[17] *Ibid.,* January, 1865, pp. 13, 139.
[18] See *ibid.,* for the speeches of Thomas T. Davis of New York, p. 154; John A. Kasson of Iowa, January 10, 1865, p. 193; Nathaniel B. Smithers of Delaware, p. 217; Green Clay Smith of Kentucky, January 12, p. 237; James S. Rollins of Missouri, p. 258; William Higby of California, January 25, p. 478; Lyman Trumbull of Illinois (1st sess.), p. 1313; John B. Henderson of Missouri, April 7, p. 1465; Charles Sumner of Massachusetts, pp. 1479–1483; Daniel Morris of New York, May 21, p. 2615; John F. Farnsworth of Illinois, p. 2979.

that the proponents of the measure intended thereby a revolution in federalism; that the opponents of the amendment understood that intended purpose and made it virtually the sole basis of their opposition to the amendment; that the amendment was passed by Congress in the face of the well-articulated fear that it would revolutionize the federal system and the publicly expressed purpose of doing so, that is, with complete agreement between proponents and opponents as to its effect. To grasp this revolution, these debates make clear, one need only appreciate the threefold meaning of the word "slavery" as it was then used and understood. What was the "slavery" which the Thirteenth Amendment would abolish?

First, the amendment would strike "the shackle...from the limbs of the hapless bondman." It would destroy slavery's "chattelizing, degrading, and bloody codes." Slavery in its narrowest and strictest sense—slavery as legally enforceable personal servitude—would thus be forever "put down and extinguished." This much the amendment would certainly do. But this much had already been done by other acts and events. With respect to slavery in this primary and limited sense, little remained to be accomplished by the amendment except to give "completeness and permanence to emancipation." And that the amendment was intended to do.

Second, slavery which was within the reach of the amendment extended far beyond the personal burden of the slaves and the characteristics of immediate bondage. The congressional debates repeated what the history of abolitionism had already made abundantly clear. The free colored person, South and North, as the abolitionists knew him and had labored for him, was only less degraded, spurned, and restricted than his enslaved fellow. He bore all the burdens, badges, and indicia of slavery save only the technical one. His freedom along with that of his enshackled brother had been an integral part of the life and work of "the great crusade." His slavery as well as that of the "hapless bondman" was to be abolished by the Thirteenth Amendment.

the Fourteenth Amendment

The opposite of slavery is liberty. The liberty which the abolition of slavery would bring about, spelled out by thirty years of antislavery controversy, was again itemized and detailed in the congressional debates. The amendment would "convert into a man that which the law had declared to be a chattel." It would be "a practical application of that self-evident truth 'that all men are created equal, that they are endowed, by their Creator, with certain unalienable rights.'" It would "bring the Constitution into avowed harmony with the Declaration of Independence." It would recognize and confirm the principle that "nature made all men free and entitled them to equal rights before the law." It would "secure to the oppressed slave his natural and God-given rights," "the sacred rights of human nature," "the rights of mankind." It would assure that these rights were "respected and protected"; it would "give to each, equal protection under the law." It would safeguard the right to be educated to the "race imbruted by long years of enforced ignorance." "The hallowed family relations of husband and wife, parent and child," would "be protected by the guardian spirit of that law which makes sacred alike the proud homes and lowly cabins of freedom." It would guarantee to the free Negro "the right to live," the capacity to acquire and hold "property," the "right to till the soil, to earn his bread by the sweat of his brow, and to enjoy the rewards of his own labor." It would make certain that all these rights would receive "the protection of the government," the protection of "equal laws," and that the Negro would be given "a status in court," especially the untrammeled right to testify.

Third, the slavery which was to be abolished by the amendment consisted of the incidents of the system which impaired and destroyed the rights of the whites. In part, the framers, sponsors, and supporters of the Thirteenth Amendment felt that, with chattel bondage abolished and the Negro elevated to legal and civil equality, the pulsing heart of the system would be stilled and all the appendages would soon atrophy and disappear. Some of the outgrowths—the "nameless woes," the "sumless agonies of civil war," the "sweltered venom" filling the hearts of the southern people, the "dark and malignant hatred of the free states"—would die automatically.

These outgrowths of slavery could not in any event be legislated out of existence, but others could, and the Thirteenth Amendment was intended as specific legislation or as authorizing specific legislation against these. It was meant to be a direct ban against many of the evils radiating from the system of slavery as well as a prohibition of the system itself. It would bring to an end the "kidnapping, imprisoning, mobbing, and murdering" of "white citizens of the United States, guilty of no offense." It would make it possible for white citizens to exercise their constitutional right under the comity clause to reside in southern states regardless of their opinions. It would carry out the constitutional declaration that each citizen of the United States shall have equal privileges in every other state. It would protect citizens in their rights under the First Amendment and the comity clause to freedom of speech, freedom of press, freedom of religion, and freedom of assembly. It would "make the future safe for the rights of each and every citizen."

This, then, was the slavery which the Thirteenth Amendment would abolish: the involuntary personal servitude of the bondman; the denial to blacks, bond and free, of their natural rights through the failure of the government to protect them and to protect them equally; the denial to whites of their natural and constitutional rights through a similar failure of government. Stated affirmatively, and in the alternative phrases and concepts used repeatedly throughout the debates, the Thirteenth Amendment would: first, guarantee the equal protection of the laws to men in their natural rights and to citizens in their constitutional rights; and/or second, safeguard citizens of the United States equally in their constitutional privileges and immunities; and/or, running a bad but nevertheless articulated third, enforce the constitutional guar-

the Fourteenth Amendment

antee to all persons against deprivation of life, liberty, or property without due process of law.

Just as the major elements of unity in abolitionist constitutional and natural rights theory emerged in the congressional debates over the Thirteenth Amendment and formed the explicitly articulated as well as the broadly historical basis of the amendment, so the divergent elements of abolitionist doctrine equally manifested themselves. They also supply a basis of the amendment and add to our understanding of it.

The question of the enfranchisement of the Negro divided antislavery men, leaders as well as the rank and file, as it had long before and did even more sharply later. Those who thought of enfranchisement as an immediately desirable goal or as a necessary consequence of the social compact or the Constitution were, however, undoubtedly a small minority. In the congressional debates, Democratic spokesmen often insisted that the Republicans intended, under the Thirteenth Amendment, to give the freed Negro the vote, "to be used throughout all time for the purpose of keeping control of the federal government, and of the [southern] states."[19] Such politically minded Jacobins as Thaddeus Stevens of Pennsylvania, Benjamin F. Wade of Ohio, and Zachariah Chandler of Michigan doubtless thought of the party advantage. That the enfranchisement of freedmen would result from the Thirteenth Amendment or could be achieved under it, whether for partisan political or more generally abolitionist ends, was, however, not avowed or admitted by even the most extreme of the radicals. If it was believed at all by those who put the amendment across, it belongs in the category of secret or conspiratorial intentions. Josiah B. Grinnell, representative from Iowa, spoke the historically correct answer of abolitionists to the charges of the Democrats:

> But we are met with another objection, that if we emancipate we must enfranchise also. I deny the conclusion; but I should not be deterred from the move, even if it were correct. A recognition of natural rights is

[19] *Ibid.*, p. 179.

one thing, a grant of political franchises is quite another. We extend to all white men the protection of law when they land upon our shores. We grant them political rights when they comply with the conditions which those laws prescribe. If political rights must necessarily follow the possession of personal liberty, then all but male citizens in our country are slaves.[20]

The principal source of disagreement among the abolitionists revealed by the debates over the Thirteenth Amendment was, of course, the very one that had served as the basis of the only important doctrinal difference on constitutional questions to develop in the movement. It had originated in the late 'thirties and persisted down through the Civil War. It had nothing to do with the scope of abolitionist objectives. It had to do only with the constitutional means of achieving those objectives. Did Congress have the power by direct action to abolish slavery in the states under the Constitution as it existed or was an amendment necessary before such action could be taken? In other words, was the Thirteenth Amendment declaratory or amendatory? Did it simply reaffirm what the Constitution already provided or did it change the Constitution or add to it?

On this question the abolitionists were split. Some hardened constitutional apostates, like Charles Sumner, unequivocally took the position that the Thirteenth Amendment would be entirely declaratory, that under the Constitution as it then stood Congress could "by a single brief statute... sweep slavery out of existence." In Sumner's view, such a statute was authorized by the common defense and war clauses, by the republican form of government guarantee, and by the due process provision of the Fifth Amendment. The last named, especially, was "in itself alone a whole bill of rights,... an express guarantee of personal liberty and an express prohibition against its invasion anywhere,... in itself... a source of power" for Congress to carry out the guarantee and to enforce the prohibition everywhere in the country.[21]

---

[20] *Ibid.*, p. 302.
[21] *Ibid.*, 1st sess., pp. 1479 ff.

Other abolitionist sponsors of the amendment leaned heavily on the declaratory theory, but were less explicit about congressional power to enforce the antislavery provisions of the Constitution and perhaps believed that it did not exist. Wilson's important speech on March 18, 1864, typified the attitude of this group.[22] It was left to James M. Ashley of Ohio, however, to state the declaratory theory in its basically nationalistic, antistate-compact constitutional ramifications.[23] In an able speech, delivered in January, 1865, he substantially recapitulated the doctrine developed by Spooner and Tiffany and, in some phases, by J. Q. Adams. "The unity and citizenship of the people," Ashley asserted, "existed before the Revolution, and before the national Constitution." In fact, it was in order "to secure" this "unity," this "pre-existing nationality," this "national citizenship," for which "life, fortune, and honor" had been periled in the Revolution, that the Constitution was formed. "The utter indefensibility of the state sovereignty dogmas, and... the supreme power intended by the framers of the Constitution to be lodged in the National Government" were particularly demonstrated by the republican form of government guarantee and the comity clause of the Constitution. The comity clause "secures nationality of citizenship," "a universal franchise which cannot be confined to states, but belongs to the citizens of the Republic."

The abolitionists who believed that the Thirteenth Amendment was amendatory, that it would revise or change the Constitution, harked back to the stand of the American Anti-Slavery Society, adopted originally in the Constitution of 1833 and copied in the constitutions of most of the state and local antislavery societies. The United States Constitution not only did not authorize Congress to uproot slavery in the states where it existed, but it protected slavery there. Elsewhere—in the District of Columbia, in the territories—Congress possessed the power and the duty to act in behalf of freedom. Moreover, Congress was bound to exercise the powers

---
[22] *Ibid.*, p. 1199.
[23] *Ibid.*, 2d sess., p. 138.

it possessed over the District, the territories, and interstate commerce to hedge slavery in, to confine it "to the spots it already polluted." But beyond that, Congress could not constitutionally go "to touch slavery in the states." "... such, Sir, was my position," said Thaddeus Stevens, the leading exponent of this view in the 1865 debates, "not disturbing slavery where the Constitution protected it, but abolishing it wherever we have the constitutional power, and prohibiting its further extension.... As the Constitution now stands... the subject of slavery has not been entrusted to us by the states, and... therefore it is reserved."[24]

Placed in the context of this constitutional divergency among the abolitionists, the function of the Thirteenth Amendment is not confused but clarified. The split between the declaratory and amendatory theorists shows that there was disagreement about how the Thirteenth Amendment affected the preëxisting Constitution but none about the meaning of the Constitution after the adoption of the amendment. To the declaratory theorists who believed both that the Constitution was antislavery and that Congress was empowered to carry out its antislavery provisions, the Thirteenth Amendment would confirm, reaffirm, reiterate; it would bring out anew the true nature of the Constitution, which had been "degraded to wear chains so long that its real character" was "scarcely known." To the declaratory theorists who believed that the Constitution was antislavery but that a power of enforcement was lacking, the Thirteenth Amendment commanded freedom all over again and provided a means "to carry it into effect," "a remedy" against disobedience.

To the amendatory theorists the Thirteenth Amendment brought about a fundamental change: it took from the states what hitherto had been constitutionally reserved to them, the power to protect or promote slavery; it abolished slavery throughout the country, nationalized the right of freedom, and made the national Congress the organ of enforcement.

---

[24] *Ibid.*, pp. 265-266.

the Fourteenth Amendment

Thus, in the eyes of all abolitionists, the Thirteenth Amendment either gave or confirmed congressional power to enforce a constitutional prohibition against slavery everywhere in the United States; and the liberty which Congress now had constitutional mandate to enforce was not just the liberty of the blacks but the liberty of the whites as well; it included not merely freedom from personal bondage but protection in a wide range of natural and constitutional rights. The revolution in federalism had been given its ultimate constitutional sanction.

CHAPTER X

The Third Congressional Debate

~~~~~~~~~~~~~~~~~~~~~~~~~~~~~~~~~

THE THIRTEENTH AMENDMENT was declared ratified and in force on December 18, 1865. Meanwhile, on December 5 the Thirty-ninth Congress had convened. The great issues of reconstruction which that Congress was to face were emerging and taking shape in men's minds: fiscal retrenchment, reëstablishing a balance between civil and military authority, rebuilding the political structure of the rebel states, finding a new basis on which to resurrect the shattered economy and society of the South.

Standing in the forefront of these problems was what to do with the freedmen, "the everlasting, inevitable Negro." This question "puzzled all brains and vexed all statesmanship." Loosened not only from the legal but the economic ties which fixed their place in society and their part in production, many of them wandering aimlessly about the countryside or huddled near northern army camps and in philanthropic centers, the victims alike of continued white oppression and of their own long past of slavery, the former bondmen constituted a vast relief and welfare problem as well as a problem of legal protection and Lockeian political theory.

All shades of Republican opinion agreed that the care of the race emancipated by the war and made by circumstances the wards of the nation was the responsibility of the nation. "We have," said Thaddeus Stevens, "turned or are about to turn loose four million slaves without a hut to shelter them or a cent in their pockets. The diabolical laws of slavery have prevented them from acquiring an education, understanding the commonest laws of contract, or of managing the ordinary business of life. This Congress is bound to look after them until they can take care of themselves."[1]

The national responsibility had been discharged in part by an earlier comprehensive act passed in the preceding March, coördinating and centralizing through the Freedmen's Bureau existing wartime organizations for the care of the liberated Negro. The bureau had been given far-reaching jurisdiction. It had been made the general guardian and, backed by the United States Army, the guarantor of the general welfare and interests of former slaves. It had been given charge of their family relations and was to supervise charitable relief and educational work among them. It was to aid them in the purchase or lease of land and to distribute abandoned lands among them. It had jurisdiction over all controversies in which freedmen were involved, whether blacks alone were concerned or whites also were parties. The whole realm of black-white labor relations in the South had been made the province of the bureau. It was to safeguard the freedmen against victimization by white employers, oppressive working conditions and unreasonably low wages, coercion, intimidation, or anything remotely approaching involuntary labor or actual slavery. The bureau had been thus empowered to play an important if not a determinative part in reorganizing and reconstituting the social and economic life of the South and in ensuring genuine freedom to the former slaves.

---

[1] *Cong. Globe*, 39th Cong., 1st sess., 1865-1866, p. 74.

But the protection afforded by the Freedmen's Bureau was at best temporary, irregularly administered, and inadequate. Broader and more explicitly statutory guarantees were regarded as necessary if freedmen were to be given both something more than parchment rights and freedom from the forms of bondage. Hardly were the doors of the Thirty-ninth Congress opened before an assortment of bills was entered for this purpose. Representative John Farnsworth of Illinois offered a resolution which, though concerned primarily with the rights of Negro soldiers, declared generally that "as all just powers of government are derived from the consent of the governed, that cannot be regarded as a just government which denies a large portion of its citizens who share its pecuniary and military burdens" the right to express their consent, "and which refuses them full protection in the enjoyment of their inalienable rights."[2] Representative Benjamin F. Loan of Missouri submitted a resolution directing the select committee on freedom to consider "legislation securing the freedmen and the colored citizens of the states recently in rebellion the political and civil rights of other citizens of the United States."[3]

Senator Henry Wilson of Massachusetts sponsored a bill confined to the rebel states and to be enforced by the army and the Freedmen's Bureau. It declared null and void all "laws, statutes, acts, ordinances, rules and regulations" establishing or maintaining "any inequality of civil rights and privileges" on account of "color or previous slavery."[4] Charles Sumner of Massachusetts introduced two bills embodying much the same program. They struck down in the Confederate states "all laws and customs... establishing any oligarchical privileges and any distinction of rights on account of color or race." They ordained that "all persons in such states are recognized as equal before the law." They gave the courts of the United States exclusive jurisdiction of all suits, criminal or civil, to which a person of African descent was a party.[5]

[2] *Ibid.*, p. 46.
[3] *Ibid.*, p. 69.
[4] *Ibid.*, p. 39.
[5] *Ibid.*, pp. 91–95.

the Fourteenth Amendment

These proposals all failed of enactment. They are significant because they show that the early statutory plans to safeguard the human rights and essential interests of the freedmen revolved about certain central ideas: "full protection in the enjoyment of their inalienable rights," "equality of civil rights and privileges," the same rights as other citizens, equality before the law. The common denominator, settled in men's minds by thirty years of abolitionist proselytization as the basis for a means of achieving Negro rights, was thus the concept of the equal protection of the laws for men's civil, that is, natural, rights.

The failure to adopt these measures was not due to any doubts about the propriety or adequacy of the basis and means. They were immediately replaced in the Republican program by other measures featuring the same elements. The principal objection made by fellow Republicans was rather that the legislation was too narrowly conceived, being based on the war power, confined to the rebel states, and aimed only at the annulment of bad laws. The great need and opportunity was to make the protection permanent, to cast it in universal form (though immediately and primarily the boon of the freedmen), to make it applicable to the whole country, and to ground it firmly not in the old Constitution but in the new amendment.

In the achievement of these wider purposes the leadership of Senator Trumbull in his capacity as chairman of the Senate Judiciary Committee soon became dominant. As he saw it, the task was to "abolish slavery, not only in name but in fact." Because "it is idle to say that a man is free who cannot go and come at pleasure, who cannot buy and sell, who cannot enforce his rights," Congress must "give effect to the provision ... making all persons free."[6] It must wipe out the remnants, badges, and indicia of slavery. It was to enable Congress to do this—or rather to remove all doubt and argument about the power of Congress to do this—that section 2 of the Thirteenth Amendment had been added. The time had come

---
[6] *Ibid.*, p. 43.

to implement that amendment and use that power. Trumbull's civil rights bill and its supplementary companion, an amendment to the Freedmen's Bureau Act, became almost immediately the heart of the Republican legislative program.

The congressional battle that raged around these two bills[7] constituted the third important debate over the Thirteenth Amendment. By the amendment, the principle of universal liberty had been established. The Freedmen's Bureau bill and the civil rights bill represented the efforts of the amendment's framers, acting contemporaneously with its ratification, to implement the amendment and define the principle. This debate, accordingly, had the distinct advantage of being evoked by specific legislative plans, of being tied down to a particular application of the liberty ensured by the amendment. As a result, not only did attention necessarily focus on section 2 of the amendment granting Congress power of enforcement, but the persons and the rights protected, the area of asserted state sovereignty invaded, and the notion of liberty itself were all given concrete significance.

Basically, the two acts proceeded upon exactly the same theory: that the way to implement the Thirteenth Amendment and secure liberty was to protect men in their "civil rights and immunities" and to do so directly through the national government—the agents of the bureau in the one case, the federal courts in the other. The rights and immunities thus to be nationalized and protected, moreover, were not to be "left to the uncertain and ambiguous language" of a general formula. They, or some of them, were to be "distinctly specified."

Section 1 of the civil rights bill and section 7 of the freedmen's bill, accordingly, contain identical lists of the civil rights of men to be guaranteed by the national government. The list is short but the rights enumerated are sweeping. The first—"the right to make and enforce contracts"—safeguards men in their labor relations,

[7] And also to some extent around the other implementing legislation, especially Senator Wilson's bill.

business affairs, and ordinary transactions. The second—the right to buy, sell, and own real and personal property—is virtually indispensable in our system to the maintenance of life itself, let alone anything like economic improvement. The third—the right "to sue, be parties and give evidence"—guarantees access to the judiciary as the normal means of maintaining rights—that is, guarantees the protection of the courts. The fourth—the right to "full and equal benefit of all laws and proceedings for the security of person and estate"—is an explicit guarantee of the "full" and "equal" protection of men in their persons and their property by laws. The right to the equal protection of the laws—the right to have other civil rights protected and equally by laws—is thus itself counted among men's fundamental "civil rights and immunities." Moreover, this is not only a matter of receiving the benefit of such laws. The detriment of the laws, the punishment under them, may not be unequal, may not be different for identical offenses, without a similar violation of civil rights.

Taken together, read in the light of their abolitionist origins and stated purposes, these bills were the practical application of the idea of equality as an essential principle of liberty. They represented the progress from abolitionist constitutional and political theory to abolitionist law, from doctrine to enactment. Consistent with those origins and purposes and with the facts of federalism as the abolitionists had learned them, in a third of a century of struggle the federal government alone was to be the agency of enforcement. Thus was effected a complete nationalization of the civil or natural rights of persons.

Neither of the bills was confined to the Negro. The Freedmen's Bureau bill extended the protection and services of the bureau to "refugees and freedmen in all parts of the United States." It dealt almost exclusively with freedmen and black refugees, contained many welfare and educational features which had special relevance to the Negro, and extended beyond the rebel states in order to permit the bureau to operate in loyal Delaware and Kentucky, where slavery had been abolished by the Thirteenth Amendment, and to aid the thousands of freedmen who had migrated into southern Illinois, Indiana, and Ohio. The civil rights bill covered "the inhabitants of any state or territory of the United States." It was intended to be permanent, truly countrywide, and inclusive of "persons of all races." The debates over these bills contain many references to loyal southern whites "who have been reduced from men almost to chattels because of their fidelity to our flag, to our constitution, and to this country" and who therefore need national "care" and "protection."[8]

Nor was either of these bills restricted to the corrective removal of discriminatory state legislation or official action. The Freedmen's Bureau bill prohibited the denial of the mentioned rights if the denial was "in consequence of any state or local law, ordinance, police, or other regulation, custom, or prejudice." The use of the word "custom" to some extent, and of the word "prejudice" altogether, removes the limitation imposed by the earlier words in the section. An abrogation of civil rights made "in consequence of any state or local . . . custom, or prejudice" might as easily be perpetrated by private individuals or by unofficial community activity as by state officers armed with statute or ordinance. Moreover, section 7 of the Freedmen's Bureau bill was part of a large and comprehensive system for the care of freedmen. That system encompassed not merely safeguarding the Negro against discriminatory state legislation but against invasions of his rights and the essential conditions of his freedom from whatever source: private outrage, employer oppression, or official action.

The language of the civil rights bill is more ambiguous. While it provides that "the inhabitants of every race and color . . . shall have the same right to make and enforce contracts," and so forth, a possibly restrictive proviso is added: "Any law, statute, ordinance, regulation or custom, to the contrary notwithstanding." If this proviso be taken to limit the category of invaders of "the same

---

[8] *Cong. Globe*, 39th Cong., 1st sess., 1865–1866, p. 438.

the Fourteenth Amendment

rights to make and enforce contracts" and so forth, and if the omission of the word "prejudice" from the list be emphasized, the case for confining the application of the bill to the nullification of state acts is put in its most favorable light. Thus to confine the bill, however, overlooks the use of the word "custom." It also disregards the fact that the proviso may not apply to the prohibition, appearing earlier in the same sentence, against any "discrimination in civil rights or immunities among the inhabitants."

In any event, the "full and equal benefit" provisions of both the civil rights bill and the Freedmen's Bureau bill immediately broadened their coverage to include state inaction as well as state action. "Full and equal benefit" of all laws and proceedings for the protection of person and property often can be afforded only by extending protection to the unprotected rather than withdrawing protection from those who have it. Invasion of civil rights made possible by the failure of the state to supply protection, consequently, falls within the language set forth.

The congressional debates make this point clear. A great deal was said about the infamous Black Codes. They were only less rigorous than the slave codes which they had replaced. Under them the freedman was socially an outcast, industrially a serf, legally a separate and oppressed class. Slavery, abolished by the organic law of the nation, was in fact revived by these statutes of the states. Knowledge of this was prominently displayed in the *Congressional Globe*. The Black Codes were read and analyzed in detail. Their obliteration unquestionably was a specific object of the Freedmen's Bureau and civil rights bills.

But the senators and representatives also had before them a sizable body of data bearing on the treatment of the Negro, the loyal white, and the northerner in the South by private individuals and unofficial groups. General Grant's report, in other respects most helpful to the conservatives, was used by the radicals for its declaration that "in some form, the Freedmen's Bureau is an absolute necessity until civil law is established and enforced, securing to the freedmen their rights and full protection." Carl Schurz's report, while conflicting with that of General Grant with respect to many aspects of national policy and conditions in the South, agreed in its emphasis on the need for protecting freedmen against both "oppressive legislation" and "private persecution."

Accounts in newspapers North and South, Freedmen's Bureau and other official documents, private reports and correspondence were all adduced to show that "murder, shootings, whippings, robbing, and brutal treatment of every kind" were daily inflicted on freedmen and their white friends.* Much of this evidence was contested as to its truth, but, true or false, it showed the realm of fact that was within the contemplation of those who framed and put across the Freedmen's Bureau and civil rights bills. Moreover, though opponents denied or minimized the facts asserted, they did not contend that the bills in question would not reach such facts if they did exist. Private outrage and atrocity were, equally with the Black Codes, evils which this legislation was designed to correct.

The persistent questions now recur: How was this vast system for the national protection of the civil rights of men "of all races" derived from the Thirteenth Amendment? Could it be sustained by a mere prohibition against "slavery and involuntary servitude"? Are these words of the amendment of such a character as to accomplish or confirm a revolution in the federal system?

The answers to these questions, abundantly and clearly supplied by the earlier debates over the Thirteenth Amendment, were now repeated by sponsors and supporters of the civil rights and Freedmen's Bureau bills. Not so, however, with those who opposed them. Democrats and a fringe of conservative Republicans now switched to a restrictive interpretation of the Thirteenth Amendment. The liberal view of its language which they had adopted in opposing its passage they now rejected as never having been correct. The evil of Negro elevation and equality which they had

---

* See, for example, *ibid.*, pp. 95, 168, 339, 340, 438, 503.

the Fourteenth Amendment 165

loudly proclaimed the amendment would bring about they now insisted it had not been intended to achieve.

In the third debate over the Thirteenth Amendment, the Democrats and some Republicans took the position that the amendment merely dissolved the relation of master and slave. Said Senator Edgar Cowan of Pennsylvania, for example, "nobody pretends that it [the amendment] was to be wider in its operation than to cover the relation which existed between the master and his Negro African slave . . . that particular relation and the breaking of it up, is the subject of the first clause of the Amendment, and it does not extend any further, and cannot by any possible implication, contortion, or straining, be made to go further . . ." Section 2, according to Saulsbury, "was intended . . . to give to the Negro the privilege of the habeas corpus; that is, if anybody persisted in the face of the constitutional amendment in holding him as a slave, that he should have an appropriate remedy to be delivered."[10]

To this narrow constructionist argument as to the meaning of "slavery" and its abolition was added weight from another source, namely, Seward's folly in labeling section 2 of the amendment a limitation on, rather than a grant of power to, Congress.[11] Though the interpretation and the motive behind it were not difficult to explain, in view of Seward's well-known conciliatory political tendency to be all things to all men, yet, coming from one with Seward's connections with the administration and former connections with the abolitionist movement, this pronouncement supplied welcome ammunition to the Democrats and reactionaries who resisted all change. It also had an effect upon the radicals. While many of them denounced it as untenable, Thaddeus Stevens accepted it as a statement of administration policy and therefore as showing the necessity for a new amendment.

---

[10] Cowan, *ibid.*, p. 499; Senator Willard Saulsbury of Delaware, *ibid.*, pp. 113, 476; Senator Thomas A. Hendricks of Indiana, *ibid.*, p. 317.

[11] Seward, as Secretary of State, telegraphed Perry, provisional Governor of South Carolina, when the latter objected that section 2 of the Thirteenth Amendment might be construed as authorizing legislation protecting civil rights, that his objection was "querlous," that the clause was restrictive in character. *Cong. Globe,* 39th Cong., 1st sess., 1865–1866, p. 43.

A third basis of the narrow constructionism now expressed by the Democrats and some Republicans related directly to the revolution in federalism brought about by the Thirteenth Amendment if it were held to sustain the Freedmen's Bureau and civil rights bills. Those measures, it was clearly recognized, were an exercise of congressional power in the regulation of the civil status of the inhabitants of the states, vested in the United States courts a jurisdiction over property, contracts, and crimes hitherto all but universally conceded to be the exclusive province of the states, and established the national government as the protector of individual rights against state oppression or against oppression due to state inaction.

To many a conservative of that day, unaware of or still resisting the great change that thirty years of abolitionism had wrought and the Civil War had confirmed, this "seemed like a complete revelation of the diabolical spirit of centralization, of which only the cloven hoof had been manifested heretofore." "Are we to alter the whole frame and structure of the laws," asked Cowan, "are we to overturn the whole Constitution in order to get at a remedy for these people?" The Thirteenth Amendment "never was intended to overturn this government and revolutionize all the laws of the states everywhere." "If under color of this constitutional Amendment, we have a right to pass such laws as these, . . . we have a right to overturn the states themselves completely."[12]

While the opponents of the Freedmen's Bureau and civil rights bills, in the third debate over the Thirteenth Amendment, thus precisely reversed their position as to the meaning and effect of the amendment, sponsors and supporters of the legislation adhered strictly to the doctrines they had expressed earlier. Senator Trumbull, a principal draftsman of both the Thirteenth Amendment and the civil rights bill, in his speech opening the debate on the latter described their relationship. The civil rights bill, he said, was intended to give effect to the Thirteenth Amendment by securing

---

[12] *Ibid.*, p. 499.

"to all persons within the United States practical freedom."[13] "Of what avail," he asked, "was the immortal Declaration" of Independence to the millions of slaves?

Of what avail to the citizens of Massachusetts, who, a few years ago, went to South Carolina to enforce a constitutional right in court, that the Constitution of the United States declared that the citizens of each state shall be entitled to all the privileges and immunities of citizens in the several states? And of what avail will it now be that the Constitution of the United States has declared that slavery shall not exist, if in the late slaveholding states laws are to be enacted and enforced depriving persons of African descent of privileges which are essential to freemen?

"It is the intention of this bill to secure those rights." What rights? The natural rights of men specified in the Declaration and the privileges and immunities of citizens under the comity clause. Trumbull implies here and makes plain elsewhere in his speech that these two sources referred to the same rights. How is the protection of these natural rights of men, these privileges and immunities of citizens—as now listed in the civil rights bill—authorized by the Thirteenth Amendment?

It is difficult, perhaps, to define accurately what slavery is and liberty is. Liberty and slavery are opposite terms; one is opposed to the other. We know that in a civil government, in organized society, no such thing can exist as natural or absolute liberty. Natural liberty is defined to be the "Power of acting as one thinks fit, without any restraint or control, unless by the law of nature, being a right inherent in us by birth, and one of the gifts of God to man in his creation, when he imbued him with the faculty of will."

But every man who enters society gives up a part of this natural liberty, which is the liberty of the savage, the liberty which the wild

---

[13] Few radicals took the cavalier view of the constitutional problem that Senator William Pitt Fessenden did. He was doubtful about the constitutionality of the bureau bill, especially the land purchase provisions. He thought he might in an extreme case go as far as Trumbull and say this was necessary to make the slave free and that Congress could do whatever was necessary for that purpose. "I cannot work the problem out and nobody else can to show that in the Constitution itself there is a clear power; but I can work the problem out to show that the power may be found when the positive necessity of the thing is apparent where the thing must be done and must be done by the government as a consequence of other things that it was compelled to do and that it had a perfect right to do." *Cong. Globe,* 39th Cong., 1st sess., p. 366.

beast has, for the advantages he obtains in the protection which civil government gives him. Civil liberty, or the liberty which a person enjoys in society, is thus defined by Blackstone: "Civil liberty is not other than natural liberty, so far restrained by human laws and no further, as is necessary and expedient for the general advantage of the public."

That is the liberty to which every citizen is entitled; that is the liberty which was intended to be secured by the Declaration of Independence and the Constitution of the United States originally and more especially by the Amendment which has recently been adopted: and in a note to Blackstone's Commentaries it is stated that "In this definition of civil liberty it ought to be understood, or rather expressed, that the restraints introduced by the law should be equal to all, or as much so as the nature of things will admit."

Then, Sir, I take it that any statute which is not equal to all, and which deprives any citizen of civil rights which are secured to other citizens, is an unjust encroachment upon his liberty; and is, in fact, a badge of servitude which, by the Constitution, is prohibited. We may, perhaps, arrive at a more correct definition of the term "citizen of the United States" by referring to that clause of the Constitution which I have already quoted, and which declares that "the citizens of each State shall be entitled to all privileges and immunities of citizens in the several States." What rights are secured to the citizens of each State under that provision? Such fundamental rights as belong to every free person.

Trumbull thus elaborated the natural rights philosophy underlying the Thirteenth Amendment and implementing legislation.[14]

---

[14] Many other speeches are to the same effect. Senator John Sherman of Ohio expressed his belief that "it is the duty of Congress to give to the freedmen of the southern states *ample protection in all their natural rights.*" The Thirteenth Amendment left "no doubt" of the power of Congress to do so. "Here," he said, "is not only a guarantee of liberty to every inhabitant of the United States, but an express grant of power to Congress to secure this liberty by appropriate legislation. Now, unless a man may be free without the right to sue and be sued, to plead and be impleaded, to acquire and hold property, and to testify in a court of justice, then Congress has the power, by the express terms of this amendment, to secure all these rights. To say that a man is a free man and yet is not able to assert and maintain his right, in a court of justice, is a negation of terms. Therefore the power is expressly given to Congress to secure all their rights of freedom by appropriate legislation. The reason why this power was given is also drawn from the history of a clause of the Constitution," namely, the comity clause, Article IV, section 2. "There never was any doubt about the construction of this clause of the Constitution—that is, that a man who was recognized as a citizen of one state had a right to go anywhere within the United States and exercise the immunity of a citizen of the United States; but the trouble was in enforcing this constitutional provision. . . . To avoid this very difficulty, that of a guarantee without a power to enforce it, this

the Fourteenth Amendment 169

While he later points to the Black Codes as instances of discriminatory state legislation which it is the aim of his bills to prevent, it is plain from this excerpt that he is also thinking of individual action based on custom or prejudice and made possible by the absence of state legislation or other restraint. Accordingly, he argues that in a state of nature all men are free to act as they please, without any restraint except such as may be imposed by the law of nature. Upon entering society, "every man ... gives up a part of this natural liberty ... for the advantages he obtains in the protection which the civil government gives him." So liberty or civil liberty is what one gets in society as a result of governmental restraint on the conduct of others. Without such governmental restraint, that is, without such laws or their enforcement, there is no civil liberty. Hence the absence of laws is a denial or withholding of the protection which was the reason for creating or entering civil society.

---

second section of the constitutional amendment was adopted, which does give to Congress in clear and express terms the right to secure, by appropriate legislation, to every person within the United States, liberty." *Cong. Globe*, 39th Cong., 1st sess.

Senator William Stewart, moderate from Nevada, said, "I am in favor of legislation under the constitutional amendment that shall secure to him [the freedman] a chance to live, a chance to hold property, a chance to be heard in the courts, a chance to enjoy his civil rights, a chance to rise in the scale of humanity, a chance to be a man. . . . we shall give him freedom, and that implies that he shall have all the civil rights necessary to the enjoyment of that freedom. The senator from Illinois has introduced two bills [the Freedmen's Bureau and civil rights bills] well and carefully prepared, which if passed by Congress will give full and ample protection under the constitutional amendment to the negro in his civil liberty; and guarantee to him civil rights, to which we are pledged." *Cong. Globe*, 39th Cong., 1st sess., p. 298. See similar remarks by Stewart, pp. 110, 111, 297, 445.

Senator Henry Wilson of Massachusetts argued, "We must see to it that the man made free by the Constitution of the United States, sanctioned by the voice of the American people, is a free man indeed; that he can go where he pleases, work when and for whom he pleases; that he can sue and be sued; that he can lease and buy and sell and own property, real and personal; that he can go into the schools and educate himself and his children; that the rights and guarantees of the good old common law are his, and that he walks the earth, proud and erect in the conscious dignity of a free man, who knows that his cabin, however humble, is protected by the just and equal laws of his country." *Cong. Globe*, 39th Cong., 1st sess., p. 111.

Senator Henry S. Lane from Indiana maintained: "They [the Negroes] are free by the constitutional amendment lately enacted and entitled to all the privileges and immunities of other free citizens of the United States. It is made your especial duty by the second section of that amendment, by appropriate legislation to carry out that emancipation. If that second section were not embraced in the amendment

All this was said so often and so earnestly, not only by Trumbull but by the rest of the sponsors of this combined constitutional and legislative program, that it cannot be doubted as the common doctrinal foundation. Constitutional historians, too, have well understood it. The reason it bears repetition and reëmphasis here is that Trumbull and the other sponsors did what constitutional historians have not so well understood: he took the next step of articulating the relationship of this natural rights philosophy to the concept of the equal protection of the laws. "Then, Sir," he said in summing up, "I take it that any statute which is not equal to all, and which deprives any citizen of civil rights which are secured to other citizens, is an unjust encroachment upon his liberty; and is, in fact,

at all your duty would be as strong, the duty would be paramount, to protect them in all rights as free and manumitted people. I do not consider that the second section of that amendment does anything but declare what is the duty of Congress, after having passed such amendment to the Constitution of the United States to secure them in all their rights and privileges.

"What are the objects sought to be accomplished by this bill? That these freedmen shall be secured in the possession of all the rights, privileges, and immunities of free men; in other words, that we shall give effect to the proclamation of emancipation and to the constitutional amendment." *Cong. Globe,* 39th Cong., 1st sess., p. 602.

See also Trumbull's remarks, *ibid.,* p. 322, and Senator Sumner's remarks, p. 91. See Representative Burton C. Cook, *ibid.,* p. 1123.

Martin F. Thayer of Pennsylvania maintained that the constitutional foundation of the Civil Rights Act was to be found in the Thirteenth Amendment, the comity clause, and that clause "which guarantees to all the citizens of the United States their rights to life, liberty, and property." *Cong. Globe,* 39th Cong., 1st sess., p. 2464.

Representative James F. Wilson of Iowa, chairman of the House Judiciary Committee, introduced the civil rights bill in the House with even more sweeping constitutional declarations than those of Trumbull in the Senate. He planted the bill squarely upon the Thirteenth Amendment, which made "a specific delegation of power to Congress." He argued, "a man who enjoys the civil rights mentioned in this bill cannot be reduced to slavery. Anything which protects him in the possession of these rights insures him against reduction to slavery." But if the bill "in its enlarged operation step out of the bounds of this express delegation of power," Wilson found it constitutional still. He said, "if citizens of the United States, as such, are entitled to possess and enjoy the great fundamental civil rights which it is the true office of government to protect, and to equality in the exemptions of the law, we must of necessity be clothed with the power to insure to each and every citizen these things which belong to him as a constituent member of the great national family. Whatever these great fundamental rights are, we must be invested with power to legislate for their protection or our constitution fails in the first and most important office of government." Wilson went on to find that these "great fundamental rights" were the natural rights of men. He defined them with Blackstone and Kent as the right to personal security, personal liberty, and

the Fourteenth Amendment

a badge of servitude which, by the Constitution, is prohibited." Civil rights which are "secured to other citizens"—"secured" how? By the only method by which rights can be secured, namely, by supplying protection, by imposing restraints on those who would invade the rights. Hence, deprivation or denial of laws "not equal to all" will occur just as much by failure to supply the protection or impose the restraints as by Black Codes imposing special burdens on a selected class.

Emphasizing the same central issue, Senator Jacob M. Howard from Michigan, cast the argument, after the manner of abolitionists for thirty years past, in terms of the rights that were denied to the slave.

---

private property. "Before our Constitution was formed, the great fundamental rights which I have mentioned, belonged to every person who became a member of our great national family. No one surrendered a jot or tittle of these rights by consenting to the formation of the government. The entire machinery of our government as organized by the Constitution was designed, among other things, to secure a more perfect enjoyment of these rights. A legislative department was created that laws necessary and proper to this end might be enacted. A judicial department was erected to expound and administer the laws. An executive department was formed for the purpose of enforcing and seeing to the execution of these laws. And these several departments of government possess the power to enact, administer, and enforce the laws 'necessary and proper' to secure these rights which existed anterior to the ordination of the Constitution.

"Upon this broad principle I rest my justification of this bill. I assert that we possess the power to do those things which governments are organized to do; that we may protect a citizen of the United States against a violation of his rights by the law of a single state; that by our laws and our courts we may intervene to maintain the proud character of American citizenship; that this power permeates our whole system, is a part of it, without which the states can run riot over every fundamental right belonging to citizens of the United States; that the right to exercise this power depends upon no express delegation, but runs with the right it is designed to protect; that we possess the same latitude in respect to the selection of means through which to exercise this power that belongs to us when a power rests upon express delegation; and that the decisions which support the latter maintain the former." *Cong. Globe,* 39th Cong., 1st sess., p. 1119.

Senator Reverdy Johnson of Maryland took a narrower view of the Thirteenth Amendment, but believed that the attributes of citizenship could be conferred on the free Negro by authorizing him under the judiciary article to sue, contract, be a witness, etc. "If I am right ... that we can authorize them to sue, authorize them to contract, authorize them to do everything short of voting, it is not because there is anything in the Constitution of the United States that confers the authority to give to a negro the right to contract, but it is because it is a necessary, incidental function of a government that it should have authority to provide that the rights of everybody within its limits shall be protected, and protected alike." *Cong. Globe,* 39th Cong., 1st sess., p. 530.

He had no rights, nor nothing which he could call his own. He had not the right to become a husband or a father in the eye of the law.... He owned no property, because the law prohibited him. He could not take real or personal estate either by sale, by grant, or by descent, or by inheritance. He did not own the bread he earned and ate. He stood upon the face of the earth completely isolated from the society in which he happened to be; he was nothing but a chattel, subject to the will of his owner, and unprotected in his rights by the law of the state where he happened to live.[15]

The opposite of the slave is the freeman; the opposite of slavery is liberty. The Thirteenth Amendment's abolition of slavery, therefore, is a declaration "that all persons in the United States should be free." But what is freedom? Freedom is the possession of those rights which were denied to the slave, that is, natural or civil rights. The radicals differed in their designation of natural rights, but they agreed that such rights included, at the least, those presented in section 1 of the civil rights bill and section 7 of the Freedmen's Bureau bill. The possession of these rights depends upon protection by government; indeed, so much so that protection by government is regarded as one of men's civil rights or as a "necessary incident" of civil rights. Governments act through laws and hence the protection which governments are instituted to supply must be by laws. Thus the Thirteenth Amendment made all men free, that is, restored civil rights to those who had been deprived of them and entitled them to the protection of the laws—in this case, according to section 2, the laws of Congress.

William Lawrence, a member of the Ohio delegation, in a carefully organized speech delivered in the House marked out the foundations of the civil rights bill in even greater detail and comprehensiveness.[16] He argued that "so far as there is any power in the state to limit, enlarge, or declare civil rights, all these are left to the states." In this sense, the Civil Rights Act merely provided that "whatever" of the listed civil rights "may be enjoyed by any shall be shared by all citizens in each state." All this, however, was

---

[15] *Ibid.*, pp. 503-504.   [16] *Ibid.*, p. 1832.

the Fourteenth Amendment 173

subject to the "limitation that there are some inherent and inalienable rights, pertaining to every citizen, which cannot be abolished or abridged by state constitutions or laws." Thus far, Lawrence is saying that, within the area of its optional operation, if the state acts at all, it must treat everyone alike. But with respect to the "inherent and inalienable rights, pertaining to every citizen" the state must refrain from passing "constitutions and laws" which "abolish or abridge."

The duty of the state, however, does not end with the observance of this negative limitation. Lawrence goes on to add: "There is in this country no such thing as legislative omnipotence. When it is said in state constitutions that 'all legislative power is vested in a Senate and House of Representatives,' authority is not thereby conferred to destroy all that is valuable in citizenship. Legislative powers exist in our system to protect, not to destroy, the inalienable rights of men." In the case of the inalienable rights of men or citizens, then, the obligation of the state is not discharged until it has given whatever protection is necessary to maintain those rights, that is, full or ample protection.

Lawrence then bears down directly on citizenship and its particular rights. The citizenship section of the Civil Rights Act, he said, was declaratory. But even if it were not, the national government, by virtue of its sovereignty and the constitutional section about a rule of uniform naturalization, has complete authority over citizenship, including the power to declare what rights appertain to it. Lawrence quotes the Declaration of Independence, the Preamble, and the Fifth Amendment to show that three of the rights of citizens are life, liberty, and property. "It has never been deemed necessary to enact in any constitution or law that citizens should have the right to life or liberty or the right to acquire property. These rights are recognized by the Constitution as existing anterior to and independent of laws and all constitutions." Furthermore, not only are these rights "inherent and indestructible, but the means whereby they may be possessed and enjoyed are equally so."

It is idle to say that a citizen shall have the right to life, yet to deny him the right to labor, whereby alone he can live. It is a mockery to say that a citizen may have a right to live, and yet deny him the right to make a contract to secure the privilege and the rewards of labor. It is worse than mockery to say that men may be clothed by the national authority, with the character of citizens, yet may be stripped by state authority of the means by which citizens exist....

Every citizen, therefore, has the absolute right to life, the right to personal security, personal liberty, and the right to acquire and enjoy property. These are rights of citizenship. As necessary incidents of these absolute rights, there are others, as the right to make and enforce contracts, to purchase, hold, and enjoy property, and to share the benefit of laws for the security of person and property.

It is not enough to note that this statement of Lawrence is an explicit articulation of the natural rights philosophy and that it identifies the natural rights of men as the rights appertaining to citizenship, important though these facts are in understanding both the significance of the Thirteenth Amendment and the concepts and clauses of the Fourteenth Amendment. Even more significant is the way in which Lawrence links all this to the equal protection concept and thus spells out the meaning of that concept. The equal protection requirement is itself a "necessary incident" of men's natural rights, and consists of a negative limitation and an affirmative command. Failure of the legislature to supply the protection which it was instituted to supply is a denial of the requirement quite as much as a legislative enactment singling out a particular group for abusive treatment. Lawrence repeats this point over and over again. "Now there are two ways in which a state may undertake to deprive citizens of these absolute, inherent, and inalienable rights: either by prohibitory laws, or by a failure to protect any one of them."[17]

---

[17] Again Lawrence said, "If the people of a state should become hostile to a large class of naturalized citizens and should enact laws to prohibit them and no other citizens from making contracts, from suing, from giving evidence, from inheriting, buying, holding, or selling property, or even from coming into the state, that would be prohibitory legislation. If the state should simply enact laws for native born citizens and provide no law under which naturalized citizens could enjoy any one of these rights, and should deny them all protection by civil process or penal enactments, that would be a denial of justice."

the Fourteenth Amendment

In the discussion of the scope and nature of the Thirteenth Amendment and the constitutionality of the Freedmen's Bureau bill and the civil rights bill the role of the idea of equality was again a dominant one. This results from the close connection between the idea of equality and the idea of governmental protection. In truth, the fact of very great importance is that these two notions often were inseparably intermingled.

Said Timothy O. Howe, abolitionist senator from Wisconsin,

> I have thought that it belonged to republican institutions to carry out, to execute the doctrines of the Declaration of Independence, to make men equal. That they are not equal in social estimation, that they are not equal in mental culture, that they are not equal in physical stature, I know very well; but I have thought the weaker they were the more the government was bound to foster and protect them. If government be designed for the protection of the weak, certainly the weaker men are the more they need its protection.[18]

So it is the protection of the laws that makes men equal. This attitude was not confined to the radicals. Senator Edgar Cowan, Pennsylvania conservative, put it thus: "What is meant by equality" is that if a man "is assailed by one stronger than himself the government will protect him to punish the assailant. It means that if a man owes another money the government will provide a means by which the debtor shall be compelled to pay, . . . that if an intruder and trespasser gets upon his land he shall have a remedy to recover it. That is what I understand by equality before the law."[19]

The usual notion of the equal protection of the laws is that it is a comparative concept. The requirement is met if one man has the same right as another. Men are protected equally if all of them are not protected. This comparative view was the one expressed by Senator Henry Wilson of Massachusetts.

> By the equality of man we mean that the poorest man, be he black or white . . . is as much entitled to the protection of the law as the richest

---
[18] *Cong. Globe*, 39th Cong., 1st sess., 1865–1866, p. 438.
[19] *Ibid.*, p. 342.

and proudest man.... We mean that the poor man, whose wife may be dressed in a cheap calico, is as much entitled to have her protected by equal law as is the rich man to have his jeweled bride protected by the law of the land.... That the poor man's cabin though it may be the cabin of a poor freedman in the depths of the Carolinas is entitled to the protection of the same law that protects the palace of a Stewart or an Astor.[20]

It is significant that these two conceptions, both identifying equality and governmental protection, but one stating the equal protection of the laws as a comparative, the other as an absolute, right of individuals, are basically identical. The first impression that they are different arises from a failure to realize that there is a constant and assumed factor in both of them, namely, the obligation of government to supply protection. When Wilson says that the poor man has the same right to protection that the rich man has, he is not saying that the poor man would have no complaint if neither he nor the rich man received protection. He is saying, in effect, that the rich man has a right to protection; the poor man has a right to protection; they have the same right to protection. Both are entitled, all men are entitled, to the protection of the laws. If some men do not receive it, they are denied the full or the equal protection of the laws. If all men receive the full protection of the laws, they equally receive the protection of the laws or they receive the equal protection of the laws. On the other hand, if men equally receive the protection of the laws, they all receive the full protection of the laws, since it is assumed that the protection of the laws will always be supplied in some form and to most people. In this context, the "equal" protection of the laws and the "full" protection of the laws are virtually synonyms. The use of both words, "full" and "equal" in the Freedmen's Bureau bill and the civil rights bill is thus highly significant. Elsewhere, throughout the discussion and in other bills, these words are used sometimes together, sometimes alternatively, but always redundantly or interchangeably.

[20] *Ibid.*, p. 343.

the Fourteenth Amendment

The equal protection of the laws, then, as an integral part of the doctrines of social compact and natural rights, and as understood by the abolitionists, was far from the simple command of comparative treatment that courts and later generations have made it. Freemen, all men, were entitled to have their natural rights protected by government. Indeed, it was for that purpose and that purpose only that men entered society and formed governments. Once slavery was abolished, the legal pretense for withholding the protection of the laws from some people was at an end. Those people, too, must then be protected fully, equally. The equal protection of the laws is thus a command for the full or ample protection of the laws. It is basically an affirmative command to supply the protection of the laws. This is its primary character. Its negative on governmental action is secondary and almost incidental. In the words of Senator Yates' resolution, it is a command that all persons "shall be protected in the full and equal enjoyment of all their civil . . . rights."[21] This view makes intelligible Senator Trumbull's otherwise odd statement that "any statute which is not equal to all, and which deprives any citizen of civil rights which are secured to other citizens, is an unjust encroachment upon his liberty, and is in fact, a badge of servitude which, by the Constitution, is prohibited."

In a revealing impromptu speech on December 19, 1865, Trumbull summed up the essential features of the Thirteenth Amendment and his purpose in sponsoring the Freedmen's Bureau bill:

I desire to give notice that I shall to-morrow, or on some early day thereafter, ask leave to introduce a bill to enlarge the powers of the Freedmen's Bureau so as to secure freedom to all persons within the United States, and protect every individual in the full enjoyment of the rights of person and property and furnish him with means for their vindication. In giving this notice I desire to say that it is given in view of the adoption of the constitutional amendment abolishing slavery. I have never doubted that, on the adoption of that amendment it would be competent for Congress to protect every person in the United States

---

[21] Senator Richard Yates of Illinois, *ibid.*, January 29, 1866, p. 472.

in all the rights of person and property belonging to the free citizen; and to secure these rights is the object of the bill which I propose to introduce. I think it important that action should be taken on this subject at an early day for the purpose of quieting apprehensions in the minds of many friends of freedom lest by local legislation or a prevailing public sentiment in some of the States persons of the African race should continue to be oppressed and in fact deprived of their freedom, and for the purpose also of showing to those among whom slavery has heretofore existed that unless by local legislation they provide for the real freedom of their former slaves, the federal government will, by virtue of its own authority, see that they are fully protected.

The bill which I desire to introduce is intended to accomplish these objects. I hope there may be no necessity for enforcing such a bill in any part of the Union; but I consider that under the constitutional amendment Congress is bound to see that freedom is in fact secured to every person throughout the land; he must be fully protected in all his rights of person and property; and any legislation or any public sentiment which deprived any human being in the land of those great rights of liberty will be in defiance of the Constitution; and if the states and local authorities, by legislation or otherwise, deny these rights, it is incumbent on us to see that they are secured.[22]

This casual utterance is a clear-cut expression of the state's affirmative duty to protect as well as its negative obligation not to pass discriminatory legislation, of the authority of Congress to protect Negroes against individual invasions of their new-found freedom and civil rights when the inaction of the state or its failure to supply protection make such invasions possible, and of the Thirteenth Amendment as the constitutional foundation upon which this radical redistribution of power rested.

Trumbull speaks of securing freedom to all persons and protecting every individual in "the full enjoyment of the rights of person and property" and the means of their vindication. Later it is plain that he is thinking entirely of blacks and is using these universal words simply because he is intent on raising the blacks to the standard of the whites. The use of the universal words thus has a significance inextricably intertwined with the idea of equality. "Full

---

[22] *Cong. Globe*, 39th Cong., 1st sess., 1865–1866, p. 77.

the Fourteenth Amendment 179

enjoyment of the rights of person and property" and the means of their vindication is the "equal" enjoyment of these rights. That enjoyment on the part of the recently freed Negroes was rendered far less than full or equal by legislative enactments, such as the Black Codes, prohibitory in their nature, which singled out the Negro for separate and abusive treatment. These accordingly fell within the ban of the amendment and of congressional power.

"Full enjoyment of the rights of person and property" was less than a reality also by reason of "a prevailing public sentiment in some of the States." By reason of the deep-rooted prejudices and attitudes toward the Negro translated into private action and community pressure, "persons of the African race continue to be oppressed and in fact deprived of their freedom." So these, too, are within the ban of the amendment and within the reach of congressional power under it. Not, however, as an original matter. The primary duty of protection is still with the states. It is only when acting they act discriminatorily or when not acting they fail to supply protection against private inroads that the federal power springs into life. Southerners are accordingly told that "unless by local legislation they provide for the real freedom of their former slaves, the federal government will by virtue of its own authority see that they are fully protected." So "full enjoyment of the right of person and property" is the same as "equal enjoyment" of those rights; and the "full enjoyment" of such rights depends upon first, the absence of discriminatory state legislative or other official action, and second, the presence of adequate affirmative protection to prevent or cope with individual invasions. This, then, is equal protection. At the very foundation of the system constructed out of the Thirteenth Amendment, the Freedmen's Bureau bill, and the civil rights bill is an idea of "equal protection" as far flung as the problem of human rights and as substantive as any guarantee of those absolute rights could well be.

The striking thing, then, about the Thirteenth Amendment is that it was intended by its drafters and sponsors as a consummation to abolitionism in the broad sense in which thirty years of agitation and organized activity had defined that movement. The amendment was seen by its drafters and sponsors as doing the whole job—not merely cutting loose the fetters which bound the physical person of the slave, but restoring to him his natural, inalienable, and civil rights, or, in other words, guaranteeing to him the privileges and immunities of citizens of the United States. Slavery and liberty were contradictory and mutually exclusive states. If slavery were abolished then liberty must exist. But liberty in society, civil liberty, consists of natural liberty restrained by human laws protecting all men in their antecedent rights and being both general and equal. Nor, carrying out this well-articulated major premise and the diplomacy of the Fathers in 1787, was any word of caste or color used in the amendment. And so within its ambit is the power "to secure freedom to all persons and protect every individual in the full enjoyment of person and property and the means of their vindication."

Thus underlying the narrow words of the amendment and imported by them into the Constitution are the theories of Locke, the Declaration of Independence, the Declaration of Rights in the state constitutions, and the fundamental principles of the common law. This was the effect of a prohibition of slavery and involuntary servitude; and a grant of power to Congress to enforce it by appropriate legislation designated the agency and imposed the responsibility for the protection of the rights thus nationalized.[23]

---

[23] Three of the justices of the Supreme Court, in opinions delivered at circuit before the post-bellum reaction and counterrevolution had set in, took this broad view of the Thirteenth Amendment and concluded that the Civil Rights Act was constitutional under it: Justice Swayne in *United States* v. *Rhodes*, 1 Abbott (U.S.) 28; Chief Justice Chase in *Matter of Elizabeth Turner*, 1 Abbott (U.S.) 84; Justice Bradley in *United States* v. *Cruickshank*, 1 Woods 308, 318. The Rhodes case involved the right of a colored woman to testify against a white man in the courts of Kentucky, denied by the laws of that state. In the Turner case, the Chief Justice struck down, under the "full and equal benefit of all laws" provision of the Civil Rights Act, a Maryland system for apprenticing freed Negro children to their former masters under conditions more rigorous than those applied to other apprentices. See also *Smith* v. *Moody*, 26 Ind. 299, 306; *People* v. *Washington*, 36 Cal. 658. Cf. *Bowlen* v. *Commonwealth*, 2 Bush (Kentucky) 5.

Part Four

RECONSUMMATION
THE FOURTEENTH AMENDMENT

CHAPTER XI

The Fourteenth Amendment

THE CHRONOLOGY of the development of the Fourteenth Amendment in Congress and the general course of the congressional debates have been covered by Dr. Flack,[1] Professor Fairman,[2] and Professor Warsoff,[3] and to a lesser extent by others. That part of the story is familiar or at least accessible and requires no retelling. Some main batches of evidence and conclusions, however, bearing on the intended scope of the amendment, need to be gathered together and restated; others added.

The one point upon which historians of the Fourteenth Amendment agree, and, indeed, which the evidence places beyond cavil, is that the Fourteenth Amendment was designed to place the constitutionality of the Freedmen's Bureau and civil rights bills, par-

---
[1] H. E. Flack, *The Adoption of the Fourteenth Amendment* (1908).
[2] Charles Fairman, "Does the Fourteenth Amendment Incorporate the Bill of Rights?" *Stanford Law Review*, Vol. 2 (December, 1949).
[3] Louis A. Warsoff, *Equality and the Law* (1938).

ticularly the latter, beyond doubt. The principal source and nature of the doubt have already been indicated in the discussion of the third debate over the Thirteenth Amendment. The doubt related to the capacity of the Thirteenth Amendment to sustain this far-reaching legislative program. The Thirteenth Amendment, it had been argued, was designed merely to free the slave from personal bondage. Section 2 restricted rather than enlarged its scope. And, in any event, the amendment could not be construed as destroying or seriously modifying the federal system as it existed hitherto. Primarily these arguments were raised by those who were basically opposed to the civil rights bill and the Freedmen's Bureau bill. But the impetus thus given a new amendment was augmented by other doubts entertained by some of the staunchest friends of the legislation.

From the very beginning of the Thirty-ninth Congress there were those who felt that the rights secured in the civil rights and Freedmen's Bureau bills, especially as they applied to the Negro, should be placed beyond the power of shifting congressional majorities. This group did not question the program by which the rights of individuals were nationalized, by which the jurisdiction of the states was ousted if not properly exercised and that of Congress and the federal courts instituted. They felt that this program should be made an inescapable obligation of the whole federal government—not merely a discretionary alternative of Congress—by fixing it in the Constitution itself. This idea, well defined at the beginning of the Thirty-ninth Congress among the radicals, gradually spread and became the conviction of the overwhelming majority of all Republicans, radicals and conservatives alike.

Thus the Thirteenth Amendment played an important part in the evolution of the Fourteenth Amendment, not as universalizing freedom, which the Fourteenth Amendment presupposes, or as the first step in a comprehensive plan of two or three steps, but because, after its passage, doubts about the adequacy of the amendment became so serious that it seemed advisable to try to do the

the Fourteenth Amendment

same job over again through another amendment. The character of these doubts, the existence of which gave rise to the new amendment and which that amendment was intended to remove, tells much about the meaning of the new amendment.

The statutory plan which the Fourteenth Amendment was to place beyond all constitutional doubt and the substantive provisions of which it was to incorporate were intended "to protect every individual in the full enjoyment of the rights of person and property." That statutory plan did supply the means of vindicating those rights through the instrumentalities of the federal government. It did intrude the federal government between the state and its inhabitants. It did constitute the federal government the protector of the civil rights, that is, the natural rights, of the individual. It did interfere with the states' right to determine disputes over property, contracts, and crimes. It did "revolutionize the laws of the states everywhere." It did overturn the preëxisting division of powers between the state and the central government.

All these things can be read in the words of the civil rights bill. Their presence can be amply confirmed by resorting to the intentions of the framers, the circumstances which brought forth the act, the historical experience which the act was designed to culminate and embody. The fact that the new amendment was written and passed, at the very least, to make certain that that statutory plan was constitutional, to remove doubts about the adequacy of the Thirteenth Amendment to sustain it, and to place its substantive provisions in the Constitution itself should place the minimum capacity of the new amendment beyond controversy, especially if its words reasonably can accommodate such a purpose. This sweeping and comprehensive meaning of the Fourteenth Amendment thus does not depend upon any single speech of one speaker or a number of speeches of many speakers, though many of these are available in confirmation. Likewise, it does not depend upon the history of the antislavery movement, though that history makes it inevitable. It turns simply upon the nature of the statutory plan which was sought to be made constitutional and constitutionally secure by the amendment.

To this all-important circumstance must be added another batch of evidence, not hitherto given proper weight, showing that the protection intended was not merely against state action. That batch of evidence consists of the emphasis, at the hearing of the Joint Committee on Reconstruction, on individual violation of the rights of freedmen and southern loyalists. The need for the continuation of the national protection then being supplied in the form of the Freedmen's Bureau and the United States Army was apparent from the great burden of evidence collected at the committee hearings. The index to the report of the hearings contains two full pages of entries on "Freedmen, evidence of general hostility and occasional cruelty towards." The number of entries listed indicates that the word "occasional" was rather too mild to be accurate. Witness after witness spoke of beatings and woundings, burnings and killings, as well as deprivations of property and earnings and interference with family relations—and the impossibility of redress or protection except through the United States Army and the Freedmen's Bureau.[4] Professor Warsoff has supplied a tally of those who testified:

Of 125 witnesses who were questioned by the committee, 89 admitted that general hostility and frequent cruelty toward the negro characterized the attitude of southern whites, whereas only 36 denied such treatment.... 73 persons were confident that the rights of the negro could be maintained in the south only through the presence of the Freedmen's Bureau and United States troops. Only 9 witnesses dissented from this belief. The testimony served not to create any new concepts as to what measures ought to be passed, but simply to confirm the belief that the four guarantees already agreed upon [by the committee] were actually indispensable.... Foremost among the majority's aims was the proposal to confer civil equality upon the negro; accordingly, it became

[4] 39th Cong., 1st sess., House Report 30 (1866), Serial 1273.

the Fourteenth Amendment 187

the function of the committee to demonstrate that no such equality then existed and that the rights of the southern freedmen were abused in consequence.[5]

The evidence of individual invasions of the rights of Negroes particularly, but also of loyalists, accordingly, was not fortuitously brought forward as an unimportant incident of other matters regarded as primary. Elicited mainly by leading questions, the evidence was deliberately adduced by the committee for its bearing upon a principal feature of the proposed amendment, the precise wording of which was at the very moment under discussion by the committee. There can be little doubt not only that the members of the committee were aware of these individual violations but that the majority of the committee took pains to get them into the record—an odd procedure, to say the least, if they were not to be comprehended within the amendment which the committee was then perfecting.

The movement to resolve, by another constitutional amendment, the doubts about the constitutionality of a far-reaching legislative program nationalizing the natural or civil rights of men got under way on the opening day of the Thirty-ninth Congress, before the legislative program had taken anything like definite shape and before the formal announcement of the ratification of the Thirteenth Amendment. Since the various forms in which the proposed amendment was cast are very revealing, they will be set forth in detail.

Stevens, December 5, 1865: "All national and state laws shall be equally applicable to every citizen, and no discrimination shall be made on account of race and color."

Bingham, December 6, 1865, empowering Congress "to pass all necessary and proper laws to secure to all persons in every State in the Union equal protection in their rights, life, liberty, and property."

---
[5] Warsoff, *op. cit.*, pp. 109–110.

Stevens, January 12, 1866: "All laws, state or national, shall operate impartially and equally on all persons without regard to race and color."

Bingham, January 12, 1866: "Congress shall have power to make all laws necessary and proper to secure to all persons in every State within the Union equal protection in their rights of life, liberty, and property."

Subcommittee of Joint Committee on Reconstruction, January 20, 1866: "Congress shall have power to make all laws necessary and proper to secure to all citizens of the United States, in every State, the same political rights and privileges; and to all persons in every State equal protection in the enjoyment of life, liberty, and property."

Subcommittee of Joint Committee on Reconstruction, January 27, 1866: "Congress shall have the power to make all laws which shall be necessary and proper to secure all persons in every State full protection in the enjoyment of life, liberty, and property; and to all citizens of the United States in any State the same immunities and also equal political rights and privileges."

Bingham, February 3, 1866: "The Congress shall have power to make all laws which shall be necessary and proper to secure to the citizens of each State all privileges and immunities of citizens in the several states, and to all persons in the several states equal protection in the rights of life, liberty, and property."

Stevens, April 21, 1866:

Section 1. "No discrimination shall be made by any state nor by the United States as to the civil rights of persons because of race, color, or previous condition of servitude."

Section 2. "From and after the 4th day of July in the year of 1876 no discrimination shall be made by any state nor by the United States, as to the enjoyment by classes of persons of the right of suffrage, because of race, color, or previous condition of servitude."

Section 3. "Until the 4th day of July, 1876, no class of persons, as

the Fourteenth Amendment

to the right of any of whom to suffrage, discrimination shall be made by any state because of race, color, or previous condition of servitude, shall be included in the basis of representation."

Section 4. "Debts incurred in aid of insurrection and of war against the Union and claims of compensation for loss of involuntary service or labor, shall not be paid by any state or by the United States."

Section 5. "Congress shall have the power to enforce by appropriate legislation the provisions of this article."

Bingham, April 21, 1866, added to Steven's draft: Section 1. "... Nor shall any State deny to any person within its jurisdiction the equal protection of the laws nor take private property for public use without just compensation."

Bingham, April 21, 1866, defeated on the foregoing addition to section 1, proposed to add as section 5 of the bill: "No State shall make or enforce any law which shall abridge the privileges or immunities of citizens of the United States; nor shall any State deprive any person of life, liberty, or property, without due process of law; nor deny to any person within its jurisdiction the equal protection of the laws."

Joint Committee on Reconstruction, April 30, 1866:

Section 1. No State shall make or enforce any law which shall abridge the privileges or immunities of citizens of the United States; nor shall any State deprive any person of life, liberty, or property, without due process of law; nor deny to any person within its jurisdiction the equal protection of the laws.

Section 2. Representatives shall be apportioned among the several States which might be included within this Union, according to their respective numbers, counting the whole number of persons in each State, excluding Indians not taxed. But whenever, in any state, the elective franchise shall be denied to any portion of its male citizens not less than twenty-one years of age, or in any way abridged except for participation in rebellion or crime, the basis of representation in such State shall be reduced in the proportion which the number of such male citizens shall bear to the whole number of male citizens not less than twenty-one years of age.

Section 3. Until the fourth day of July, in the year 1870, all persons who involuntarily adhered to the late insurrection, giving aid and comfort, shall be excluded from the right to vote for representatives in Congress, and for electors for President and Vice-President of the United States.

Section 4. Neither the United States nor any State shall assume or pay any debt or obligation already incurred, or which may hereafter be incurred, to aid in insurrection or of war against the United States, or any claims for compensation for loss of involuntary service or labor.

Section 5. The Congress shall have power to enforce, by appropriate legislation, the provisions of this article.

Set out thus in chronological order, the evolutionary stages in the development of the Fourteenth Amendment immediately disclose a number of important facts. It is apparent that the deletions, changes, and additions are far less significant than the factors which remain constant. The basic idea, the recurrent idea, which appeared in all these drafts is that of "equal protection." Both Stevens' narrow line of development and Bingham's broad line of development began exclusively with that idea and retained it without exception to the end. To both lines, other elements were later added—privileges and immunities of citizens, due process of law, political rights. These were all either addenda to the basic notion or an elaboration of it.

The basic idea was phrased in many different forms. The narrowest simply forbade discrimination on account of race or color in state or national laws. The broadest was an allocation of power to Congress to secure all persons "full protection in the enjoyment of life, liberty, and property." The narrow form developed through various stages: first it forbade discrimination in the laws, on their face presumably; then, in the operation of the laws, in their administration; and, finally, by government in any form. The narrow form first specifically protected "citizens"; later, "persons." In one draft "the civil rights" of persons were particularly mentioned; in others the antidiscrimination provision was not thus expressly confined. The broad form used alternatively "full" protection and

the Fourteenth Amendment 191

"equal" protection, always extended to "persons" even when citizens were also mentioned, and almost always enumerated the natural rights of life, liberty, and property as the rights to be secured.

The competition between the narrow and the broad line of equal protection was also a competition between a flat constitutional prohibition or requirement and a simple grant of power to Congress. Both ideas of a constitutional guarantee and a grant of power to Congress prevailed in the end. Moreover, the constitutional and congressional guarantee as it finally evolved was stated in the broad equal protection form, not in the narrow antidiscrimination form.

CHAPTER XII

The Fourteenth Amendment
(Continued)

~~~~~~~~~~~~~~~~~~

THE CONGRESSIONAL debates over the Fourteenth Amendment re-emphasize the "full" or "equal" protection of men in their natural or civil rights—by the national Constitution and legislature—as the predominant element in section 1. Frequently, these natural or civil rights of persons are referred to also as the privileges or immunities of citizens of the United States. Constitutional historians have commented upon the spareness of these debates. Considering the character of the contemplated action and the fact that a constitutional amendment was at stake, very little was said on the floor of either House, and what was said related primarily to the more obviously political sections of the proposal. But meager though these debates were with respect to section 1, and though they left many fine points unanalyzed and unanswered, they yet were sufficient to show a predominant trend. Their central, almost exclusive concern was, on the part of the proponents, with the national protection of persons or citizens in their natural rights; and, on the

Fourteenth Amendment

part of antagonists, with the destructive impact of this notion upon the federal system. This is seen with particular force in the floor debate upon Bingham's draft of February 3. That draft empowered Congress to make laws "necessary and proper to secure to the citizens of each State all privileges and immunities of citizens in the several states, and to all persons in the several states equal protection in the rights of life, liberty, and property." This is the so-called positive draft.

William Higby, Republican of California, in opening the debate, argued that the proposed amendment would be entirely declaratory. Congress already had power to make all necessary and proper laws; the comity clause already guaranteed the privileges and immunities of citizens; and the Fifth Amendment, life, liberty, and property. "The language of this proposed amendment" was "very little different." But it did give "force, effect, and vitality" to the comity clause, which had "been trampled under foot and rendered nugatory."[1]

William D. Kelley, Republican from Pennsylvania, also thought the amendment declaratory, that it would merely "reinvigorate a primitive and essential power of the Constitution" which had lain "dormant" for eighty years, a power now in the Constitution "by which the general government may defend the rights, liberties, privileges, and immunities of the humblest citizen wherever he may be upon our country's soil."[2] In line with approved abolitionist doctrine, Kelley thought that this power was the power to enforce the comity clause and the republican form of government guarantee; eccentrically, however, he believed that the power derived from the constitutional section "granting Congress power to determine who should be electors of federal officers."

According to Frederick E. Woodbridge, Republican from Vermont,

[the amendment] merely gives the power to Congress to enact those laws which will give to a citizen of the United States the natural rights

---
[1] *Cong. Globe*, 39th Cong., 1st sess., p. 1054.
[2] *Ibid.*, p. 1057.

which necessarily pertain to citizenship. It is intended to enable Congress by its enactment when necessary, to give to a citizen of the United States, in whatever state he may be, those privileges and immunities which are guaranteed to him under the Constitution of the United States. It is intended to enable Congress to give to all citizens the inalienable rights of life and liberty, and to every citizen in whatever state he may be that protection to his property which is extended to the other citizens of the state.[8]

In Woodbridge's view the slaves, when freed, became United States citizens.

Freely admit as we must that these statements are full of confusion and imprecision; that it takes something more than a mention of the comity clause to find United States citizenship in it and something more than assertion to establish natural rights as the privileges and immunities appertaining to United States citizenship; that Higby tied the necessary and proper, the comity, and the due process clauses together in a way that disregarded everything except abolitionist history; that Kelley had a novel theory as to the source of congressional power over the states; that Woodbridge wobbled badly in the last sentence of the quotation—freely admit all these things, yet they do not in the slightest diminish the importance of the fact that, in a debate over a constitutional amendment authorizing Congress to secure to all persons "equal protection in the rights of life, liberty, and property," the qualifying word "equal" was almost entirely forgotten and "protection" treated as if it stood alone.

The language of the "equal protection" clause was held to be "very little different" from a command in the due process clause to protect men in the rights of life, liberty, and property or, in the comity clause, to protect citizens in their natural rights. It was simply declaratory of the existing constitutional power "by which the general government may defend the rights, liberties, privileges and immunities of the humblest citizen." It was an expression that "merely gives the power to Congress to enact those laws

---

[8] *Ibid.*, p. 1088.

the Fourteenth Amendment 195

which will give to a citizen of the United States the natural rights which necessarily pertain to citizenship." The essential element of the "equal protection" which Congress was empowered to provide was thus protection, and equality was subordinate.[4]

This view of the equal protection clause was not confined to the miscellaneous rank and file of congressional radicals. It was the view taken also by leading Republicans, not all of whom were members of the radical camp and not all of whom favored the amendment. This is strikingly illustrated by the well-known speeches of Hale and Bingham in the debate over the February 3 draft. It is the most important point to emerge from those speeches.

Hale was the most able and effective spokesman in the House of Representatives of the conservative Republican opposition to the amendment. His principal ground was federalism. The amendment, he thought, was "in effect a provision under which all state legislation in its codes of civil and criminal jurisprudence and procedure, affecting the individual citizen, may be repealed or abolished, and the law of Congress established instead." But how did the amendment make this possible? The equal protection clause was the answer. It was the equal protection clause which empowered Congress "to legislate upon all matters pertaining to the life, liberty, and property of all of the inhabitants of the several states." Said Hale,

Reading the language in its grammatical and legal construction, it is a grant of the fullest and most ample power to Congress to make all laws "necessary and proper to secure to all persons in the several states protection in the rights of life, liberty and property," with the simple proviso that such protection shall be equal. It is not a mere provision that when the states undertake to give "equal" protection which is unequal Congress may equalize it; it is a grant of power in general terms—a grant of the right to legislate for the protection of life, liberty, and property, simply qualified with the condition that it shall be equal legislation.[5]

[4] Nor should it be ignored that these speeches exhibited the common understanding that the privileges and immunities of citizens of the United States are the natural rights of men.

[5] Representative Robert S. Hale of New York, *Cong. Globe*, 39th Cong., 1st sess., pp. 1063, 1064.

Could there be a clearer statement of the double-barreled nature of the equal protection clause, of the idea that an authorization to Congress to secure the equal protection of the laws is at one and the same time a grant of power and a limitation upon power, that is, a grant of the power to protect, and a limitation that the protection must be equal?[6]

In his speech of February 27, as well as elsewhere during this debate, Bingham marked out the area of his disagreement with Hale and indicated his understanding of his own proposal. This speech of Bingham's has probably been read more, analyzed more, and misunderstood more than any other important piece of evidence in the entire background of the Fourteenth Amendment. Yet in it the author of section 1 of that amendment does little more than recapitulate the traditional abolitionist doctrines which he had spelled out in his congressional speeches of 1856, 1857, and 1859.

The proposition pending before the House is simply a proposition to arm the Congress ... with power to enforce the Bill of Rights as it stands in the Constitution today ... gentlemen admit the force of the provisions in the Bill of Rights, that the citizens of the United States shall be entitled to all the privileges and immunities of citizens of the United States in the several states, and that no person shall be deprived of life, liberty, or property without due process of law; but they say, "We are opposed to its enforcement by act of Congress under an amended Constitution as proposed." Why are gentlemen opposed to the enforcement of the Bill of Rights, as proposed? Because they aver it would interfere with the reserved rights of the states! Who ever before heard that any state had reserved to itself the right, under the Constitution of the

---

[6] Thaddeus Stevens apparently did not accept this broad reading of the clause. He interrupted Hale to ask: "Does the gentleman mean to say that, under this provision, Congress could interfere in any case where the legislation of a state was equal, impartial to all? Or is it not simply to provide that, where any state makes a distinction in the same law between different classes of individuals, Congress shall have power to correct such discrimination and inequality?" Of course Congress would not and could not interfere where "the legislation of a state was equal, impartial to all." In that event there would be no occasion to interfere. The latter half of the sentence shows, by its reference to "a distinction in the same law between different classes of individuals," at least that Stevens has a mind fixed primarily on the narrower interpretation of equal protection.

the Fourteenth Amendment

United States, to withhold from any citizen of the United States within its limits, under any pretext whatever, any of the privileges of a citizen of the United States, or to impose upon him, no matter from what state he may have come, any burden contrary to that provision of the Constitution which declares that the citizens shall be entitled in the several states to all the immunities of a citizen in the United States?

What does the word immunity in your Constitution mean? Exemption from unequal burdens. Ah! say gentlemen who oppose this amendment, we are not opposed to equal rights; we are not opposed to the Bill of Rights that all shall be protected alike in life, liberty, and property; we are only opposed to enforcing it by national authority, even by the consent of the loyal people of all the states. . . . The gentleman did not utter a word against the equal right of all citizens of the United States in every state to all privileges and immunities of citizens . . . If a state has not the right to deny equal protection to any human being under the Constitution of this country in the rights of life, liberty, and property, how can state rights be impaired by penal prohibitions of such denial as proposed? . . . There never was even colorable excuse, much less apology, for any man North or South claiming that any state legislature or state court, or state executive, has any right to deny protection to any free citizen of the United States within their limits in the rights of life, liberty, and property.[7]

So, according to Bingham, the purpose of the amendment is to authorize Congress to enforce the Bill of Rights. What Bill of Rights? Certainly not the first eight amendments to the Constitution. The answer is not left open to conjecture: the Bill of Rights that contains (1) the comity clause (Art. IV, sec. 2, of the body of the Constitution), which guarantees the privileges and immunities of citizens of the United States; (2) the due process clause of the Fifth Amendment; and (3) the requirement "that all shall be protected alike in life, liberty, and property," not explicitly mentioned in either body or amendments. Today, this may not be the Bill of Rights known to the United States Supreme Court, to citizens, and to schoolchildren. But it was the "immortal Bill of Rights" of John A. Bingham, long-time representative from the abolitionized Western Reserve of Ohio.

---

[7] *Cong. Globe,* 39th Cong., 1st sess., p. 1088.

Once it is firmly grasped that this is the Bill of Rights Bingham is talking about, no constitutional legerdemain is necessary to make it binding on the states or to render fruitless, if not absurd, the federalism argument of Hale and the Democrats. To deny this, one must deny that the rights guaranteed to citizens of the United States by the comity clause and to all persons by the due process clauses are the natural rights of life, liberty, and property—a manifest impossibility. This being so, there is indeed no "colorable excuse for any man North or South" to claim "that any state legislature ... court ... or executive, has any right to deny protection to any free citizen of the United States within their limits" or to any "human being." This being so, well might Bingham ask with shocked incredulity: "Who ever before heard that any state had reserved to itself the right, under the Constitution of the United States, to withhold from any citizen of the United States within its limits, under any pretext whatever, any of the privileges of a citizen of the United States ... ?"

The "immortal Bill of Rights" not binding on the states! How can one refute an axiom? The puzzlement expressed by constitutional historians that Bingham could have maintained this proposition and at the same time, elsewhere in his speech, have quoted and discussed, in fact relied upon, *Barron* v. *Baltimore* is thus resolved with amazing ease. Chief justices of the United States Supreme Court cannot successfully refute an axiom any more than other mortals. The Bill of Rights, that is, the list of men's natural rights, would be binding on the state, on all governments, if there never had been the first eight amendments or even a Constitution of the United States. Marshall might hold that the federal government wanted authority to enforce the Bill of Rights on the states. He could not, by any pronouncement of his, diminish the obligation of the states to protect men in their natural rights to life, liberty, and property. Nor could the Fourteenth Amendment create that obligation. That amendment could give what Marshall could withhold—any enforcement power to the national government.

the Fourteenth Amendment

Even more significant than all this in its bearing on the meaning of the Fourteenth Amendment, however, is the fact that, while Bingham disagreed with Hale as to the alteration his draft would work in the federal system, there was no disagreement between them on the import of the equal protection clause. Bingham sometimes, as in the extracts above, ties up the equal protection concept with the comity clause. Later in his speech he connects it with the due process clause.[8] The reason for this shifting or, more correctly, interchangeable usage is that the concept really derives from the natural rights referred to by both comity and due process clauses and that the essential notion of the concept is protection. Bingham, in fact, in the extracts quoted above, speaks of equal protection and protection as but a single expression—"A state has not the right to deny equal protection..."; no state has "any right to deny protection..."; "all shall be protected alike..."; "equality in the protection of the rights of life, liberty, and property..."; "the equal right of all citizens of the United States in every state...."[9] It is noteworthy also that Bingham uses such words as "withhold" and

---

[8] Bingham says, "Representatives, to you, I appeal, that hereafter, by your action and the approval of the loyal people of this country, every man in every State of the Union, in accordance with the written words of your Constitution, may by national law, be secured in the equal protection of his personal rights. The Constitution provides that no man . . . shall be deprived of life, or liberty or property without due process of law—law in its highest sense, that law which is the perfection of human reason, and which is impartial, equal, exact justice; that justice which requires that every man shall have his right . . ."

[9] Other language of Bingham is to the same effect. "The gentleman seems to think," says Bingham, speaking of Hale, "that all persons, could have remedies for all violations of their rights, of life, liberty, and property in the federal courts.

"I ventured to ask him yesterday when any action of that sort was ever maintained in any of the federal courts of the United States to redress the great wrong which has been practiced and which is being practiced now in more States than one of the Union under the authority of State laws, denying to citizens therein equal protection or any protection in the rights of life, liberty, and property." "Denying citizens equal protection or any protection"—the latter only occurs when the state fails to act. Hence this expression covers all violations of the rights of life, liberty, and property. And Congress is to be authorized to remedy this situation, namely, the denial of equal protection or any protection of life, liberty, and property. Again Bingham says, "It stands . . . as the universal ruling of the United States Supreme Court, concurring with the continued action of the other departments of the government from the year 1789 'til this hour, there being no law anywhere upon our State books to punish penally any State official for denying in any State to any citizen of the United States protection in the rights of life, liberty, and property."

"deny" both when referring to the absence of protection and to equal protection. And, in his usage, a state denies protection or denies equal protection whenever it fails to safeguard men in their natural rights. Bingham and Hale thus completely agree that the equal protection clause was "a grant of the right to legislate for the protection of life, liberty, and property simply qualified with the condition that it shall be equal legislation."

In all likelihood, there never would have been any historical question about the revolution in federalism worked or confirmed by the Fourteenth Amendment were it not for the shift from the positive to what at first glance appears to be a negative form of the amendment. The rejection of the "Congress shall have power" form in favor of the "no state shall" and "Congress shall have power" form is the significant fact relied upon to give plausibility to an interpretation of the amendment "consistent with our federal system." This point of view was summed up soon after the ratification of the amendment by Congressman J. A. Garfield of Ohio speaking in the K. K. K. debates of 1871. Compare the adopted and rejected forms of the amendment, he said:

> the one exerts its force directly upon the states laying restrictions and limitations upon their power and enabling Congress to enforce these limitations. The other, the rejected proposition, would have brought the power of Congress to bear directly upon the citizens, and contained a clear grant of power to Congress to legislate directly for the protection of life, liberty, and property within the states. The first limited but did not oust the jurisdiction of the state over the subjects. The second gave Congress plenary power to cover the whole subject within its jurisdiction, and, as it seems to me, to the exclusion of the state authorities.

In part, Garfield's conclusion is based on the language employed in the rejected and the adopted proposals, but it is based even more on congressional history. The "Congress shall have power" form, so runs the argument, was introduced and sponsored in the House by John A. Bingham, who, together with Thaddeus Stevens, con-

the Fourteenth Amendment

stituted the Republican leadership most actively concerned about a second amendment. It was reviewed, carefully analyzed, and reported out by the Joint Committee of Fifteen. Thereafter, it was recommitted by a vote of 110 to 37, after a debate in which not only Democrats but also conservative Republicans sharply criticized it as effecting a radical redistribution of powers of the states and the national government by empowering Congress to legislate directly upon the citizen with respect to his rights of life, liberty, and property.

Two months later the joint committee reported out the "no state shall" and "Congress shall have power" version. When it did so, Thaddeus Stevens opened the debate with these words: "The proposition is not all that the committee desired. It falls far short of my wishes, but it fulfills my hopes. I believe that it is all that can be obtained in the present state of public opinion." In these circumstances, it is concluded, "We cannot, by any reasonable interpretation, give to the section, as it stands in the Constitution, the force and effect of the rejected clause."

The three mainstays of this argument, consequently, are the difference in the language employed in the final and earlier forms, the significance of the congressional history which attended the change in forms, and the remarks made upon the final draft by Thaddeus Stevens, active sponsor of the new amendment and by the time of the final debate indisputedly in control of the House of Representatives.

Examining these mainstays in reverse order, it is obvious that the third rests upon too excerpted an account of what was said. A few minutes with Stevens' speech reveal that the amendment in its final form fell far short of Stevens' wishes, as Garfield asserts, but not his wishes with respect to section 1. Stevens wished to see the Negro constitutionally enfranchised and the adherents of the rebellion sharply punished. These two matters, however, were treated in sections 2 and 3 of the amendment—not in section 1 at all—and it was their mildness that disappointed Stevens. Moreover, section 1 not only contained the elements of a draft amendment which Stevens had introduced and advocated from the beginning of the session, but broadened and strengthened his own proposal, hardly a source of dissatisfaction to him. Finally, even if the portion of the speech alluded to expressed the position attributed to it, which clearly it does not, at least equal weight must be given to another part of the same speech dealing directly with section 1 which, as will be shown presently, created a strongly contrary inference.

The second mainstay is no less flimsy. Assuming the possibility of determining congressional intent from the formal record of congressional proceedings, the particular mechanics of enactment here emphasized, if anything, tends to produce a conclusion opposite to that claimed. The destruction of the federal system certainly was pressed as an objection to the positive form. It was also pressed, however, as an objection to the final so-called negative form. It was after the change had been made that Representative Rogers, Democratic member of the Joint Committee of Fifteen, charged that section 1 "consolidates everything into one imperial despotism; it annihilates all the rights which lie at the foundation of the Union of the states." It was after the change that Representative Aaron Harding of Kentucky asked, "Will not Congress then virtually hold all power of legislation over your own citizens and in defiance of you?" It was after the change that Representative George S. Shanklin of Kentucky asserted that the amendment struck "down the reserved rights of the states" and "reserved all power in the general government."[10]

Since the amendment was adopted in the teeth of this criticism, might we not as reasonably conclude, if we are to give weight to the procedural record, that the amendment was intended to do the very thing objected to? Not all changes in legislative proposals are aimed at conciliating or removing objections. Some are made to

[10] *Cong. Globe,* 39th Cong., 1st sess., 1865–1866. See also Samuel Jackson Randall, *ibid.,* p. 2530; Representative Andrew J. Rogers, p. 2538; George S. Shanklin, p. 2500; and Aaron Harding, p. 3147.

strengthen a proposal in order better to achieve an objective, the sponsors having determined to proceed despite the consequences predicted by critics, or perhaps even for the very purpose of bringing those consequences about. This second mainstay of the restrictive interpretation of the Fourteenth Amendment thus presents an instance of the elementary fallacy of *post hoc, ergo propter hoc*. The mere fact that the so-called negative form emerged after the federalism objection does not necessarily mean that the federalism objection was the cause of the change or that the new language was intended to obviate the objection. There were other objections to the positive form—objections more relevant to the purpose and attitudes of the radical sponsors of the amendment. Principal among these was, of course, the point that the positive form made national protection of life, liberty, and property only as certain as Republican control of Congress.

It must be remembered, too, that from the last half of February to the middle of May the congressional fight with the President had intensified and that the conservative Republicans had by the later date pretty well merged with the radicals and come to adopt their program. Consequently, the radicals were no longer under the same pressure from colleagues in their own party.

From the beginning, the program for the national protection of men in their civil rights encountered the destruction-of-federalism argument. The Thirteenth Amendment, the first constitutional expression of that program, was proposed, encountered the federalism objection, and was adopted anyway. Next, the civil rights bill, designed to implement the Thirteenth Amendment, had heaped upon it the same charge. It was adopted notwithstanding. Then, at last, came the Fourteenth Amendment. Created to accomplish what the Thirteenth Amendment had been designed to do but had failed to do because of the continuation of the federalism objection, intended to remove from the Civil Rights Act the constitutional doubts arising from the federalism objection to it, the Fourteenth Amendment was itself, in turn, subjected to the very same criticism. Despite that criticism, it too was adopted.

Is it anything less than a colossal historic irony that, after three times adopting a program to nationalize the natural rights of men—twice by solemn constitutional amendment and once by legislative enactment over a presidential veto—each time over the bitter criticism that it would destroy the federal system, the nation should then—particularly through the instrumentality of the Supreme Court—without benefit of formal repeal, adopt the objection and reject the program by a refusal to carry it out?

Finally, the third of the mainstays—that built upon the difference of the wording in the two principal drafts—is superficially a better support for the restrictive interpretation of the Fourteenth Amendment than the other two. But only superficially! "No State shall..." at first looks like a negative on state action; and section 5, granting enforcement power, would accordingly authorize Congress to impose only such restraints as would prevent states from taking the forbidden action. Section 5 would thus authorize nothing more than a corrective removal of prohibited state acts, a vastly different thing, so it is argued, from a positive grant of power to Congress, itself directly and affirmatively, to protect men and citizens in their civil rights.

Does not this interpretation render section 5 altogether nugatory? Precisely how could Congress operate to enforce a prohibition on state action? What would "appropriate legislation" for such a purpose be? Congress could not by legislation either prevent the legislature of a state from passing an act or compel it to pass an act. Congress might pass a law declaring null forbidden state acts, and might do so either before or after their passage. But, since the judges would in any event strike down state acts transcending the prohibitions of the amendment, a law by Congress to this effect would serve no purpose. It would, in fact, be in the nature of legislative adjudication.

The only possible method by which Congress could by appropriate legislation enforce section 1 would be itself to supply the protection to individuals which the state had withheld. If individuals are deprived of life, liberty, or property without due process of law, Congress might supply the due process and see that persons are not deprived without it. If persons are not protected in their natural rights at all, or are not as well protected as others, or if citizens are not protected in their privileges and immunities, then Congress might make up the state's deficiency and give the protection. From this, however, it would follow that, even granting that section 1 does nothing more than forbid state acts, if section 5 is to be given any meaning at all it must authorize Congress to legislate affirmatively for the protection of individuals. Thus, considering sections 1 and 5 literally and grammatically, the final so-called negative form has virtually the same meaning as the earlier and abandoned positive form, unless we are to conclude that section 5 is utterly pointless, a mere redundancy in the Constitution.

Aside from the redundancy argument, the restrictive inference based on the change in language fails to hurdle another and an even more important obstacle. So far, we have been concentrating on the words "No State shall...." Certainly much will depend upon what follows those words. What are the states forbidden to do, in this final form? If the states are merely forbidden to take certain actions, to move in given directions, then the restrictive interpretation is beyond challenge, except by the redundancy argument. But if the negative on the states is a prohibition to remain inactive, if they are forbidden to fail to act as well as to act in particular directions, the restrictive interpretation is untenable, and that textually, or as a matter of the words used. "No State shall" (1) "make or enforce any law which shall abridge the privileges or immunities of citizens of the United States"; (2) "deprive any person of life, liberty, or property, without due process of law"; (3) "deny to any person within its jurisdiction the equal protection of the laws."

The restrictive interpretation is least justified by the wording of the third of these clauses. Since government alone may provide the protection or the equal protection of the laws, the state does deny them when it withholds or fails to supply them. An exact equivalent of "No State shall...deny" is "No State shall withhold or fail to provide," or "Every State shall supply." "Every State shall supply" what? "The equal protection of the laws." But the basic notion of this phrase is protection; equality is the condition. The equal protection of the laws cannot be supplied unless the protection of the laws is supplied; and the protection of the laws, at least for men's natural rights, being the sole purpose for which governments are instituted, must be supplied. The clause is thus understood to mean: "Every State shall supply to all persons within its jurisdiction the protection of the laws and the protection shall always be equal to all." Once "protection of the laws" is recognized as the basic idea of the phrase, made inevitable by its natural rights usage, the rest follows easily.

The due process clause is similar in nature and construction to the equal protection clause. The word "deprive" is the main point of difference. Can a state deprive one of anything other than by a positive act? A state having a monopoly of legal protection denies such protection when it withholds it. In these circumstances, does the state not also deprive one of protection? Is due process of law different in this light? The state alone can supply the due process of the laws. Life, liberty, and property can be taken with due process of law, consequently, only if the state supplies it. If life, liberty, and property are taken without due process of law, has not the state failed to supply due process of law or deprive persons of it?

This is clear when the state itself is doing the taking of life, liberty, and property. But suppose it is done by private persons or unofficial groups? Does the state then, by failure to provide the due process of law, itself deprive persons of life, liberty, and property at all, with or without due process of law? The answer must be the same. Since the state has a monopoly on the due process of law, it deprives persons of life, liberty, and property

the Fourteenth Amendment

without such process whenever by failing to supply and insist upon it, the state allows persons to have their lives, liberties, and property taken without it. Essentially, the due process clause, like the equal protection clause, rests upon the obligation of the state to protect men in their lives, liberties, and property, to see that persons are not deprived of these rights unless in very special circumstances, that is, by due process of law.

The privileges and immunities clause is the most obviously favorable to the restrictive interpretation. "No State shall make or enforce any law which shall abridge the privileges or immunities of citizens of the United States." The thing forbidden is a clear-cut positive act—"make or enforce any law." Yet, even here, if the privileges or immunities of United States citizens are the natural rights of men, then the obligation of the states "to make or enforce laws" protecting them underlies the clause. By the lights of the drafters, indeed, this underlying presupposition was already affirmatively stated in the comity clause of the Constitution. They merely reëxpressed it here in the privileges or immunities clause of the Fourteenth Amendment.

The speeches thus far commented upon were made in connection with the so-called positive form of the amendment—the form in which Congress was directly authorized to secure to all persons the equal protection of the laws and to all citizens their privileges and immunities. Those speeches indicate that the equal protection clause is primarily a reference to the obligation of government to supply protection to men in their natural rights, and secondarily is a requirement that such protection, when supplied, must be equal to all.

Does this conception of the equal protection clause shift when stated with particular reference to the states? Is the dominance of protection in the clause lost when it is preceded by what appears to be a negative on state power, though made enforceable by Congress? If the clause was mainly a confirmatory reference to an affirmative obligation of government, would its meaning be changed, would the character and ultimate location of power be different, if the words preceding it were: (1) Congress shall have power to secure . . . or (2) no state shall deny . . . and Congress shall have power to see that the states do not deny . . . ?

Thus far we have examined the argument from congressional history and the changes in the wording of the draft which traditionally have been relied upon to justify the conclusion that the Fourteenth Amendment was not intended to nationalize the civil rights of men. We now turn our attention briefly to the congressional debates upon the final so-called negative form of the amendment to see how they bear upon this question.

Like the February debates, those of May and June were preoccupied mainly with the patently political sections of the amendment, sections 2 and 3. Yet, despite this fact, and despite the common criticism of their vagueness and imprecision, the May and June debates, like those of February, do illuminate the scope and purpose of section 1. The illumination is derived from two sources. First, the May and June debates provide a fairly consistent and undisputed explanation of the reasons for section 1 and the change from the positive to the so-called negative form. Section 1 was designed, said speaker after speaker, to make certain the constitutionality of the Civil Rights Act, an act, it must be remembered, extending national protection to persons in their civil rights against state or private invasion. "I regard as very doubtful, to say the least," said Henry J. Raymond, conservative Republican from New York, "whether Congress, under the existing Constitution, had any power" to enact the civil rights bill. "Now, it is again proposed so to amend the Constitution as to confer upon Congress the power to pass it."[11]

It was not enough, however, to make certain of the constitutional

---

[11] *Ibid.*, p. 2501. See also Stevens, p. 2549; Garfield, p. 2462; Boyer, p. 2467; Kelley, p. 2468; Broomall, p. 2498; Raymond, p. 2501; Spalding, p. 2509; Eliot, p. 2511; Eckley, p. 2534; Rogers, p. 2538; Farnsworth, p. 2539; Poland, p. 2961; Henderson, p. 3031.

the Fourteenth Amendment

power of Congress to enact the civil rights bill. As the radical leaders realized from the beginning of the Thirty-ninth Congress, Republican control of Congress would not last forever, probably would not even last long. Stevens, especially, brooded over the day when "that side of the House will be filled with yelling secessionists and hissing copperheads" and "if not a Herod, a worse than Herod elsewhere to obstruct our actions." If the Democrats should come to power, the civil rights bill could be repealed as easily as a Republican majority could enact it.

Constitutional protection in addition to congressional protection was the one means of guarding against this contingency. The Republican leadership therefore determined to place the provisions of the Civil Rights Act beyond the power of shifting congressional majorities by writing them into the Constitution itself. To accomplish this, a change in the form of the proposed amendment was necessary. Instead of a simple grant of authority to Congress, a constitutional prohibition was called for—this time on the states, since such prohibitions were already imposed on Congress by the Constitution—together with the grant of enforcement power to Congress. Thus the shift was made from the positive to the so-called negative form.

This simple, unsophisticated, and convincing explanation of the change in the forms, the implications of which later generations of judges and constitutionalists have systematically rejected, was offered repeatedly by the Republicans during the May and June debates. The statement of Representative J. A. Garfield of Ohio was more colorful but not more in point than many others.

The Civil Rights Bill is now a part of the law of the land. But every gentleman knows that it will cease to be a part of the law whenever the sad moment arises when that gentleman's [Mr. Finck] party comes to power. It is precisely for that reason that we propose to lift that great and good law above the reach of political strife, beyond the reach of the plots and machinations of any party, and fix it in the serene sky, in the eternal firmament of the Constitution, where no storm or passion can shake it and no cloud can obscure it. For this reason, and not because I believe the Civil Rights Bill unconstitutional, I am glad to see that first section here."[12]

Second, the speeches in the May and June debates which deal with the meaning of section 1 (whether for or against) other than by specific allusion to the Civil Rights Act do so precisely in the terms employed in the February debate. The natural rights foundation is once more made explicit. Emphasized again is the declaratory nature of the substantive provisions. National protection of men in their civil rights is identified as the great need; investing Congress with power hitherto lacking, the specific means. Protection or equal protection recur as the all-important expressions. Would all this have been possible if the significance attributed to the change from the positive to the so-called negative form were correct?

Farnsworth of Illinois pointed to the fact that the privileges or immunities and due process clauses were already in the Constitution. The equal protection clause was therefore the new addition. "Equal protection of the laws . . . can there be any well-founded objection to this? Is not this the very foundation of a Republican government? Is it not the undeniable right of every subject of the government to receive 'equal protection of the laws' with every other subject? How can he have and enjoy equal rights of 'life, liberty, and the pursuit of happiness' without 'equal protection of the laws'?" How indeed? Or without the protection of the laws? The Declaration of Independence, natural rights, protection, equal protection—all this is tied together in one neat little package in the equal protection clause of section 1 of the Fourteenth Amendment.

Said Garfield, "This first section . . . proposes to hold over every American citizen, without regard to color, the protecting shield of law."[13] ". . . the principle of the first" section, observed Raymond,

---
[12] *Ibid.*, p. 2462. See also p. 2501.
[13] *Ibid.*, p. 2462.

the Fourteenth Amendment

"secures an equality of rights among all citizens of the United States."[14] ". . . we propose, first," maintained Broomall from Pennsylvania, "to give power to the government of the United States to protect its own citizens within the states."[15] The first section, said George F. Miller from Pennsylvania, "is so just that no state shall deprive any person of life, liberty, or property without due process of law, nor deny equal protection of the laws, and so clearly within the spirit of the Declaration of Independence of the 4th of July, 1776, that no member of this House can seriously object to it."[16]

In his speech of May 15 Stevens said that "our Fathers had been compelled to postpone the principles of their great Declaration [of Independence] and wait for their full establishment until a more propitious time. . . . That time ought to be present now." The provisions of section 1 of the amendment, he maintained, were not only just; "they are all asserted in some form or other, in our Declaration or organic law. But the Constitution limits only the action of Congress, and is not a limitation on the states. This amendment supplies that defect, and allows Congress to correct the unjust legislation of the states, so far that the law which operates upon one man shall operate equally upon all." Stevens goes on to speak of discriminatory state acts; but the equal protection which Congress was to be authorized to enforce and which was "asserted . . . in our Declaration or organic law" could only be that requiring governmental protection of life, liberty, property, and pursuit of happiness.

Bingham in his May 10 speech repeated what he had commenced saying in Congress ten years earlier. The amendment, he argued, would give Congress the power which hitherto it did not possess,

> to protect by national law the privileges and immunities of all the citizens of the Republic and the inborn rights of every person within its jurisdiction whenever the same shall be abridged or denied by the unconstitutional acts of any state. [The amendment took] from no state any right that ever pertained to it. No state ever had the right, under the

---
[14] *Ibid.*, p. 2501.
[15] John M. Broomall, *ibid.*, p. 2498.
[16] *Ibid.*, p. 2510.

forms of law or otherwise, to deny to any free man the equal protection of the laws or to abridge the privileges or immunities of any citizen of the Republic, although many of them have assumed and exercised the power, and that without remendy.... The great want of the citizen and stranger, protection by national law from unconstitutional state enactments, is supplied by the first section of this amendment.

So we are back to this: the "citizen and stranger" are again put on the same footing; "the inborn rights of every person" and "the privileges and immunities of citizens" are coupled together and refer to the same rights; "no state ever had the right" either under the Constitution of the United States or because of the nature of government "to deny to any free man the equal protection of the laws or to abridge the privileges or immunities of any citizen." Ideas of protection and equal protection in their intermingled form and connected with natural rights thus reappear. Moreover, though Bingham twice in the passage above refers to abridgment or denial by unconstitutional state enactments, he also says that "no state ever had the right, *under the forms of law or otherwise,* to deny to any free man the equal protection of the laws or to abridge the privileges or immunities of any citizen," a denial or abridgment, consequently, which cannot depend on state enactments. In another sentence, Bingham confirms this inference as well as specifically says that the privileges and immunities of citizens are the natural rights of men: "... the words of the Constitution that 'the citizens of each state shall be entitled to all privileges and immunities of citizens in the several states' included, among other privileges, the right to bear true allegiance to the Constitution and laws of the United States, and to be protected in life, liberty, and property." Protection is thus again made the essential part of equal protection, and the rights protected—men's natural rights—make this inevitable.

Senator Howard, a member of the Joint Committee on Reconstruction, began his long speech[17] presenting the amendment to the Senate with his much-quoted remarks about the meaning of the

---

[17] Senator Jacob M. Howard of Michigan, *ibid.*, p. 2765.

the Fourteenth Amendment 213

privileges and immunities clause of section 1. That clause, he maintained, guaranteed to citizens of the United States the privileges and immunities already secured by the comity clause. For a list of these, though they could not be "fully defined in their entire extent and precise nature," Howard went to *Corfield* v. *Coryell*.[18] To these, Howard continued, "should be added the personal rights guaranteed and secured by the first eight amendments of the Constitution." In stating why these already existing guarantees should be repeated, Howard says, "They do not operate in the slightest degree as a restraint or prohibition upon state legislation."

State acts are thus expressly indicated; but what followed shows that Howard thought that the reach of the amendment extended beyond them. "The states," he said, "are not restrained" by the United States Constitution "from violating the principles embraced" in these guarantees. "The great object of the first section of this amendment is, therefore, to restrain the power of the states and compel them at all times to respect these great fundamental guarantees." Disrespect might be shown by states for these principles, "these great fundamental guarantees," by failure to protect them, especially since one of them—listed by *Corfield* v. *Coryell*— was the right "to protection by government." Howard then described section 5 as "a direct affirmative delegation of power to Congress to carry out all the principles of all these guarantees," not simply to remove state abridgments.

All this was in connection with the privileges and immunities clause, which forbids states "to make or enforce any law which shall abridge . . ." If anything, the due process and equal protection clauses seem to state more broadly the limitation imposed. In turning to the latter of these clauses, Howard said:

> This abolishes all class legislation in the states and does away with the injustice of subjecting one caste of persons to a code not applicable to another. It prohibits the hanging of a black man for a crime for which the white man is not to be hanged. It protects the black man in his funda-

[18] *Corfield* v. *Coryell* (1823), 4 Washington (U.S.) 377.

mental rights as a citizen with the same shield which it throws over the white man. Is it not time, Mr. President, that we extend to the black man, I had almost called it the poor privilege of the equal protection of the laws? Ought not the time to be now passed when one measure of justice is to be meted out to a member of one caste while another in a different measure is meted out to the member of another caste, both castes being alike citizens of the United States, both bound to obey the same laws, to sustain the burdens of the same government, and both equally responsible to justice and to God for the deeds done in the body.

Section 5 gave Congress power "appropriate to the attainment of the great object of the amendment," that is, the supplying with equal protection of the laws. Is this only a power to correct state legislation? That it is not, the following passage makes even plainer:

I look upon the first section, taken in connection with the fifth, as very important. It will, if adopted by the states, forever disable every one of them from passing laws trenching upon these fundamental rights and privileges which pertain to citizens of the United States, and to all persons who may happen to be within their jurisdiction. It establishes equality before the law, and it gives to the humblest, the poorest, the most despised of the race the same rights and the same protection before the law as it gives to the most powerful, the most wealthy, or the most haughty. That, sir, is Republican government as I understand it, ... without this principle of equal justice to all men and equal protection under the shield of the law, there is no Republican government and none that is really worth maintaining.

If section 1 and section 5 "establish equality before the law" and "give to the humblest . . . the same protection before the law as . . . to the most powerful," if this is the "principle of equal justice to all men and equal protection under the shield of the law," then certainly the power of Congress may be exercised whenever there is not equality before the law, whether because of state acts of commission or of omission; whenever the humblest and the most powerful do not have the same rights and protection before the law; whenever there is not "equal justice to all men and equal protection under the shield of law." This would appear to be about

the Fourteenth Amendment 215

as "direct" and "affirmative" a delegation of power to Congress as could be made; and in Howard's theory it was tied up with the equal protection and the privileges and immunities clauses of section 1.

Senator Poland of Vermont[19] thought that the privileges and immunities clause "secures nothing beyond what was intended" by the comity clause, which had become a dead letter because "no express power was by the Constitution granted to enforce it." "The residue" of section 1 "is the very spirit and inspiration of our system of government, the absolute foundation upon which it was established. It is essentially declared in the Declaration of Independence and in all the provisions of the Constitution." The power of Congress to legislate for these purposes, as expressed in the civil rights bill, having been doubted, Poland thought it "desirable that no doubt should be left existing as to the power of Congress to enforce principles lying at the very foundation of all Republican government if they be denied or violated by the states . . ." Denial by the states of principles "lying at the very foundation of all Republican government," "essentially declared in the Declaration of Independence and in all provisions of the Constitution" could be nothing if not a refusal to protect men in their natural rights.

Senator John B. Henderson[20] of Missouri stressed the privileges and immunities clause together with the definition of citizens. In his view, those provisions left "citizenship where it now is," merely making plain what had been "rendered doubtful by the past action of the government." The remaining provisions of section 1, he thought, would "merely secure the rights attached to citizenship in all free governments."

This indeed was the aim of the Civil Rights Act. Its purpose was "to give the right to hold real and personal estate to the Negro, to enable him to sue and be sued in courts, to let him be confronted by his witnesses, to have the process of the courts for his protection,

---
[19] Luke Poland, *Cong. Globe*, 39th Cong., 1st sess., 1865–1866, p. 2961.
[20] *Ibid.*, p. 3031.

and enjoy in the respective states those fundamental rights of person and property which cannot be denied to any person without disgracing the government itself." The Civil Rights Act was "simply to carry out" the comity clause. This is no doctrine limited to the corrective removal of state acts. Securing "the rights that attach to citizenship in all free governments," protecting the enjoyment "in the respective states of those fundamental rights of person and property which cannot be denied to any person without disgracing the government itself," is the very description of the purpose for which governments are instituted; this, according to Henderson, was now, by a new declaration of the Constitution, made the explicit duty of the national government.

This was the sweeping view of those who sponsored and spoke for the adoption of the Fourteenth Amendment on the floor of Congress after it had achieved its final form. The very same arguments were adduced in its support that had been used to sustain the positive draft. Both forms were held to be almost entirely declaratory of the great natural rights of men already embodied in the Declaration of Independence, lying at the foundations of all Republican governments, and expressed in the Constitution itself.

The comity clause, guaranteeing these fundamental rights to United States citizens as their privileges and immunities, was the particular provision of the existing Constitution, most speakers agreed, the systematic violation of which had made necessary a new constitutional confirmation. The privileges or immunities and equal protection clauses were the duplicatory provisions by which this was done. Protection or equality in the protection of these fundamental rights of men and citizens was the common refrain throughout.

The spokesmen were not entirely in agreement in their designations of the natural rights protected. Life, liberty, property; life, liberty, and the pursuit of happiness; the rights contained in the Civil Rights Act—these were accepted and reiterated by everybody.

the Fourteenth Amendment

To these Howard added the whole of the first eight amendments; others added one or another of them. But most of these additions were made casually, without systematic development. The due process clause slipped into a subordinate, almost forgotten position, being commonly read and frequently discussed as if it were a part of the equal protection requirement.

While section 1 of the Fourteenth Amendment was thus declaratory and confirmatory, section 5 corrected the one great constitutional defect, the one pressing want which years of systematic violation of men's natural rights had demonstrated. It gave Congress power to protect those rights. The violations and denials most often mentioned were, of course, those occurring under state laws and carried on by state officials. These were the sources, the perpetrators, of flagrant, commonly observed, and systematic invasions of those rights. But the absence of and need for protection against private invasions were adverted to almost as frequently.

This comprehensive view of the meaning of sections 1 and 5 of the Fourteenth Amendment, expressed by its supporters, was not repudiated by the Democrats. In fact, their argument of the destruction of the federal system and the creation of a consolidated national government accepts and presupposes it. Understood merely as investing Congress with a power to correct or remove forbidden acts done by the states—a power to equalize unequal state legislation—the amendment created little danger of obliterating the states or rendering them useless. It is only when the amendment is read as authorizing Congress itself affirmatively to protect men in their natural rights of life, liberty, and property if the states do not do so or do not do so equally that a real threat of the foreshadowed result exists or is possible. In this sense, the case of the Democrats was built on the very interpretation of the amendment, sections 1 and 5, which ever since has been rejected on the grounds then put forward by them as the basis of their opposition.

CHAPTER XIII

Conclusions

THE ANTISLAVERY background of the Civil War amendments is conceded by all. The nature of that background, however, has been almost entirely forgotten.

In its bearing on the Constitution and the Civil War amendments, the antislavery movement must be viewed, first, as a great historic experience in the national life of the United States. The Civil War amendments were the culmination and embodiment of that experience. As such, their meaning is to be gathered from the comprehensive goals of the abolitionist crusade; from the abrogation of the natural rights of men, bond and free, black and white, which were the active cause of that crusade; from the unmistakable nationalistic implications of the abolitionist movement; and from the constitutional theory which the abolitionists evolved to fit those goals, causes, and implications. Read in this way, the Thirteenth and Fourteenth amendments can only be taken to assure national constitutional and governmental protection of men in their natural rights or of citizens in their privileges and immunities, fully and

Fourteenth Amendment 219

equally and regardless of federal principles—natural rights which accordingly government could never allow others to abrogate and could itself abrogate only when such rights were forfeited by crime proved by established legal procedures.

The antislavery origins of the Civil War amendments may be viewed, second, in the much narrower framework of the immediate political and legislative history—say from 1861 to 1866—which encompassed the actual translation of crusading goal into constitutional amendment, of abstract doctrine into concrete enactment. The short-range history and the limited context show the manner in which the translation was made, and confirm and repeat conclusions derived from the long-range history and the broad context.

The Republican party, operating through its eventual control of Congress, propelled by an internal machine made up of radicals and downright abolitionists moving forward under a platform whose antislavery constitutional principles and statements were directly traceable through Giddings and Chase to organized abolitionist origins—having achieved political power and capitalizing on the outcome of the Civil War—carried through a combined constitutional and legislative program consisting of the Thirteenth Amendment, the Freedmen's Bureau and civil rights bills, and the Fourteenth Amendment. In doing so, Republicans employed the constitutional ideas, the very concepts and clauses which, a quarter of a century earlier, had been evolved by Birney and Weld, Stanton and Wright, Stewart and Tiffany, Goodell, Gerrit Smith, Chase and Olcott.

The Thirteenth Amendment nationalized the right of freedom. It thereby nationalized the equal right of all to enjoy protection in those natural rights which constitute that freedom. The Freedmen's Bureau bill and the Civil Rights Act supplied national government protection to the rights of contract, of property, of the equal protection of the courts, and of the "full and equal benefit of all laws for the security of person and property." These two measures were legislative implementations of the Thirteenth Amendment as authorized by its second section.

The Fourteenth Amendment reënacted the Thirteenth Amendment and made the program of legislation designed to implement it constitutionally secure or a part of the Constitution. The Fourteenth Amendment added again, as the Thirteenth Amendment had done earlier, a power and duty of congressional enforcement.

The national protection of men in their natural rights or of citizens in their privileges and immunities, the basic idea of this whole repeatedly reënacted program—expressed in its language, reiterated in the debates upon it, emphasized in the circumstances which brought it forth stage by stage, and made inevitable by the historic experience and movement which it culminated and embodied,—extended to individuals without regard to the private or governmental character of the violator, and was both constitutional and congressional.

It is but to repeat this to give the answers to the five specific questions posed at the outset of this book.

1. The privileges or immunities of citizens of the United States, guaranteed by the first of the three famous clauses of section 1 of the Fourteenth Amendment, were the natural rights of all men or such auxiliary rights as were necessary to secure and maintain those natural rights. They were the rights to life, liberty, and property. They were the right to contract, and to own, use, and dispose of property. They were the right to the equal protection of the courts and to the full and equal protection of the laws. They were the rights of unrestricted travel, sojourn, and residence. These were the irreducible minimum.

The privileges or immunities clause was regarded as reënacting the comity clause of Article IV into which United States citizenship and natural rights had been read. It was a constitutional reaffirmation of a principle binding without constitutional mention, the reciprocal relationship of allegiance and protection. The language of the clause, cast in negative form and confined to a prohibition of state abridgment, is most plausibly understood as a by-product of the move to achieve constitutional as well as con-

the Fourteenth Amendment 221

gressional protection. The circumstances and explanations of the change from the positive to the final form make that fairly clear. The language, in any event, cannot be abstracted from the natural rights and national citizenship doctrines which constituted the foundation upon which it was based and which prompted its use.

Finally, two other conclusions follow from the fact that the privileges and immunities of citizens of the United States were the natural rights of all men. First, the fact that citizens of the United States alone were protected by the clause, whereas the immediately preceding sentence in the amendment declared both who were national citizens and who were state citizens, does not justify the inference that the privileges or immunities of United States citizens consisted only of rights which did not also belong to state citizens.

Second, there was no occasion to assert the power of Congress, under the amendment, to add without limit to the list of the privileges or immunities of citizens of the United States.

2. The clause on equal protection of the laws had almost exclusively a substantive content. As the basic conception underlying the Thirteenth Amendment and involved in the debates upon it, as the heart of the Freedmen's Bureau and civil rights bills and the debates upon them, as the common denominator of the drafts of the Fourteenth Amendment, as the pith and substance of section 1 in its final form, this was the meaning understood and accepted by friend and foe alike. Protection of men in their fundamental or natural rights was the basic idea of the clause; equality was a modifying condition. The clause was a confirmatory reference to the affirmative duty of government to protect men in their natural rights. This established its absolute and substantive character, though the use of the word "equal" would seem to give the clause a comparative form. Equal denial of protection, that is, no protection at all, is accordingly a denial of equal protection. The requirement of equal protection of the laws cannot be met unless the protection of the laws is given; and to give the protection of the laws to men in their natural rights was the sole purpose in the

creation of government. This being so, the phrase "No State shall . . . deny" becomes a simple command: "Each State shall supply"; and the whole clause is thus understood to mean: "Each State shall supply the protection of the laws to men in their natural rights and the protection shall always be equal to all men." It was because the protection of the laws was denied to some men that the word "equal" was used. The word "full" would have done as well.

3. There are three possible meanings of the due process clause. First, it may be read as if the words "without due process of law" were not appended, that is to say, as if the state were forbidden to deprive persons of life, liberty, or property. This is the familiar substantive connotation which absolutely prohibits the doing of certain things, no matter by what procedure.

Second, the clause may be read as a declaration that only in certain circumstances may life, liberty, and property be taken away. Those circumstances are a prescribed procedure. But the procedure is exclusively in the hands of the government, as is the inherent duty to protect men in their lives, liberty, and property. Read in this manner, the clause is an affirmative command that the state shall see that no person is deprived of life, liberty, or property except when the condition is met, that is, except when the state itself does it by the prescribed procedure. Only thus can the state discharge its inalienable duty to protect and maintain or carry out its monopoly of the procedure for determining forfeitures of natural rights.

Third, the clause may be read as a simple statement that whenever the state by its own acts deprives persons of life, liberty, or property it shall adhere to certain procedural safeguards, which are designed to assure at least judicial regularity.

These three possible interpretations are not necessarily mutually exclusive. They may, in fact, be regarded as merely different points of emphasis in a single concept. The first meaning has its roots deep in abolitionist constitutional history. It was only occasionally

the Fourteenth Amendment 223

employed in the later days of the congressional history. The second meaning goes back as far as the first, but only as an implicit assumption. It never was so well or so firmly articulated as the first. Like the unmixed substantive meaning, however, it is suggested in the congressional debates on the Thirteenth and Fourteenth amendments by the undifferentiated association, in a fair number of speeches, of due process and equal protection ideas. The third meaning was generally accepted as at least the minimum content of the clause.

4. The Fourteenth Amendment was not intended to apply the Bill of Rights to the states. The rights sought to be protected were men's natural rights, some of which are mentioned in the first eight amendments and some of which are not. Life, liberty, and property, substantively guaranteed by the due process clause of the Fifth Amendment, were certainly such. The Fifth Amendment's procedural guarantee of judicial process and jury trial, like the Fourth Amendment's guarantee of personal security and the First Amendment's guarantee of speech, assembly, and religion, perhaps also were. These had commonly been claimed as natural rights during thirty years of abolitionist activity, but they were rarely mentioned in the final stages of congressional history. To the extent that the rights of the first eight amendments are natural rights, those amendments were regarded as already binding on the states. The state governments, like other governments, were under a duty to protect such rights. The Fourteenth Amendment confirmed that duty and imposed it also on Congress. The rights of the Bill of Rights, however, which are of a lesser order were not within its scope.

5. The three clauses of section 1 of the Fourteenth Amendment are mostly but not entirely duplicatory. The due process clause has a procedural content not necessarily present in the others. The due process and equal protection clauses refer to persons; the privileges or immunities clause, only to citizens of the United States. The privileges or immunities clause mentions laws and their enforcement; the equal protection, only laws; the due process, neither. All

three, however, refer to the protection or abridgement of natural rights. Section 5 authorizes Congress to supply that protection if the states do not do so, or do not do so fully or equally. Section 5 thus confirms or effects a revolution in federalism by nationalizing the natural or civil rights of men or citizens.

Table of Cases

Barron *v.* Baltimore, 53 n, 72, 91 n, 107–108, 198
Birney, James G., *v.* State of Ohio, 39 n
Bowlen *v.* Commonwealth (Kentucky), 180 n
Bushnell, Simeon, *Ex Parte,* 55 n
Commonwealth (Massachusetts) *v.* Aves, 77 n
Corfield *v.* Coryell, 213
Crandall, Prudence, *v.* State of Connecticut, 73
Dred Scott *v.* Sandford, 54 n, 91 n, 101
Forsyth *et al. v.* Nash, 9 n
Harry and others *v.* Decker and Hopkins, 9 n
Jack *v.* Martin, 37 n
Jones *v.* VanZandt, 54 n
Merry *v.* Chexnaider, 9 n
People (California) *v.* Washington, 180 n
People of the State of New York *v.* Lemmon, 77 n, 79 n
Perkins, *In re,* 55 n, 77 n
Prigg *v.* Pennsylvania, 36, 41 n, 54 n, 82
Roberts, Sarah C., *v.* City of Boston, 55 n
Smith *v.* Moody, 180 n
State (New Jersey) *v.* Post, 46 n, 55 n
State (New Jersey) *v.* VanBeuren, 46 n, 55 n
Taylor *v.* Porter, 91 n
Turner, Elizabeth, Matter of, 180 n
United States *v.* Cruickshank, 180 n
United States *v.* Rhodes, 180 n
Willard *v.* Illinois, 77 n

Source Materials

Adams, John Quincy. *An Oration Addressed to the Citizens of the Town of Quincy, July 4, 1831*, 63 n.; *An Oration Delivered before the Inhabitants of the Town of Newburyport at Their Request, July 4, 1837*, 63 n.

Allen, Charles. "Speech of the Honorable Charles Allen at City Hall, Worcester, Massachusetts, November 5, 1850," *Chronotype*, November 9, 1850, 38 n. 10, 40 n.

American Anti-Slavery Society. *Declaration of Sentiments of the American Anti-Slavery Society* (New York, 1833), 34; *Fourth Annual Report* (1837), 11, 13 n.; *Twenty-eighth Annual Report* (1861), 129 n., 131 n. 3, 132 n.6; *Twenty-sixth Annual Report* (1856), 131 n. 2

Anti-Slavery Record, August, 1837, 11 n. 4, 37 n. 8

Birney, James G. Articles, *Albany Patriot*, May, June, 1847, 54–65

Chase, Salmon P. *Speech in the Case of the Colored Woman Matilda Who Was Brought before the Court of Common Pleas of Hamilton Co., Ohio, by Writ of Habeas Corpus, March 11, 1837* (Cincinnati, 1837), 37 n. 7

Chronotype, editorial, November 26, 1850, 40 n.; "Defence of Fugitive Slaves," December 4, 1850, 38 n. 9

The Emancipator, June 3, 1834, 8; July 22, 1834, 12 n. 6, 101 n.; November 4, 1834, 37; December 16, 1834, 17–18 n. 2; March 24, 1835, 34, 35 n. 3; May 19, 1835, 15–16

Farley. "Speech of Mr. Farley at Faneuil Hall," *Chronotype*, November 15, 1850, 40 n.

"A Farmer." *Serious Address to the Rulers of America* (1783), 48 n.

A Full Statement of the Reasons Which Were in Part Offered to the Committee of the Legislature of Massachusetts on the Fourth and Eighth of March, 1836, etc., Published by Order of the Managers of the Mass. ASS (Boston, 1836), 13 n.

Giddings, Joshua. *Speeches in Congress* (Boston, 1853), 36 n., 124 n.

Goodell, William. "An Appeal on Behalf of the American Anti-Slavery Society Addressed to the People of the City of New York," *The Emancipator* (special edition), August, 1834,13 n., 99; "Constitution of the U. S. vs. Slavery," *The Emancipator*, November 4, 1834, 37 n. 6; articles, *Albany Patriot*, vols. 6 and 7, 51 n. 8; *Slavery and Anti-Slavery: A History of the Great Struggle in Both Hemispheres; with a View of the Slavery Question in the United States* (1852), 51 n.; *Views of American Constitutional Law in Its Bearing upon American Slavery* (Utica, N. Y., 1844), 51 n. 8, 76 n.

Honeoye Liberty Mass Meeting, held on the Twenty-nine December, and the three succeeding days. Declaration of Sentiments, 1846, 118 n., 121 n. 7

Hopkins, Samuel. "Dialogue concerning Slavery," *Works* (1776), Vol. 2, p. 576, 48 n.

Jay, William. *Miscellaneous Writings on Slavery* (Boston, 1853), 76 n. 4

Lovejoy, Joseph C., and Owen Lovejoy. *Memoir of the Rev. Elijah Lovejoy; Who was Murdered in Defence of the Liberty of the Press, at Alton, Illinois, Nov. 7, 1837* (New York, 1838), 13 n.

Macedon Convention, Platform, 1847, 117–118 n., 122–123 n.

Manchester meeting, November 6, 1850. Report, *Chronotype*, November 12, 1850, 40 n.

Mann, Horace. *Slavery: Letters and Speeches* (Boston, 1851), 24 n. 10, 38 n. 10, 76 n. 5.

Massachusetts. Legislature. Resolve and Declaration of a Joint Special Committee of the Legislature of Massachusetts, February 3, 1845, 76 n. 6

Mellen, George. *An Argument on the Unconstitutionality of Slavery, Embracing an Abstract of Proceedings of the National and State Conventions on This Subject* (1841), 52 n. 11

"Memorial to the Congress of the United States on the Subject of Restraining the Increase of Slavery in New States to Be Admitted to the Union," 1819, 76 n. 4, 78 n.

New England Anti-Slavery Society. Address, *The Emancipator*, September 30, 1834, 37 n. 6

Ohio Anti-Slavery Society. *Report*, fourth anniversary meeting, Putnam, Muskingum County, May 29, 1839, 70 n.

Olcott, Charles. *Lectures on Slavery and Abolition* (1838), 18; *Report on Laws of Ohio* (1835), 73

Palfrey, John. "Papers on the Slave Power," *Boston Whig* (1847), 76 n. 6

Parrish, John. *Remarks on the Slavery of the Black People* (1806), 48 n.

"Petition of the American Anti-Slavery Society *re* Slavery in the District of Columbia," *The Emancipator*, December 16, 1834, 18 n. 2

Quarterly Anti-Slavery Magazine, Vol. 2 (1837), 11 n.

Quincy, Joshua. Letter to J. Ingersoll, Esq., *Chronotype*, October 15, 1850, 38 n. 10, 40 n.

"Resolution Passed by a Meeting in Faneuil Hall, October 15, 1850," *Chronotype*, October 15, 1850, 38 n. 10

Rogers, N. P. "The Constitution," *Quarterly Anti-Slavery Magazine*, Vol. 2 (1837), 11 n.

Seneca Falls national reform meeting. Resolution, March 22, 1847, 118 n.

"Seventy-six," *The Emancipator*, January 4, 1838, 63 n.

Smith, Gerrit. Letter to Salmon P. Chase, *Albany Patriot*, Vol. 6, No. 52 (November 10, 1847), p. 206, 51 n. 7; Speech in New York state capitol, 1850, 90 n. 10; Speech in Peterboro', October 22, 1834, 13 n.

Spooner, Lysander. *A Defense for Fugitive Slaves against the Acts of February 12, 1793, and September 18, 1850* (Boston, 1850), 38 n. 9, 40 n.; *The Unconstitutionality of Slavery* (Boston, 1845), 36, 49 n. 5, 86

Stanton, H. B. *Remarks in the Representatives Hall on 23 and 24 February before the Committee of the House of Representatives of Massachusetts* (Boston, 1837), 13 n., 18, 27; Speech,

American Anti-Slavery Society, *Sixth Annual Report* (1839), 68 n.
Stewart, Alvan. *The Friend of Man* (New York, 1837), 43; Letter to Gamaliel Bailey, *Albany Patriot*, Vol. 7, No. 26 (May 10, 1847), 49 n. 4
Tappan, Lewis. *Address to the Non-Slaveholders of the South on the Social and Political Evils of Slavery* (1843), 76 n. 5
Thomas, William (Defensor). *Enemies of the Constitution Discovered* (New York, 1835), 13 n.
Tiffany, Joel. *A Treatise on the Unconstitutionality of American Slavery: Together with the Powers and Duties of the Federal Government in Relation to That Subject* (Cleveland, 1849), 36, 49 n. 6, 86, 106
Treadwell, S. B. *American Liberties and American Slavery Morally and Politically Illustrated* (Rochester, N. Y., 1838), 13 n.
Weld, Theodore Dwight. *The Power of Congress over Slavery in the District of Columbia* (New York, 1838), 12 n. 5, 18, 21–23
Wright, Elizur. *Chronicles of Kidnapping* (New York, 1834), 34

Index

Abolitionist movement: clash of constitutional theories in District of Columbia, 16, 68–70; definition of citizenship, 72–75, 87 ff.; demand for protection of civil liberties, 11–14; history of early movement, 7–14; judicial and legislative action, 54 n.; objectives, 42, 102–105

Allegiance and protection, reciprocal doctrines: Birney's view, 61–65; Weld's view, 22–23

Amendments. See United States Constitution

Antislavery movement: Civil War amendments, 218–220; history, 48 n., 94–96, 113; in Republican party, 120–124, 129–134

Anti-Slavery Society of Booneton, N.J., preamble and constitution of 1834, 7–8

Ashley, James M., evils of slavery, 147

Bill of Rights, binding on states, 198

Bingham, John A.: 14th Amendment empowers Congress to enforce Bill of Rights and Constitution, 196–197; work in development of 14th Amendment, sec. 1, 125–128, 193

Birney, James: District of Columbia as slave territory, 15–16; federalism and slavery, 54–65; Fugitive Slave Act, 38 n. 10

Black Codes, 163–164, 169, 179

Chase, Salmon P., view of due process, 37 n. 6, 38, 39, 116–117 n. 1

Citizens: abolitionist definition, 72–75, 87 ff.; Attorney General Bates' opinion, 91 n.; federal power to protect, 59–61, 87–90; free colored seamen, 56–57, 76 n. 6, 81–82; rights under 14th Amendment, 185–186, 211–212; of states, 77–80, 82–83. See also Comity clause; Paramount national citizenship

Civil Rights bill and Act: carrying out comity clause, 215–216; 14th Amendment as constitutional guarantee, 207–210; implementation of 13th Amendment, 160–164, 166–176

Comity clause: applicable only to citizens of states, 77–78; conflict with states' rights, 82–84; development of paramount national citizenship, 73–74, 77–81, 84–85; enforcement, 193–194; federal power not suggested, 80–81; free colored seamen as citizens, 56–57, 76 n. 6, 81–82; history of, 75–76 n. 4; inapplicable to stationary citizens, 77; natural rights of men, 195 n. 4; slavery as violation of, 18–19, 61–65; weaknesses of, 78, 83–84

Common law, no toleration of slavery, 20 n. 5, 45

Congress: debates on 13th Amendment, 141–155, 160–180; debates on 14th Amendment, 183–217; rejection of "Congress shall have power" clause, 200–203; split on direct action, 68–70

Congress, power to abolish slavery: Birney's view, 55; under comity clause, 83; under common defense and general welfare clause, 18, 23 n. 8; in District of Columbia, 16, 18–31, 69, 70, 153; under 5th Amendment, 43–48; under Preamble of Constitution, 22; in southern states, 68; under 13th Amendment, 141 ff., 152–155, 168 n.; without just compensation, 19–20 n. 4, 20 n. 6, 21, 23–24 n. 9

Constitution. *See* United States Constitution

Declaration of Independence, constitutional theory of abolitionists, 62–63 n.

Discrimination forbidden by 14th Amendment, 190–191

District of Columbia: constitutional limitation on power of Congress to legislate for, 24–25; power of Congress to abolish slavery in, 16, 18–31, 69, 70, 153

Due process of law: abolitionist interpretation, 25–28, 98–101; Chase's interest in, 37 n. 6, 38, 39, 116–117 n. 1; "deprives" when government fails to supply protection, 61 n. 19; fugitive slave clause, 40, 44; grant of power, 40–41; James' argument, 39–40; meaning, 222–223; positive duty of states, 205–207; slavery in District of Columbia, violation of, 25; Stewart's definition, 40, 44, 48; use in antislavery cases, 54–56 n. 17

Ellsworth-Goddard-Olcott argument, 73–81, 84; and comity clause, 77 ff.

Enfranchisement, 151–152

Equal protection of laws: abolitionist constitutional theory, 26, 96–98; absence allowing slavery, 20–21, 22–23; agreement between proslavery and antislavery men, 30–31; arguments for, 210 ff.; comity and due process clauses, 194–196, 199–200; duty of government to enforce, 26–29, 207; guarantee of civil rights against state action, 187–191, 199 n., 205–206; identified with equality, 175–179; substantive content, 221–222

Federalism: abolitionist constitutional theory, 108–109; attack on principles of, 54–65; power of Congress under 14th Amendment, 200–207; "revolution" proposed by 13th Amendment, 142–148

Freedmen: benefits under 13th Amendment, 143, 148–149; equality opposed, 143; free colored seamen as citizens, 56–57, 76 n. 6, 81–82; need for protection, 32–33, 143–144, 156–158, 168 n., 186–187; rights in North, 14, 73–81

Freedmen's Bureau: bill, 160–164, 166–176; organization, 157–158, 177–178

Free Soil Democratic party, antislavery platform, 1852, 120

Free Soil party, antislavery platform, 1848, 119–120

Fugitive Slave Act: abolitionist action against, 32–36, 36 n.; absence of grant to Congress to enforce, 37 n. 6; Birney's view, 38 n. 10; denial of due process, 40, 44; denial of protection to free Negroes, 32–33; jury trial denied by, 33, 38 n. 10, 40–41; Liberty party platform, 36 n.; operation in New York, 34; state action forbidden, 36–37; violation of Constitution and federal character of government, Chase argument, 38–39

Index

Garfield, J.A.: civil rights bill set in Constitution, 209–210; power of Congress, 200–201
Goodell, William: right to protection, 12–13 n. 6; theory of federal authority, 51–52
Grinnell, Josiah B., enfranchisement, 151–152

Habeas corpus, guarantee of liberty, 45, 49–50
Hale, Robert S., equal protection clause, 195–196
Harlan, James, objectives of 13th Amendment, 146
Higby, William, proposed declaratory 14th Amendment, 193
Howe, Timothy O., equal protection, 175

Ingersoll, E. C., meaning of 13th Amendment, 146

James, Francis, Fugitive Slave Act, 37, 39–40
Jury trial, denied by Fugitive Slave Act, 33, 38 n. 10, 40–41
Just compensation, power of Congress to abolish slavery without, 19–20 n. 4, 20 n. 6, 21, 23–24 n. 9

Kelley, William D., amendments, 147, 193

Lawrence, William, foundations of civil rights bill, 172–174
Liberty party: constitutional aspects of 1843 platform, 118; platform on Fugitive Slave Act, 1843, 36 n.; tariff and land monopoly, 117–118
Lincoln, Abraham, antislavery principles, 129–130
Lovejoy, E. P., demand for protection of rights as citizens, 13 n.

Mallory, Robert, freedmen under 13th Amendment, 143

"Needful rules and regulations" clause, incompatibility with slavery in territories, 58–60

Negroes: citizenship status as defined by Pinckney, 79 n.; enfranchisement, 151–152; plans to safeguard rights, 158–160. *See also* Black Codes; Freedmen; Fugitive Slave Act; Slavery.
Nullification, used by abolitionists against Fugitive Slave Act, 35–36

Olcott, Charles: equal protection, 26; rights denied slaves, 26–28; slavery hostile to Constitution, 18–19

Paramount national citizenship: abolitionist development, 71–73, 85–86; and comity clause, 73–74, 77–81, 84–85; conflict with states' rights, 82–84; doctrine of Ellsworth-Goddard-Olcott argument, 73–81, 84; legal protection, 73–74 n. 3; liberty guaranteed by Constitution, Birney's view, 57
Party platforms, political action, 115–124
"Person," Stewart's definition, 43–44, 47
Pickens, F. W.: just compensation argument, 20 n. 6; proslavery constitutional system, 16–17
Pinckney, H. L.: citizenship status of Negroes, 79 n.; proslavery constitutional system, 16–17
Poland, Luke, "privileges or immunities" clause secures comity clause, 215
"Privileges and immunities." *See* Comity clause
"Privileges or immunities" clause: Bingham's contribution, 127–128, 193; Howard's interpretation, 212–214; meaning, 220–221; obligation of states, 207

Rayner, Kenneth, denial of citizenship aspects of comity clause, 81–83
Republican party: fruition of antislavery action, 129–134; platforms, 1856–1860, 120–124
Rights: of citizens under 14th Amendment, 174, 185–186, 211–212; constitutional protection, Mellen's view, 52–53; denied to slaves, 20–23, 27–28, 103–106, 171–172; guaranteed by 13th Amendment, 144–148. *See also* Equal protection of laws

Sherman, John, duty of Congress to protect freedmen's rights, 168 n.

Slave codes, definition, 103 n.

Slavery: applied to whites with impaired or destroyed rights, 148–151; incompatible with republican form of government, 50; legally enforceable personal servitude, 148; no toleration of, under common law, 20 n. 5; rights denied under, 20–23, 27–28, 103–106, 171–172; slaves as property, 16–17, 31; status in Congress during Civil War, 141; violation of comity clause, 18–19, 61–65; violation of due process, 25; violation of natural law, 90–91 n. 16. *See also* Congress, power to abolish slavery; Fugitive Slave Act

Smith, Gerrit, Preamble as argument against slavery, 51

Spooner, Lysander: constitutional views, 49–50; contribution to paramount national citizenship, 86–91

Stanton, Henry B.: denial of rights to slaves, 27–28; power of free states to abolish slavery, 68 n.; protection of laws violated by slavery, 18, 20

States' rights: limited by 14th Amendment, 185, 187–189, 199–207; violated by 13th Amendment, 141–143, 187–191. *See also* Comity clause

Stewart, Alvan: definition of "person," 43–44, 47; due process clause, 40, 44, 48; federal power to end slavery, 43 ff.; historical data supporting arguments, 46–47

Supremacy clause, allocation of power under, Birney's view, 57–58

Territories, slavery in, 21–22, 58–60, 69, 153

Tiffany, Joel: constitutional views, 49–50; contribution to paramount national citizenship, 86–91

Trumbull, Lyman: duties of Freedmen's Bureau, 177–178; relation of civil rights bill and 13th Amendment, 166–171

United States Constitution: first eight amendments applied, 105–108; instrument against slavery, 11 n., 18–19, 66–68; paramount national citizenship, Spooner's view, 86–91; slavery under, Stewart's view, 43 ff.

United States Constitution, Fourteenth Amendment: debates, 183–217; discrimination forbidden, 190–191; limitation on states' rights, 185, 187–189, 199–207, 211–212; not intended to apply Bill of Rights to states, 223; personal rights under, 185–186; power of Congress, 204, 213, 214, 217, 224; preliminary drafts, 187–191; questions on meaning, 1–4; relation to 13th Amendment, 184–185. *See also* Equal protection of laws; Privileges or immunities clause

United States Constitution, Preamble: and slavery, 22, 51; use in citizenship doctrine, 86–87

United States Constitution, Thirteenth Amendment: benefits to free colored persons, 143, 148–149; debates, 141–155, 160–180; declaratory or amendatory, 152–155; evolutionary stages, 187–190; limited construction, 165–166; opposed as invasion of states' rights, 141–143, 187–191; origins, 137–139; rights guaranteed by, 144–148

Ward, Elijah, objection to Negro equality, 143

Weld, Theodore Dwight: power of Congress to abolish slavery in District of Columbia, 18, 21–23; protection and equal protection, 27–28; rights of slaves, 27–28, 104–105

Wilson, Henry: abolition of slavery by 13th Amendment, 145–146; equality, 175

Wilson, James F., slavery violation of Constitution, 144–145

Winthrop, Robert C., report making comity clause basis of citizenship, 81–83

Wood, Fernando, opposition to 13th Amendment as unconstitutional, 142

www.ingramcontent.com/pod-product-compliance
Lightning Source LLC
Chambersburg PA
CBHW021704230426
43668CB00008B/718